THE GOD MARKET

THE GOD MARKET
How Globalization is Making India more Hindu

by MEERA NANDA

MONTHLY REVIEW PRESS
New York

Originally published as *The God Market*
by Random House Publishers India Private Limited, 2009

Library of Congress Cataloging-in-Publication Data
Nanda, Meera.
  The god market : how globalization is making India more Hindu / by Meera
Nanda.
    p. cm.
  Includes bibliographical references.
  ISBN 978-1-58367-250-1 (cloth : alk. paper) — ISBN 978-1-58367-249-5
(pbk. : alk. paper) 1. Globalization—Religious aspects—Hinduism. 2.
Globalization—India. 3. Hinduism—India. 4. India—Religion. I. Title.
  BL1151.3.N35 2011
  306.60954—dc23

                              2011041134

Monthly Review Press
146 West 29th Street, Suite 6W
New York, NY 10001
www.monthlyreview.org

5 4 3 2 1

CONTENTS

A Note to the Readers

All quotations and facts and figures cited in the book are backed by complete references provided in the Notes at the end of the book. Readers are invited to follow along by matching the first few words of a sentence with the correct page number listed in the notes. Those interested in further reading will find the Bibliographic Essay useful.

Introduction
to the Monthly Review Press Edition

The defeat of the Bharatiya Janata Party (BJP) in India's last general elections in 2009 was greeted with relief by secularists and democrats everywhere. Not entirely unreasonably, many saw it as evidence that Indian voters have rejected the toxic idea of India as a Hindu nation peddled by the BJP and the rest of the Hindu right "family" (or the Sangh Parivar). The consensus among political pundits is that piety is no longer driving politics, as it did during the mass mobilizations through the 1990s that led to destruction of a 500-year-old mosque in Ayodhya and brought the BJP to power. The forces of secularism and communal harmony are said to have won the day, at least for now.

Market reforms and globalization are singled out as the stars of this saga. Both the friends and critics of the BJP have come to agree that the fervour for making money in India's roaring economy has doused the flames of Hindu nationalism in the hearts of the middle-class voters who were the mainstay of Hindu nationalism in the past. The market economy, energized by global tie-ups and foreign investments, we are told, will not only rid India of the menace of communal violence, it will also dissolve caste and other hierarchies that have shackled it for ages.

The God Market challenges this gospel of globalization. Far from eroding the public presence and political power of religion, this book argues, globalization and neoliberalism in India are bringing the state and the business world closer to Hinduism, the religion of the majority. The state-temple-corporate complex is enabling a resurgence of popular religiosity that is brimming with majoritarian and nationalistic sentiments.

This extended introduction for the Monthly Review Press edition of *The God Market* is written with a hope that it will help international readers connect India's story with worldwide trends. I have taken this opportunity to bring in new data and new political developments to update the basic argument of the book, which was first published in India in 2009.

•   •   •

Let us begin with India's last general election in 2009, which was in progress when the Indian edition of *The God Market* went into print. The BJP-led National Democratic Alliance (NDA) lost votes, and the Congress-led United Progressive Alliance (UPA), with Manmohan Singh as the prime minister, came to power.

The story about how the markets defeated the BJP in these elections goes as follows: Hindutva (literally, Hinduness), the ideology of India as a Hindu nation, used to appeal to the urban middle classes and youth back in the bad-old days of the 1980s and 1990s. Those were the days when these groups were feeling beleaguered and angry due to the failures of Nehruvian socialism and "pseudo-secularism," which, in their view, gave undue privileges to the lower castes and Muslim and Christian minorities. But in the nearly two decades of economic liberalisation and foreign investments that began in the early1990s, India has witnessed a great burst of economic growth. As a result, the Hindu middle classes are angry no more. Far from feeling beleaguered and discriminated against, they have become more cosmopolitan, more self-confident, and more willing to take on global challenges and seek out global opportunities. Indeed, so confident is the Great Indian Middle Class that it has claimed the twenty-first century as India's century. And so the critics ask: What use can such forward-looking people possibly have for the past glories of Hinduism that the stodgy old men in khaki shorts keep harping upon?

This explanation of why BJP lost has been articulated most forcibly by Swapan Dasgupta, a prominent center-right public intellectual.[1] Dasgupta leads a new breed of conservative journalists and intellectuals who oppose whatever remains of the Nehru-Gandhi brand of socialism and secularism. They are keen on popularizing a strident defence of the virtues of capitalism within a socially conservative Hindu cultural matrix, which they accept as a way of life that binds the country together. They want the BJP to "drop the H-word," since Hindutva has become too loaded with bigotry and has lost all appeal for the middle classes. They would like BJP to tone down the openly anti-minority rhetoric and turn Hindutva into a vaguely emotional idea without any concrete political demands. Only this, they believe, will enable BJP to evolve into a "normal" pro-market, pro-defence, anti-appeasement (of religious and caste minorities), socially conservative, right-of-center party.

By now, the notion that the ideology of Hindutva is passé, and that India has "moved on" to bigger and better things has become a standard trope in the mainstream media and public discourse. There are, of course, supporters of the Sangh Parivar who don't buy this story. They think that BJP lost because it *betrayed* Hindutva, and that it was not "Hindu chauvinist enough."[2] This remains a minority view, popular among true believers, but not often heard in the mainstream.

A similar story about the liberating potential of neoliberalism is being told from the opposite end of the political spectrum, made up of ex-untouchable (or Dalit) intellectuals, most of whom are no friends of the BJP. Influential members of this circle, notably the journalist-activist Chandra Bhan Prasad, have claimed that economic liberalisation, fostered by globalization, is improving the living standards of Dalits, liberating them from the caste norms that consigned them to degrading work for generations.[3] They derive their evidence exclusively from two districts of Uttar Pradesh that have access to labour markets for semi-skilled work in Delhi, Lucknow, and other cities, while ignoring significant evidence that the incorporation of Dalits in the unorganised sector is taking place only on extremely exploitative terms, without any legal protection to speak of. The markets' blow against caste norms in employment is naturally seen as a victory for secularism, because by destroying the material conditions of caste hierarchy, the markets are seen as loosening the hold of Brahminical justifications for caste. Thus at least some friends of Dalits, like the friends of BJP, have come to embrace the gospel of globalised markets in the name of upward mobility and annihilation of caste barriers.

India is not the only country where the global spread of market capitalism is supposed to be exorcising the demons of religion- inspired fanaticism and retrograde, time-worn traditions.

The globalization of Islam, along with the globalization of democratic aspirations and new technologies, is said to have ushered in the Arab Spring, the movement for democratic rights and economic justice that is sweeping through the Arab world. The largely secular nature of the Arab Spring and the relative marginalization of al-Qaeda and radical Islamic parties in the mass demonstrations are seen as evidence that a new "global generation" has emerged in the Arab world that is more interested in living under Islamic laws than in creating an Islamic state.[4] Global movements of people, ideas, and markets are credited with defeating political Islam, while energizing a more personalized, less dogmatic, and more experiential version of Islam in the civil society. This new popular Islam accepts the legitimacy of secular states and limits itself to the personal and cultural realms alone. This thesis of "post-Islamism" is advocated most energetically by the renowned French scholar Olivier Roy in his influential books including *Globalized Islam* and the more recent, *Holy Ignorance*. (Notice the parallels between Roy's post-Islamism and the post-Hindutva argument described above.)

Others single out neoliberal economic policies for defeating political Islam. Parts of the Islamic world—Dubai, Turkey, Malaysia, and even Egypt and Iran—are cited to support the proposition that "global capitalism is the single best hope for combating Islamic extremism," as the American-Iranian author Vali Nasr put it in his recent book, *The Forces of Fortune*. Nasr holds up Turkey under the

Islamist AKP (Justice and Development Party) as the model for the rest of the Islamic world. The secret of Turkey's success, in Nasr's opinion, lies in its embrace of IMF-imposed market reforms back in the 1980s. The opening up of markets found great support from the deeply pious and deeply capitalist-minded middle-class entrepreneurs from small towns. It is thanks to these "Islamic Calvinists" that the ruling AKP has been able to embrace a soft Islam, a middle path between the extremes of radical secularism and radical Islamism. Nasr believes that a greater opening of the entire Arab world to global markets, combined with the dismantling of command economies, is the key to fighting Islamic extremism. (Nasr completely ignores the fact that it is the *failure* of IMF-imposed market reforms, especially the corruption and inequities left in their wake, that have fuelled the Arab Spring.) In a reversal of the idea that McWorld begets jihad, as put forth by Benjamin Barber in his well-known 1995 book *Jihad vs McWorld*, Nasr hails the charms of McWorld for seducing potential jihadis into shopping malls.

Those who believe in the moderating powers of markets assure us, as the political scientist Alan Wolfe did in a 2008 essay, that "religion's priority of belief and secularism's commitment to individual rights are not in opposition," as most religions are adapting to the capitalist world by becoming "prosperity religions."[5] The aim of these prosperity religions is not to question the morality of acquiring wealth, but rather to bless the believers into thinking that they can become rich as well by the grace of god. Thus, Wolfe assures us, the rising religious fervour in many parts of the world is nothing to worry about, as it safely feeds into the fervour for making money and getting rich.

The new evangelists of prosperity religions cheer the fact that, from China to Russia to Turkey, *God Is Back*, as the title of a 2009 book by two writers for *The Economist*, John Micklethwait and Adrian Wooldridge, declares. The same two forces—namely, competition and choice—that have let loose a "hurricane of capitalism" upon the world are also creating conditions where more and more people are "taking cover under the canopy of religion." Those turning to religions are not the meek and the desperate who are seeking "the heart in a heartless world" of oppression and soulless commerce, as Karl Marx had predicted. Rather, even the most successful and prosperous are *choosing* to embrace religions as "a go-ahead thing to do." The old secular pieties about modernization leading to secularization have been rendered obsolete by the force of markets and competition, as organized religions have adopted the competitive ethos of the markets and individual choice, and as people have learned to blend their spiritual and material aspirations. Gods and organized religions that celebrate them, Micklethwait and Wooldridge insist, are perfectly compatible with modernity, as long as they are freely chosen and as long as they don't get mixed up with politics and state power. The authors admire greatly the American genius for creating a right balance between freedom *of* religion and freedom *from* religion. They welcome the global spread of American style capitalism as a force for universalizing the American style securlarism, with its religion-friendly public sphere.[6]

A similar theme of celebration is struck by Timothy Shah and Monica Toft in their 2006 *Foreign Policy* essay, "Why God Is Winning." They look at the resurgence of religiosity around the world as a sign of "global expansion of freedom" showing that whenever and wherever "people get a voice, they want to talk about God." They acknowledge that the growth in religiosity is not without significant political influence on all levels of politics, from voting choices, welfare, and health policies at home, to issues of war and peace abroad. But this, they believe, is as it *should* be: democracies should reflect people's values, including their religious beliefs.[7]

Others, such as Robert Wright, the author of *The Evolution of God*, go even further, proclaiming that globalization is carrying out the expansion of moral imagination that was kick-started by the Abrahamic God. Just as Christianity and Islam learned to assimilate pagan gods and tribes, global economy is setting up "non-zero-sum games" that allow people to include distant strangers in faraway lands in their circle of moral concern.[8] So, according to this line of thought, when the whole world becomes interlinked through trade, we will all learn to become more tolerant, and a great concord of civilisations will ensue. Globalization, in other words, is doing God's work. (This celebration of global tolerance fails to account for the fact that globalization is not a non-zero-sum game: it produces very clear winners and losers.)

From this very brief overview, one can safely surmise that most observers of contemporary religions tend to converge on the following two propositions:

- One, that the current round of globalization is accompanied with a resurgence of religions all around the world. The world today is practically bubbling with religious passions, which have put all existing secularisms on the defensive.

- Two, that this religious revival is politically benign. The resurgence of religiosity worldwide is not a threat to secular democracies because most organized religions are learning to adapt to—and exploit—the new institutional opportunities created by modern democratic capitalism and modern communication technologies for their own self-propagation. As Harvey Cox, the well-known Harvard scholar of religion put it, in this era when the market has taken on the attributes of God, "traditional religions seem content to become its acolytes or to be absorbed into its pantheon, much as the old Nordic deities ... eventually settled for a diminished but secure status as Christian saints."[9]

This process of adaptation to the markets and popular culture is seen as *de-politicizing* religions, reconciling them with secular states and consumer cultures. So, even if globalization is bringing about a resurgence of religions, it is also able to tame them.

•   •   •

The God Market challenges this celebratory perspective on God and globalization, as it applies to India.

It acknowledges that in India, too, as in most of the world, secularism is retreating, the "gods are back" in ever greater force in the private and public spheres, and that "globalization is making India more Hindu" as the subtitle of the book declares. Using recent facts and figures, this book illustrates how the new, largely Hindu middle classes are successfully blending their religiosity with growing appetites for wealth and profits. It grants the proposition that neoliberal globalization is indeed proving to be good for the gods in India.

But this book does not celebrate the growing visibility of Hinduism in the Public Square, or the blending of piety and capitalism. Instead, it questions the naïve faith that market fundamentalism can and will tame religious fundamentalism. It challenges the complacent idea that the "return" of faith in public life will revive the traditional sources of tolerance, community, and belonging that secularism is said to have driven out. It raises critical questions about the appropriateness of a Public Square saturated with the sacred signs and symbols of the majority religion in a country as multi-religious as India.

The God Market demonstrates that neoliberal globalization is, in fact, creating an institutional matrix that is enabling Hindu nationalism to embed itself deeper into the pores of the civil society, the state, and the business sector. Despite the recent electoral setback, neoliberalism and globalization are friends of Hindu nationalism, and not its foes, as is often made out by some.

The main theses of the book can be summed up in three simple propositions:

- First, the *demand* for religious services—from worship ceremonies at home and in public, visits to temples, pilgrimages, etc.—is growing, especially among the urban, educated, and largely Hindu middle classes who are benefitting the most from neoliberalism and globalization.

- Second, the *supply* of these religious services that cater to the majority community is being facilitated by the neoliberal policies of the state. The pro-market reforms have brought the state and the corporate sector in a closer collaboration with the religious establishment, giving a great boost to the already thriving God market. Economic liberalization, in other words, is altering state-religion relations in a way that is making India less secular.

- Third, the net *result* of this is the mindset of majoritarianism, which identifies the national culture of India with Hinduism. Gods and goddesses sacred to Hindus have come to stand for the nation itself, while the line between political and religious rituals is being eroded. An uncritical adoration of Hindu heritage, along with barely concealed contempt for non-Hindu minorities, especially Muslims, has become the norm in public culture. Hindu nationalism, this book argues, is becoming a banal, everyday affair in the public life of the country.

This is not to say that neoliberal reforms and globalization are creating these circuits of demand and supply where none existed before. The process of domesticating and Hinduizing modernity did not begin with the current phase of globalization: it goes back to the Hindu Renaissance that started in the nineteenth century. The mixing up of Hindu idiom and political mobilizations is nothing new either: Mahatma Gandhi himself refused to recognize any wall separating his faith from his politics. The middle-class religiosity that revels in ritualism, idol-worship, fasts, pilgrimage, and other routines of popular theistic Hinduism was by no means absent from the cultural milieu of the educated middle and upper classes that came of age in the more "socialist" and "secular" era that was ended by market-friendly reforms in the early 1990s.

So, all these aspects of contemporary Hinduism that *The God Market* describes existed before the market reforms. However, market reforms have opened up more spaces in the public sphere into which popular and nationalistic expressions of Hinduism and traditional Hindu "sciences" can penetrate. Contemporary Hinduism, both in its more spiritualist and more devotional forms, can thus be seen to have adapted quite well to the new consumer lifestyles, exploiting the new institutional spaces opened up by the public-private partnerships in higher education, tourism, and health and welfare schemes. It is this synergy between a nationalistic Hinduism, capitalism, and globalization that this book aims to capture.

The rest of this introduction briefly summarizes the four myths about India's much vaunted democratic secularism that this book challenges.

•   •   •

First, let us look at the myth of Hindutva's decline.

Has Hindu nationalism been defeated by the new cosmopolitanism ushered in by global markets? Is the Sangh Parivar really ready and willing to bid farewell to the "H-word"? If Hindutva is really a dying ideology, should Indian secularists learn to love neoliberalism as a friend and ally?

Well, it depends. It depends upon what we mean by religious nationalism in the Indian context.

If we see Hindu nationalism primarily through the prism of communalism—that is, mutual antagonism between religious communities which has historically expressed itself in violent riots—then the answer to above question is a qualified "yes." Overt, large-scale rioting on the streets, the kind that erupted in Mumbai after the demolition of the Babri mosque in Ayodhya in 1992, or in Gujarat after the train-burning in Godhara in 2002, has decidedly gone down. Even serious provocations like the Pakistan-backed terrorist attack on Mumbai in 2008 failed to provoke Hindu-Muslim violence. Indeed, social scientists predict that "with rising politics of aspirations, which India is beginning to see as it moves economically forward . . . communal riots will be a matter of India's past, not its future. It will be a great surprise if communal riots return to India in a big way, as the nation rises up the income ladder."[10]

Any overt violence that leads to a breakdown of law and order is not good for business, and no one knows that better than those who make a living through business. Thus those upwardly mobile Indians who are benefiting from offshored, information-technology jobs and the expanded consumer choices made possible by foreign investment and trade definitely do not want to create an impression of religious bigotry and political volatility in India. Little wonder, then, that the largely Hindu middle classes deserted the BJP in the last election: they do not want to risk bloody riots in Bombay, Ahmedabad, Delhi, and other centres of commerce by flogging the dead horse of the Ram temple in Ayodhya, or by getting exercised over a *dargah* in Karnataka or Christian-versus-Hindu issues elsewhere. That is the reason that even those who admire Gujarat's chief minister Narendra Modi—which includes captains of Indian industry, well-known journalists, Bollywood stars, and even Gandhian activists like Anna Hazare—advise him to showcase his state's economic development but tone down his anti-Muslim invective. That is the reason why the business press cheered when the Congress-led United Progressive Alliance (UPA) coalition won in 2009.

But as any careful India-watcher will be able to ascertain, the decline of large-scale mass violence has not ruled out smaller-scale acts of violence, and even acts of terrorism planned and carried out by small gangs hidden from the public view. For example, barely within a month of Congress winning all the seven parliamentary seats from Delhi in May 2009, handing BJP one of its worst defeats from India's capital, Hindus came out in large numbers to violently oppose the construction of a mosque in a middle-class suburb of Delhi.[11] Sporadic attacks on churches, too, have continued in Delhi, Karnataka, and other parts of the country.

An even more dangerous development is that of Hindutva terrorism aimed at Muslim shrines, mosques and residential areas that has been gaining momentum through the last decade or so—the glory days of "India Shining" when radical Hindu nationalism is supposed to have lost momentum. With the arrest of bomb-makers and activists drawn from the ranks of Hindu holy-men and women, ex-servicemen, and radical Hindus, it is clear that Hindutva is by no means renouncing its heritage of communal violence.[12] Yet, such is the power of stereotypes that pervade the public consciousness in India— "All terrorists are Muslims," "Hinduism is a religion of peace," and "Hindu terrorism is an oxymoron"—that Muslims are held responsible for attacking their own mosques and neighbourhoods! There are always ready-made answers for why Muslims would bomb their own communities—they could be Pakistani agents trying to foment communal riots, they could be Wahabi purists who hate India's tolerant Islam, and so on. Scores of Muslim youth have had their lives ruined on these flimsy grounds for crimes that were later found to have been the handiwork of Hindu terrorists.

The God Market takes the view, however, that communal violence, whether overt or covert, is not an adequate measure of Hindu nationalism. Hindu nationalism is a much bigger project, which is not exhausted by communalism, even though it provides the soil in which the communal virus grows. Hindu nationalism can continue to gain ground, even when it is not openly channelled into religious violence. It is when Hindu nationalism is seen through a wide-angle lens, this book argues, that globalization and neoliberalism appear as its allies and enablers.

What is the wide-angle view of Hindu nationalism that this book offers? Here Hindu nationalism is understood not primarily, or solely, as a political or a religious project, but rather as a cultural project. The primary aim of Hindutva is to Hinduize the public culture, to embed a "modern" understanding of Hinduism (derived largely from the nineteenth-century anti-Enlightenment, Theosophical, and Orientalist perspectives) into the pores of the state and civil society, without directly overturning the secular democratic laws enshrined in the Constitution of India. It is cultural hegemony at home, and recognition of India as a spiritual, economic, and military "superpower" abroad, that the Hindu nationalists seek: electoral victories, religio-political mobilizations (the many *yatras* or pilgrimages, fasts-unto-deaths, yoga camps, and such) are merely means to that end.

Hindu nationalism understood as a project for cultural hegemony has two enduring features that are finding great resonance with globalization. One, to make the majority religion the basis of the nation's collective identity and the source of its ultimate values and purposes; and two, to allow the institutional space of the majority religion—the networks of temples, ashrams, religious schools, universities, and *gurukuls*, charitable hospitals, etc.—to take on the public functions of the state, while retaining their distinctive religious nature. The idea is to erase the line between the ritual and political spaces, or to remove any distinction between the worship of gods and the worship of the nation.

These features of religious nationalism depend upon the institutional arrangements between the state, religions, and other dominant institutions of the society, including, of course, the amorphous domain of the market. A major thesis of *The God Market* is that liberalization is changing the state-temple relations and aligning both of them with businesses and corporate interests. Chapter 3 in this book describes many instances of how Hindu places of worship and Hindu educational institutions that propagate more "secular" Hindu traditions such as Vedic astrology, priest-craft, yoga, Ayurveda, and such, are aided by public subsidies and corporate sponsorship. This book refers to this three-sided relationship as the "state-temple-corporate complex."

Hindu nationalism in the wider sense used in this book, complete with the state-temple-corporate complex, was on display in the recent anti-corruption campaigns that rocked the UPA government through much of 2011. A group calling itself "India Against Corruption," whose inner circle was made up largely of lawyers and middle-class professionals, managed to launch a nationwide movement demanding stricter legislation against corruption. IAC turned to two men to rally support for their cause— Baba Ramdev, a prominent tele-yogi and Ayurvedic healer with millions of admirers, especially among the lower-middle classes in small towns, and Anna Hazare, the Gandhian ex-army man turned social reformer, whose core support came from urban middle classes and idealistic youth. Both men exemplify how smoothly and almost imperceptibly religion blends with politics and business in India these days.

Baba Ramdev's proximity to the Sangh Parivar was so obvious that the leadership of IAC got nervous about turning off their "apolitical" constituency and quickly replaced him with Anna Hazare.[13] Anna Hazare, a veteran of many "fasts unto death," went on two fasts through the summer of 2011 to force the government to pass his version of the anti-corruption law, which contains many anti-democratic elements. The mainstream English media, Bollywood stars, and Twitter and Facebook–savvy professionals all gravitated more toward the Gandhian Hazare than the rustic, Hindi-speaking Ramdev.

While Hazare tried to maintain a distance from the organized Hindu Right, his saffron slip kept showing: His campaign freely used slogans and images, including the highly divisive image of Bharat Mata (literally, Mother India).

Bharat Mata is no ordinary mother, but revered as an avatar of the Goddess, or Devi. The traditional Bharat Mata image superimposes the body of the Goddess—imagined as a sari-clad woman with all the traditional divine insignia—on the map of "Greater India," which includes all of Kashmir and even the rest of the subcontinent. This literal sacralization of the nation has been a staple of Hindu nationalism from the early years of the twentieth century when the extremist nationalists led by Sri Aurobindo and Bipin Chandra Pal popularized the idea originally derived from a popular novel (*Anandmath*) written by the Bengali man of letters, Bankim Chandra Chattopadyaya.[14]

Hazare opened his first fast with the Bharat Mata image as the backdrop to where he was fasting. (The closest equivalent in the United States would be a Christian cross painted red, white, and blue—a visual representation of wrapping the cross in the flag that is quite popular among the Christian nationalists. Yet it is hard to imagine the Occupy Wall Street movement, which has been compared to Hazare's anti-corruption drive by some, adopting the flag-draped cross as its insignia.[15]) In his second fast, this image was replaced with an image of Gandhi, but the slogans invoking Bharat Mata continued throughout both fasts. Many secularists, Muslims, and others refused to join Hazare's campaign at least in part because of these Hindu nationalist motifs.[16]

Ramdev and Hazare exemplify the workings of what this book describes as the state-temple-corporate complex.

Ramdev built his multimillion-dollar empire through his ashram complex, helped along by generous land-grants and tax breaks from various state governments, and accreditation for his Divya brand of medicines, many of highly dubious quality, from the central government and the medical establishment.[17] What the first edition of *The God Market* missed, and what became apparent during Ramdev's role in the anti-corruption agitation, are the many new ways that businesses, large and small, have come to underwrite his Hindu nationalist agenda. It appears that the huge cost of Ramdev's popular yoga camps and his yoga cruises, which cater to the very rich Indians and NRIs or nonresident Indians, are borne by pious businessmen who see it as an act of piety, or dharma. Likewise, it is the devout businesses that pay hefty sums to have their gurus and godmen appear on religious TV channels, including Aastha, India's most well-known and lucrative spiritual channel, which is owned by none other than Ramdev's proxies.[18]

Despite his Gandhian aura, Anna Hazare, the other mascot of the anti-corruption movement, is not without corporate supporters either. According to Arundhati Roy, India Against Corruption has received funds from "Indian companies and foundations that own aluminium plants, build ports and SEZs and run real estate businesses and are closely connected to politicians who run financial empires that run into thousands of crores [one crore is 10 million] of rupees."[19] That is perhaps why the anti-corruption bill pushed by Hazare exempts private businesses and nongovernmental organizations from the scrutiny of an otherwise omnipotent ombudsman.

The anti-corruption movement exemplifies what this book is about, namely, the growing banalization, or the everydayness, of Hindu nationalism in polite society.

Corruption *per se* is not a communal issue—not even the most rabid Hindu extremists are suggesting that corruption is the handiwork of Muslims, or that there is "foreign hand" behind it. Yet Hindu nationalist motifs with a terrible history of communal divisions and Hindu-traditionalist discourse of ancient and forthcoming glories of Bharat Mata managed to take center stage. The same segments of high-tech savvy, market-friendly global Indians who are supposed to have turned their backs on BJP are quite at home with the symbols and idiom of Hindu nationalism. It is almost as if these symbols and idioms make up their unexamined political unconscious.

• • •

The second myth that this book examines is the *myth of the prosperous non-believer,* the idea that religiosity declines with the existential security that economic prosperity provides.

The modernists among India's founding fathers, especially Jawaharlal Nehru and Bhimrao Ambedkar, believed in the inevitable decline of religion that modernization would bring. The Constitution they helped write includes provisions that try to limit the sway of religion on the social and intellectual life of the country. India's doctrine of secularism is a valiant attempt to balance freedom of religion with reform and rationalization of religion through democratic means.

Indian Constitution-makers were hardly alone: the idea of the inevitable decline of religion with modernization has constituted the central plank of nearly all the major theories of modernization. It is only in the waning years of the twentieth century that secularization has come under serious challenge. The details of the rise and fall of secularization theory, however, do not concern us at this point. (The interested reader can turn to the final chapter of this book, which connects the Indian debates on secularism to social-scientific theories.)

The classic secularization theory, to put it simply, predicted that growing prosperity and existential security would make people less concerned with God and otherworldly matters. On a macro level, when different countries with different levels of economic prosperity and social welfare are compared, the inverse relationship between prosperity and religiosity still seems to hold true. A well-known study by two Harvard sociologists, Pippa Norris and Ronald Inglehart, of nineteen countries covering most of Europe, North America, Brazil, and Japan, showed clearly that the level of religiosity declined more sharply in those societies that were less unequal and provided greater "existential security" through better welfare measures. They explain the exceptionally high religiosity in the United States as a consequence of it "being the most unequal post-industrial society under comparison. . . . Americans face far greater anxieties than citizens of other advanced industrialized countries" about medical insurance, job security, and balancing work with family life. What is even more interesting is that the inverse correlation between income inequality and religiosity shows up not just across different countries, but *within* each country as well: in all of the nineteen countries they studied, Norris and Inglehart found that the poor are nearly twice as religious than the rich. In the United States, for example, two-thirds (66 percent) of the least well-off attend church regularly, compared to 47 percent of the higher income groups.[20]

One of the themes of *The God Market* is how India complicates what social sciences tell us about the connections among poverty, prosperity, and religiosity. Following the logic of Norris and Inglehart's cross-country study, one would expect a country like India—with its high levels of inequality and its mass poverty, with almost no social-safety net—to have high levels of religiosity. But the Indian data turn the other part of the picture on its head: it is not the poor but the rich in India who are more religious, and those who get richer are likely to become more, not less, religious.

India, it turns out, is not alone in posing a challenge to the trends predicted by Norris and Inglehart, and by the classical secularization theory more generally. Studies from other newly emerging market economies—especially China, Brazil, Turkey, and other Islamic countries—also show that growing prosperity under the current round of globalization seems to be making people more religious. The authors of *God Is Back* seem to have it right when they say, "The growth in faith has coincided with a growth in prosperity. . . . In much of the world, it is exactly the sort of upwardly mobile, educated middle classes that Marx and Weber presumed would shed such superstitions who are driving this expansion of faith."[21] There is no agreement why rising levels of prosperity, education, and exposure to the rest of the world should encourage religiosity: causal explanations are bound to vary with the nature and history of religions and their relationship with the state in different countries. But the fact of the growing de-secularization of the world under the current economic regime is hard to ignore.

The Indian edition of *The God Market* provides plenty of data and case studies to show that it was the growing ranks of the new-rich middle classes who were experiencing the "rush hour of the gods" (chapter 2). It describes the growth of popular Hindu devotionalism, of *murti-pujas* (idol worship), temples, and pilgrimages, and the time-honoured passion for miracle-working god-men and -women, all combined with the growing craze (and market) for *yagnas* (fire sacrifices), astrology, palmistry, and other occult arts among the middle classes. It describes how the statues of popular gods are getting taller, temples are becoming grander, and the lines of well-heeled devotees outside temples and ashrams in posh suburbs are getting longer.

Since the Indian edition appeared in 2009, new data on religiosity based upon the National Election Survey (NES) carried out during the 2009 and 2004 general elections have been released.[22] Conducted by the highly regarded data-gathering group, Lokniti, at the Center for Study of Developing Societies in Delhi, NES is considered the most authoritative survey of Indian voters. These data confirm the findings of *The God Market* that the rich, the upper castes, and the educated in India are significantly more religious than the poor, the lower castes, and those who are less educated.

When in 2004 the National Election Survey asked a representative sample of the Indian population how often they prayed, 60 percent of rich and middle-class Hindus said they offered puja every day in temples or in family shrines, while only 34 percent of the very poor and 42 percent of the poor did so. This trend held up across caste and educational level. The "twice-born" castes were the most religious, with 58 percent doing puja daily, while Dalits and Adivasis were found to be the least religious, with only 35 percent of each category reporting the habit of daily pujas. When the data are mapped onto educational levels, those with college degrees are more given to daily pujas (at 53 percent) than those who are illiterate (38 percent) or with only a primary education (46 percent). The higher the income levels, the caste status, and education, the greater the religiosity — this seems to be the trend.

When measured again in 2009, the trend has held up. The rich, the upper castes, and the more educated continued to pray more often than other social groups. But there was one surprising result: Dalits and Adivasis seem to be praying more than they used to do. In the 2009 NES survey, 40 percent of Dalits and 43 percent of Adivasis said they offered daily pujas, a significant jump from the 2004 survey.[23]

It is not entirely clear how this rise in religiosity of the subaltern castes and groups has come about. It could be related to rising living standards: there are reports (cited in the book) that suggest that Dalits who are trying to break out of their caste ghettos are beginning to undertake ostentatious religious rituals such as *kathas* and *jagratas* in order to "pass" as upper castes in their neighbourhoods. If true, this recourse to showy Hindu rituals would be a sad commentary on the prevalence of caste-ist prejudices in the larger society. Even if there is some economic trickle-down in places, as the advocates of "Dalit capitalism" have claimed, economic betterment is not weakening the hold of the beliefs that justify caste hierarchies.

· · ·

The book explores yet another myth that is proving to be false in the contemporary God-drenched world, namely, the *myth of privatisation of faith*.

Those who believe in secularisation theory expect that as societies become modern, religion will recede from the public sphere into private lives. But the reality has belied this expectation. In fact, religions all over the world are becoming less private, more visible in the public sphere, and more influential on policies on everything from medical research, women's reproductive choices, and sexuality to environment, terrorism, and armed conflicts.

In India, too, there is sufficient evidence of the growing presence of religion in the public sphere. *The God Market* describes how many rituals and pujas that used to be simple domestic affairs are now becoming more public and more ostentatious. Indeed, many of these public rituals are becoming full-blown political events, where holy men and political figures join forces. It is common for campaigning politicians to organise "political *darshans,*" using public money, and representatives of all parties seem to think nothing of using the state machinery for organising large-scale Hindu rituals for political gain. The Congress party's Digvijay Singh's order to hold public prayers and *yagnas* for his victory in the 2003 elections in Madhya Pradesh was more than a match for the BJP chief minister of Karnataka, B. S. Yediyurappa, who used up INR 1.1 million in just five months for his pilgrimages to temples. Even the communist government in West Bengal thought nothing of ritually worshipping the land (*bhoomi* puja) it wanted to gift to the Tata industrial group for the Nano car factory.

Participation in public rituals like *kathas, kirtans*, and *satsangs* is also growing among ordinary people—or rather, these events and rituals are moving out of the family and into the public square, while also becoming more ostentatious and expensive affairs. The trends for engagement in public religious activities, again as measured by the National Election Surveys in 2004 and 2009, are following the trends for private pujas, with the wealthy, the upper castes, and the educated leading the way. Close to 30 percent of upper-caste and wealthy respondents were found to have a high level of participation in public rituals, with Dalits and Adivasis generally falling around 16 percent. In recent years, both the upper castes and Dalits have shown an increase in public religious events, with 18 percent of Dalits reporting higher participation in 2009, as compared to 16 percent in 2004.[24]

Privatization of religion, it must be pointed out, was never on the horizon of possibilities in India. Even though liberal-minded secularists cherish it as an ideal, modern Indian secularism is not premised upon a "wall" that would separate religion from public life. In part this has to do with the nature of Hindu religion itself. Hinduism, famously, is not a religion primarily of beliefs or faith, but of rituals. Many rituals that used to be performed at home or in neighbourhood temples were turned into public spectacles during the freedom movement with an express intention of nationalizing the masses. The connection with anti-colonial nationalism has sanctified the public expression of religiosity, which shows no signs of abating.

• • •

Finally, this book examines the decline and near-death of the secularist hope for the spread of scientific temper and disenchantment of worldviews. The classical theorists of secularisation believed that modernity would "melt all that is solid " (Marx) and remove mystery from the world, leaving it disenchanted (Weber). The basic idea is that as the stock of scientific knowledge grows, the scope of "god's will," or fate, will diminish. To some extent this has happened, with people around the world increasingly accepting naturalistic explanations for natural disasters. But this process seems to have hit its limits already, and religions are learning to use the language of science and tools of technology and markets to celebrate god's powers.

The expectation that religions will learn to scale down their claims about their "timeless Truth" in the face of the growth of scientific knowledge has been belied. In fact, the language of science is now used to justify religious beliefs. Modern Hindu gurus have finessed the art of justifying the spirit-centred metaphysics of Brahminical Hinduism in modern, scientific terms. This "scientistic" Hinduism sells better among those urban sophisticates who make a living in scientific and technological fields.

India provides a treasure trove of examples of this phenomenon, from the growing trend of "e-pujas," remote *darshans*, and computer-generated horoscopes, to Disney-like theme parks cropping up inside temples. But even at a more basic level, which may or may not deploy modern technology, the belief in the efficacy of prayer and ritual (like *yagna*) to change the course of events in the natural world is growing—and to add insult to injury, such superstitions are claimed to be explicable through laws of modern science! This belies the hopes of nineteenth-century neo-Hindu reformers from Ram Mohan Roy of the Brahmo Samaj and Dayananda Saraswati of Arya Samaj to Swami Vivekananda, who stressed the textual and spiritual elements of the Vedas and Vedanta over the more ritualistic practices.

The God Market provides many examples of the re-ritualization and scientization of contemporary Hinduism.[25]

•   •   •

To conclude this extended introduction, we return to the fundamental question from which we started out: Is Hindu resurgence benign as long as it does not translate into communal violence, or into votes for the Hindu nationalists?

There are those who see no connection between the explosion of mass religiosity and religious nationalism, and hold up "true" religiosity as an enemy of religious nationalism. In the same vein as Olivier Roy, who celebrates the growth of popular Islam defeating political Islam, India's best-known public intellectual, Ashis Nandy (2009), has argued that "the BJP's electoral defeat is a sign that Hinduism has probably defeated Hindutva."[26] What he means is that the "true" Hinduism of the traditional masses has defeated the "laptop Hinduism" of the middle classes, which they share with the Hindu right. *Traditional* Hinduism, from this perspective, is tolerant, pluralistic, and deeply embedded in a way of life, whereas the *neo-Hinduism* of English-educated middle classes is homogenized, decontextualized, and nationalistic. For Nandy and other postcolonial intellectuals, the modern, nationalistic expressions of Hinduism are products of Nehruvian secularism, which (supposedly) delegitimized religion in public life to such an extent that it took the pathological form of fanaticism and bigotry. But now that the Nehruvian project has lost its prestige and there is no more secular finger-wagging, the Indian masses are going back to their original "good Hinduism." And that is what has defeated "bad Hindutva."

Drawing such hard and fast distinctions between Hinduism and Hindutva and between traditional and modern Hinduism, simply will not do. Modern manifestations of Hinduism are not created out of nothing: they gain their emotional content from reverence for the symbols of traditional Hinduism.

It is easy to scoff at the religiosity of the middle classes as inauthentic and shallow, as portable as a laptop, because it is not connected to any tradition or history worth its name. This turns traditional, premodern Hinduism into a sacred fossil, denying it the right to evolve. All the later stages of Hinduism's evolution, the many adaptations it has made through its long and sustained coexistence with Islam, its encounter with British colonialism and its integration into the modern world of science, technology, and markets are discredited as somehow lacking in authenticity and integrity.

This idealization of old-style religion overlooks one simple fact, namely, *all religions change all the time.* For all their claims to "eternal and timeless Truth," adaptation to changed circumstances and new social contexts is as basic to religions as it is to any other social institution. Hinduism, in particular, has shown an exceptional flexibility in accommodating to modernity and globalization. Its eagerness to deny and cover up glaring contradictions with modern science, for example, is a part of its attempt to maintain its plausibility and relevance in the modern era. These adaptations do not make today's Hinduism any less emotionally and spiritually satisfying to modern-day believers than the traditional Hinduism was in its own time.

Likewise, the good-Hinduism, bad-Hindutva distinction does not hold up to closer scrutiny. Hindu militants choose their symbols, rituals, and even their history and cosmology from the traditional stock. For these symbols to work, they must be held in reverence by a sufficient number of people. Everyday religiosity creates a common sense, a political unconscious, which can become readily available for nationalistic and communal causes when it encounters sacred sounds, sights, and stories mobilized in religio-political campaigns. It is at this gut-level, which is beyond words, reason, and evidence, that popular religiosity serves the ends of religious extremism. In the aforementioned case of Bharat Mata, for example, it is the deep reverence Hindus—modern as well as the traditional—hold for the figure of the Devi, the goddess, that spills over into reverence for the landmass of India. No one has to openly declare that India is a Hindu land, or that Muslims and Christians are not fully Indians—the image of Bharat Mata says all there is to be said. Thus to welcome the unchecked growth of popular Hinduism as an antidote to Hindu extremism, as Nandy does, is simply disingenuous.

There is an even more direct connection between popular religiosity and political choices. Just as in the United States, where the degree of religiosity is the surest predictor of his or her political affiliation, in India, too, a similar co-relation can be established. According to National Election Study data, up until 2004, there was a clear correlation between religiosity and voting behaviour: those Hindus who participated in public religious activities more frequently tended to vote for the BJP (38 percent) over the Congress (25 percent). In the 2009 elections, this relationship broke down, and this category of the highly religious showed the greatest decline (11 percent) in support for the BJP. According to Sanjay Kumar of Lokniti, one of the authors of the National Election Study, part of the reason why the more religious Hindus deserted the BJP in 2009 was because the party failed to assert strong Hindutva positions: the more religious Hindu voters were not embracing secularism when they did not vote for BJP; they were looking for more rabid Hindutva, not less.[27] This gives some support to the Hindu militants' own explanation for why BJP was defeated.[28]

Even more troublesome is that those who are more strongly and openly religious are also more majoritarian in their thinking. *The God Market* provides ample evidence of the growing majoritarianism in India today. Such individuals believe that Hinduism is not just a religion, but rather the soul or the life force of the nation itself, a "way of life" for all Indians—a position that clearly overlaps with that propagated by the Sangh Parivar. It appears that the more ardent Hindus, such as those who pray more often and who participate in religious rituals more often, are twice as likely as others to hold the belief that India is a Hindu country. Thus even though Hindu nationalist parties are not always able to win the Hindu votes—or "harvest the Hindu souls," as one commentator put it after the 2009 elections—a shared ground of understanding does exist between Hindu religiosity and Hindutva politics.

A final evidence of why a religion-soaked public culture is detrimental to a good society came last year in a legal judgment over the disputed structure in Ayodhya where a sixteenth-century mosque was destroyed on the pretext that it stood on the exact spot where the Hindu god Rama was supposedly born, thousands or even hundreds of thousands of years ago. On September 30, 2010, the High Court in Allahabad granted two-thirds of the disputed land to Hindus, leaving the rest to Muslims, even though the Muslim Wakf Board was the original owner. This was a very complex lawsuit involving more than thirty different issues, the details of which do not concern us here. What was most stunning about this judgment was how it disregarded evidence and legal reasoning in favour of the faith of the Hindus. It was clear even to the presiding judges that it was "an impossible task" to decide if Lord Ram was born on the disputed spot. Rather than dismiss the case as an "impossible task," the judges simply changed the question to whether "the property in suit is the site of birth of Sri Ramchandraji *according to tradition, belief and faith of Hindus in general.*"[29] Furthermore, invoking the faith and tradition of Hindus, the judges declared not just the idol of baby Ram stealthily installed in the mosque in 1949, but even the *site* where the idols were installed, the status of legal persons and admitted them as parties to the dispute.[30] This judgement is currently under review with the Supreme Court.

That the judicial system could so effortlessly—and not for the first time—substitute faith for evidence is a sign of the cultural dominance of faith in modern India. How this faith-based legislation subverts the constitutional guarantee of equal protection of all before law regardless of their faith is obvious: the court simply accepted the presumed faith of the majority community at its face value, while completely ignoring the faith of the Muslims in this dispute.

• • •

It is true that markets might be able to save us from violent religious extremism, and that is part of the reason for why the middle classes deserted the Hindu nationalist BJP and its allies in 2009. But the markets also deepen the reach of religion into the institutional spaces of society. The only real response to religious nationalism is to actively cultivate a secular culture that can displace the majority faith as the national culture. This would require an active demolition of the truth claims of all faith-based ways of thinking—including the faith in the gospel of globalization and "free" markets.

NOTES

1. Swapan Dasgupta, "A change of priorities," *Times of India*, June 4, 2009; and Dasgupta, "A 'dying' party?" *Seminar*, no. 605, 2010.
2. Koenraad Elst, "BJP apes Congress, fails," *Daily Pioneer*, May 19, 2009.
3. Chandra Bhan Prasad, "Markets and Manu: Economic reforms and its impact on caste in India," CASI (Center for Advanced Study of India) Working Paper, 2008; available at http://casi.ssc.upenn.edu/system/files/Markets+and+Manu+-+Chandra+Bhan+Prasad.pdf.
4. Olivier Roy, "The paradoxes of the re-Islamization of Muslim societies," 2011; available at http://essays.ssrc.org/10yearsafter911/the-paradoxes-of-the-re-islamization-of-muslim-societies/.
5. Alan Wolfe, "And the winner is... The coming religious peace," *The Atlantic*, March 2008.
6. John Micklethwait and Adrian Wooldridge, *God Is Back* (London: Penguin Press, 2009).
7. Timothy Shah and Monica Toft, "Why God Is Winning, *Foreign Policy*, June 9, 2006.

8. Robert Wright,*The Evolution of God*, (New York: Little, Brown, 2009).
9. Harvey Cox, "The Market as God: Living under the new dispensation," *The Atlantic*, March 1999.
10. Ashutosh Varshney, "Rethink the communal violence bill," *Indian Express*, July 16, 2011.
11. Subhash Gatade, "Hindu Rashtra in Delhi?" *Mainstream*, September 19, 2009.
12. Praveen Swami, "The Rise of Hindutva Terrorism," *Outlook*, May 11, 2010; Christophe Jaffrelot, "Abhinav Bharat, the Malegaon blast and Hindu Nationalism: Resisting and emulating Islamic terrorism," *Economic and Political Weekly*, Sept. 4, 2010.
13. Mehboob Jeelani, "The Insurgent," *The Caravan*, August 2011.
14. Sumathi Ramaswamy, "The Goddess and the Nation: Subterfuges of Antiquity, the Cunning of Modernity," in *The Blackwell Companion to Hinduism*, ed. Gavin Flood (Oxford: Blackwell, 2003); Barbara Southard, "The political strategy of Aurobindo Ghosh: The utilization of Hindu religious symbolism and the problem of political mobilization in Bengal," *Modern Asian Studies* 14, 1980: 353–76.
15. Hari Bapuji and Suhaib Riaz. "Occupy Wall Street: What businesses need to know," *Harvard Business Review* blog, October 14, 2011, available at http://blogs.hbr.org/cs/2011/10/occupy_wall_street_what_business.html.
16. For more details on the convergence between the IAC and the Hindu right, see Bhanwar Megwanshi, "The communal character of Anna Hazare's movement," trans. Yoginder Sikand, 2011, available at http://www.sacw.net/article2266.html; and Rohini Hensman, "Converging agendas: Team Anna and the Indian Right," *Perspective*, Sept. 19, 2011.
17. Meera Nanda, "Ayurveda under the scanner," *Frontline*, April 8, 2006.
18. Supriya Menon, "Press Button, change religion," *Tehelka*, July 3, 2011; Rahul Bhatia, "Origins of Ramdev," *Open*, July 2, 2011.
19. Arundati Roy, "I'd rather not be Anna," The hindu, August 21, 2011.
20. Pippa Norris and Ronald Inglehart, *Sacred and Secular: Religion and Politics Worldwide* (Cambridge: Cambridge University Press, 2004).
21. Micklethwait and Wooldridge, *God Is Back*, 16, 18.
22. National Election Study, *Economic and Political Weekly*, special issue, Sept. 26, 2009; Sanjay Kumar, "Religious practices among

Indian Hindus: Does that influence their political choices?" *Japanese Journal of Political Science* 10/3, 2009: 313–32.
23. All figures are from Kumar, "Religious practices among Indian Hindus."
24. Ibid.
25. For more recent work on these themes, see Meera Nanda, "Madame Blavatsky's Children: Modern Hindu Encounters with Darwinism," in *Handbook of Religion and the Authority of Science,* ed. James R. Lewis and Olav Hammer (Lieden: Brill, 2010), 279–344; and in the same volume, Kathinka Frøystad, "From Analogies to Narrative Entanglement: Invoking Scientific Authority in Indian New Age Spirituality," 41–66.
26. Ashis Nandy, "Defeat of an Idea." *Tehelka,* June 2009, (see note 2).
27. Kumar, "Religious practices among Indian Hindus."
28. See Elst, "BJP apes Congress, fails."
29. Anupam Gupta, "Dissecting the Ayodhya Judgment." *Economic and Political Weekly,* Dec. 11, 2010. Emphasis added.
30. Gautam Patel, "Idols in Law," *Economic and Political Weekly,* Dec. 11, 2010.

Introduction

God and Globalization in India

India had its own 'why do they hate us?' moment after the city of Mumbai came under attack in November 2008 by a bunch of gunmen with links to terrorist outfits in Pakistan. Many in India answered the question much the same way George Bush famously explained the 9/11 attacks on the United States: Islamic terrorists hate us because we are good and they are evil; we are free and democratic and they hate freedom and democracy.

This 'us–them' divide was further linked to globalization, a word that got bandied about a great deal in the aftermath of the Mumbai attacks. Pakistanis hate us, many argued in India, because we are winning in the global economy race, while they are a bunch of sore losers bent upon dimming the bright glow of our economic miracle. The terror attacks were seen as a conspiracy meant to destroy the confidence of global investors, slow down the outsourcing of IT and other jobs to India, and stop foreign tourists from coming.

India is seen as winning the globalization race not only on the economic front, but on the civilizational front as well. As Robert Kaplan, a well-known foreign policy expert, wrote in *The New York Times* shortly after the Mumbai attacks, globalization has led Indians to look for roots of their 'vibrantly free' democracy in Hinduism, while Muslims of India and Pakistan are looking for roots in the 'Islamic world community… and withdrawing into beards, skull-caps and burqas in some cases; and self-segregating into ghettos in other cases'. A similar sentiment was echoed in India as well. M.V. Kamath, a commentator well known for his strong Hindutva views, wrote in *The Organiser* that while 'indestructible India, wearing a cheerful smile and forgiving countenance is

1

busy sending rockets to the moon', its 'sick' Muslim neighbour and many Indian Muslims are bent upon isolating themselves by 'wearing skull-caps, forcing women to wear burqas, and otherwise refusing to join the mainstream'.

Something rather strange is going on here. The extreme conservatism of some Muslims, who are indeed withdrawing into traditional attire and symbols of their faith, is made to stand for the entire 'Islamic world community'. But on the other hand, the accomplishments of India—of *all* Indians, belonging to *all* of India's many faiths and creeds—are happily claimed for the glory of Hinduism. India, with its Hindu civilization, is presented as the bright, forward-facing side of globalization, while Pakistan—and indeed, Islam itself —becomes its dark, demonic, and backward-facing underside. The world gets divided into two: the winners who have the right kind of civilizational resources to play and win in the global economy, and the rest who are deemed to be laggards, if not total losers.

What this Book is about

This book challenges this 'us' and 'them' narrative. It sets out to show that India is not free from the forces of politicized religiosity which expresses itself in a growing sense of Hindu majoritarianism.

Indeed, politicized religiosity seems to be the order of the day everywhere. Globalization is making the whole world more religious—and all religions more political. Even as they are drawing closer economically, people all over the world are becoming more self-conscious of their religious and civilizational heritage. One can say that globalization has been good for the gods—and often, sadly, for gods' warriors as well who incite conflict and violence in the name of their faith.

India is no exception to this global trend.

2

This book aims to explore the changing religious landscape of India as it globalizes. It not only describes the changing trends and texture of everyday expressions of Hinduism, it connects these trends to the larger political, economic, and institutional shifts that the country is experiencing as it emerges as a major player in the global economy and world affairs. The overall aim of this book is to describe how modern Hindus are taking their gods with them into the brave new world and how Hindu institutions are making use of the new opportunities opened up by neo-liberalism and globalization.

The following, in broad brushstrokes, is the picture this book presents:

- As India is liberalizing and globalizing its economy, the country is experiencing a rising tide of popular Hinduism which is leaving no social segment and no public institution untouched. There is a surge in popular religiosity among the burgeoning and largely Hindu middle classes, as is evident from a boom in pilgrimage and invention of new and more ostentatious rituals.

- This religiosity is being cultivated by the emerging state temple–corporate complex that is replacing the more secular public institutions of the Nehruvian era. In other words, the deregulatory regime put in place to encourage a neo-liberal market economy is also boosting the demand and the supply for religious services in India's God market.

- Aided by the new political economy, a new Hindu religiosity is getting ever more deeply embedded in the everyday life, both in the public and the private spheres. Use of explicitly Hindu rituals and symbols in the routine affairs of the state and electoral politics has become so commonplace that Hinduism has become the *de facto* religion of the 'secular' Indian state which is constitutionally bound to have no official religion.

- Given India's growing visibility in the global economy, Hindu religiosity is getting fused with feelings of national pride and dreams of becoming a superpower. The country's economic success is being attributed to the superiority of Hindu values, and India is seen as entitled to the Great Power status because of its ancient Hindu civilization. Thus the hard-won achievements of all of India's many diverse religious traditions and cultures are being absorbed into the religion of the majority community.
- This new culture of political Hinduism is both triumphalist and intolerant in equal measures: while it wants the entire world to admire the superior tolerance and non-violence of the Hindu civilization, it tolerates intolerance and even violence against religious minorities at home.

This, in short, is the case this book will make.

Two caveats need to be added right away so that the readers don't have unrealistic expectations. This book will focus exclusively on the changing trends in popular Hinduism, the majority religion of the country. Changes in India's minority religions will be acknowledged where and when needed, but not investigated in any detail.

The other point to keep in mind is that this book is about Hinduism and not about organized movements for Hindutva, or Hindu nationalism. The trends in popular and public religiosity it describes cut across the secular–communal and left–right divides in the political domain. The cultural habit of imaging India in explicitly religious symbols of the majority community is not the exclusive preserve of the Sangh Parivar, even though the latter uses it more explicitly and more often for communal and electoral purposes.

At the end of it all this book poses this question: What room does this India that dreams saffron-tinged superpower dreams have for non-Hindu minorities? What happens to

4

the India that Muslims, Christians, non-believers, and other non-Hindus *also* call home as the country begins to see itself as India@superpower.OM? Can the country deliver on the promise of secularism without cultivating a secular culture and a secular polity?

Method of Enquiry: Sources of Data and Modes of Explanation

This book is not an academic report on a specific research project. But neither is it a book of polemics or ideological argumentation. Rather, this book combines political analysis and philosophical reflection with hard data, painstakingly collected from a vast variety of sources available in the public domain. The idea is to present the reader with the most cutting-edge social theories about globalization and resurgence of religion, backed with the best available facts and figures about everyday Hindu religiosity from the ground up. It is an attempt to breach the walls between the Ivory Tower of academic social sciences and the home, the street, the café, and wherever else non-academic intelligent readers live, work, and read. In short, this is a work of honest and rigorous scholarship meant to enlighten the reader and to make her think.

Like any work of contemporary social history, this book tries to connect the dots between many diverse sources of information. It uses material obtained from the mass media, opinion polls, scholarly studies, government reports, research reports of think tanks, and websites of temples/ashrams. This data will show that:

• The newly prosperous middle classes are turning away from the more philosophical, neo-Vedantic form of religiosity and embracing a more ritualistic and superstitious form of popular Hinduism centred on temples, pilgrimages, and popular saints or god-men/women. The signs of the rising religiosity are all around us: there is a boom in construction of temples and mega temples, some of which house gentrified gods and goddesses, while others offer newly invented 'ancient' rituals. The number of people undertaking pilgrimages is rising, as is the fellowship of gurus and god-men.

- This religiosity is becoming more and more public and political. Religious observances like homas (or yagnas), jagrans, and kathas that used to be relatively simple domestic affairs are becoming more and more ostentatious, expensive, and public. In addition, religious rituals like yagnas and yatras (pilgrimages) are becoming mobilizing tools for political causes of all sorts, from benign ones like protecting the environment and preventing AIDS to the more sinister shobha yatras and samaj mahotsavas (social festivals) which are meant to consolidate a majority Hindu consciousness.
- The rise in religiosity has the support of the leading institutions of the state, the temples, and the business sector, often working in a three-sided partnership.

The last issue brings us to the task of explaining the rising Hindu religiosity. There are some who say that Indians are innately more other-worldly and that Hinduism is a 'total way of life' in which the spiritual motive cannot be separated from other spheres of life. While the rest of the world might be expected to become less religious with modernity, India will always be religious.

This book will steer clear of these we-are-like-that-only kinds of theories. Instead, it will treat religiosity as any other cultural phenomenon which ebbs and flows, and changes with changing time. This book argues that the rise in Hindu religiosity can be explained by the emergence of the 'state–temple–corporate complex' that is filling the space that the 'socialist' state of the Nehruvian era has ceded to the private sector.

In one sense, the existence of the nexus between the state, temples, and the private sector is nothing new. The supposedly secular state of India has never shied away from celebrating Hindu religious symbols in the public sphere—all in the name of propagating Indian culture. Merchants and business houses, too, have a long history, going back many centuries, of sponsoring temples and monasteries devoted to their own chosen god or gurus.

But the current neo-liberal economic regime, this book will argue, is bringing the state, the religious establishment, and the business/corporate elite in a much closer relationship than ever before. As the Indian state is withdrawing from its public sector obligations, it is actively seeking partnership with the private sector and the Hindu establishment to run schools, universities, tourist facilities, and other social services. As a result, public funds earmarked for creating public goods are increasingly being diverted into facilitating the work of these private charitable institutions which bear a distinctly Hindu traditionalist bias. This, in turn, is helping to 'modernize' Hinduism: many of the newly minted, English-speaking, and computer-savvy priests, astrologers, vastu shastris, and yoga teachers who service the middle classes' insatiable appetite for religious ritual, are products of this nexus between the state, the corporate sector, and the temples.

Structure of the Book

The book opens and closes with two big ideas, namely, globalization and secularism. Sandwiched between these bookends are three chapters the contents of which are described below:

The opening chapter is titled '*India and the Global Economy: A Very Brief Introduction*'. This chapter provides an extended introduction to the phenomenon of globalization as it pertains to India. It provides a brief economic history of post-Independence India and charts its path to market reforms and integration into global markets. It pays special attention to the stark socio-economic inequalities which are worsening under the new economy. It also provides fair amount of detail regarding the privatization of higher education which has opened up fresh opportunities for religious institutions to enter the education market. This chapter is meant to set the stage for the rest of the book.

Chapter 2 is titled '*The Rush Hour of the Gods: Globalization and Middle-Class Religiosity*'. This chapter examines the 'rush hour of the gods' in contemporary India. Piecing together media reports, opinion polls, and academic studies, this chapter describes the many ways in which the new Hindu middle classes are becoming more religious and how the texture of the public sphere is becoming more distinctively Hindu than ever before.

Chapter 3 is titled '*The State–Temple–Corporate Complex and the Banality of Hindu Nationalism*'. This chapter looks at the institutional underpinnings of the rising Hindu religiosity and Hindu nationalism. It describes the nexus between the state, the temples, and the private sector in three broad areas: training of Hindu priests, creation of 'deemed universities' by religious endowments, and religious tourism. This chapter also looks at the phenomenon of banal or ordinary, everyday Hindu nationalism. It describes how the worship of the nation is becoming indistinct from the worship of Hindu gods and goddesses.

Chapter 4 is titled 'India@superpower.com: *How We See Ourselves*. It describes how India's success in the global economy is being ascribed to the Great Hindu Mind. It examines the dark side of this triumphalism which shows up as prejudice against non-Hindu minorities, especially Muslims, and, to a lesser extent, Christians. This chapter also examines the role of Voice of India, a New Delhi-based publishing house that specializes in producing Hindu triumphalist literature that openly derides the god of monotheistic religions.

Chapter 5 is titled *Rethinking Secularization (with India in mind)*. It looks at India's experience of secularism through the prism of social theories of secularization and de-secularization. It tries to understand why the god market has continued to boom under the peculiarly Indian brand of secularism and why it is flourishing under neo-liberal economic reforms.

A personal note

This book is an unplanned by-product of a much bigger enterprise that I have been engaged with for the last few years. But precisely because it emerged so unexpectedly, and yet made a lot of sense when it did come together, this book is all the more dear to me.

In 2005, I was awarded a fellowship by the John Templeton Foundation to work on a book-length study of the relationship between modern science and Hinduism in contemporary India. I was especially keen to explore the career of 'scientific temper'—an idea which was dear to Jawaharlal Nehru, Bhim Rao Ambedkar, and other secular humanists among the founding fathers of independent India. Indeed, to cultivate the temper of science is one of the fundamental duties of citizens laid out in the Constitution of India.

Like anyone trying to understand the cultural impact of modern science in India, I was immediately confronted with a paradox: there is 'science' everywhere, but hardly any sign of the critical spirit of science. India is practically drowning in 'science': gurus in their ashrams and on TV, and even professors in government-aided colleges and universities, have honed the art of casting every conceivable superstition, from astrology to vastu, as 'science'.

Since it is the educated, English-speaking, urban moneyed classes who are the biggest consumers of Hindu pseudo-science, I naturally wanted to understand the cultural and religious world-view of this growing section of the Indian population. My attempt to understand the religious beliefs and practices of middle-class Indians resulted in a long essay I called 'The Rush Hour of the Gods'. This essay became the nucleus for the present book.

Once I started focusing on middle-class religiosity, I had no choice but to look at the growing globalization of the Indian economy. It is impossible to understand the mindset of Indian middle classes today without first understanding the quantum leap in their aspirations and dreams brought about by market reforms and trade liberalization that India embraced in the early 1990s.

Well, once I began to place religiosity in the changing political economic context, one bit of evidence led to another discovery and soon a picture began to emerge. I began to understand better how liberalization had increased both the demand and the supply of religious services in the private and the public sphere. Before I knew it, I had developed a thesis that could stand on its own.

I took leave of absence from my original research project. The research and writing of this book was done entirely on my own time and without any financial support from the Templeton Foundation. The Templeton Foundation bears no responsibility either for the existence of this book or for the ideas it expresses.

With this book in print, I look forward to returning to where I started from. My original project is nearing completion and will soon appear in print under the title *Tryst with Destiny: Scientific Temper and Secularization in India.*

1

India and the Global Economy: A Very Brief Introduction

India everywhere

> India's promotional slogan, Davos, 2006

When you talk of 9.2 per cent growth rate, it becomes a statistical abstraction: 0.2 per cent of our people are growing at 9.2 per cent per annum. But there is a very large number whose growth rate is down to 0.2 per cent.

> Mani Shankar Aiyar

The ideology of Hindutva and the economics of liberalization are not only reconcilable but complementary.

> Aijaz Ahmad

India is becoming increasingly Hindu as it globalizes. But what do we mean by globalization? Why is it that whenever any country opens up to global trade these days, it invariably ends up adopting a package of neo-liberal economic policies? What is 'neo-liberalism' anyway?

This chapter will first explain, in layperson's terms, what buzzwords like 'globalization' and 'neoliberalism' mean. It will then tell the story of how India came to embrace the gospel of free markets and global trade and how it is setting the stage for the growth of Hinduism.

One note of caution is in order: the economic story told in this chapter is only meant to orient the reader to the rest of the book, which is less about Indian economics and more about politicization of Hinduism, and Hinduization of politics. Those looking for a more fine-grained analysis of economic facts and figures may want to consult the many excellent texts on these matters written by professional economists mentioned in the bibliographic essay that appears at the end of this book.

What is Globalization?

We live in a globalized world—who amongst us has not heard this statement repeatedly, endlessly, and mindlessly? But for all the monotonous repetitiveness, this statement is not a mere mantra. On the contrary, the technological infrastructure and the economic logic of globalization are beginning to touch the lives of a growing number of ordinary people in very real ways. The following two examples—the first recently reported by *The New York Times* and the second narrated by Gurcharan Das, India's leading cheerleader for liberalization —are quite revealing.

G.P. Sawant is an elderly man, a professional letter-writer who is losing his livelihood to cellphones. All his life, he earned a living sitting outside Mumbai's main post office, writing letters for his illiterate clients for a fee. But with easy access to cellphones, his services are no longer in much demand. And yet, the technological revolution that has made him jobless has also propelled his family into the ranks of the middle class: three of his four children are working in India's booming information technology sector. When *The New York Times* talked to him in December 2007, one of his daughters was on assignment in New Jersey for Infosys, India's leading software company. When the *Times* journalist graciously offered to carry a letter from the father in Mumbai to his daughter in New Jersey, Mr Sawant, the professional letter-writer, was puzzled: 'Why would I send her a letter? I'll just call her on the phone,' he said.

Raju, a teenager in Pondicherry, works in a restaurant in his summer break to save money to go to 'computer classes'. He tells Gurcharan Das, the author of *India Unbound*, that he has seen on TV 'this man, Bilgay [sic] who runs a software company and he is the richest man in the world'. Raju wants to be Bill Gates.

It is true that for each one of these upbeat stories, one can find many more stories of terrible deprivation and wasted lives. The much celebrated IT sector is tiny compared to the size of the workforce, elite led and not open to the vast majority who can't speak American-accented English. One cannot therefore get carried away, as some market enthusiasts tend to.

And yet, one cannot deny that something new is afoot. New possibilities are beginning to take hold of people's imagination: the mental horizons of ordinary working people in India now include 'Bilgay', 'New Jersey', and other distant people and lands. What is more, for the first time in human history, it has become technologically feasible for ordinary people, using everyday, household gadgets, to communicate across oceans almost as easily as it is to talk to their neighbour across the street. Even those who lack the resources and the opportunities are becoming aware of the possibilities.

So how do we define globalization that is sensitive to both its possibilities and the pitfalls? Anthony Giddens, the guru of the New Labour in the UK, described it best in his acclaimed book, *The Consequences of Modernity:*

> Globalization can thus be defined as the intensification of worldwide social relations which link distant localities in such a way that local happenings are shaped by events occurring many miles away and vice versa.

The same idea is also expressed eloquently by Ulrich Beck, one of globalization's staunchest critics:

Globality means that from now on, nothing which happens on our planet is only a limited local event; all inventions, victories, and catastrophes affect the whole world, and we must reorient and reorganize our lives and actions, our organizations, and institutions along a local–global axis.

Critics and advocates can—and do—disagree over how best to regulate this intensification of local–global connections. But no one denies that the condition of globality, as Giddens and Beck call it, is real. Local events—the ups and downs of stock markets, changes in climate, the spread of Avian flu, for example—are becoming ever more intertwined with what happens many miles away in distant lands. The world is indeed getting smaller. But this is not all: more and more people are realizing that the world is getting smaller—and organizing their lives in light of this realization. As the awareness of globality begins to influence the decisions people make about their careers and businesses, it begins to act as a material force in society.

This small-ing of the world has been described as space–time compression by David Harvey (1990) in his well-known work *The Condition of Postmodernity*. Harvey and other scholars believe that this compression of space and time is what lies behind the change from the old-fashioned, assembly-line industrial production to flexible production in which the different stages of production—research and development, manufacture, financing, marketing, customer services, and the final consumption—are spread all over the world in search of higher profits or less regulation. The production process is broken apart into pieces, scattered to practically any corner of the globe, and coordinated through the new technologies of communication and transportation.

Globalization can be understood as the sum total of processes that have brought about this space—time compression to the point when, at least in principle, anyone, from any place on earth, can instantaneously communicate with anyone, anywhere on this planet. Globalization is not new: it began the day our human ancestors left Africa and spread to all the continents some 120,000 years ago. But the creation of trans-planetary communication networks in the last thirty years or so is something radically new. Never before in human history have people been able to engage with each other, in real time, wherever on the habitable parts of planet earth they may be. For the first time in human history, another dimension of space —'super-territorial space', or space that is not linked to any specific physical territory on the map—has become widely available for carrying out all kind of activities, from buying and selling of goods to exchanging cultural and political ideas. Because the super-territorial space exists only in the communication networks, territorial boundaries provide no particular impediment to commerce carried out in this dimension.

The Internet is obviously the best example of this new dimension of globalization. But the Internet was made possible by quantum leaps in other technologies in the later half of the 20th century, including telecommunication satellites, fibre optics and telephony. We are only now beginning to get used to some of the social-cultural manifestations of these new technologies: the global media, electronic banking, and global commerce are only some of the examples.

What is Neo-liberalism?

One can rhapsodize all one wants about the fantastic possibilities of this interconnected world. But the condition of globality is a product—and a faithful servant— of a particularly ruthless, dog-eat-dog variety of global capitalism.

At one level, the space–time compression is an unadulterated public good: news and views cross national boundaries at the speed of light and enrich public debate everywhere. But it is the owners and the managers of global capital who are benefiting the most out of globalization. It is the giant transnational corporations that are using the new technologies to scrounge the globe for cheap labour, tax breaks, and lax environmental laws. New technologies have given big businesses the physical ability to break down the production process into smaller and smaller units and move them to any corner of the world that can offer them a better deal. The threat of offshoring jobs to cheaper and more docile workers serves as a threat to discipline workers, especially in relatively high-wage countries.

Globalization, in other words, is helping capitalism to become hyper-capitalism—that is, more global, more entrenched, more exploitative, and more unjust than ever before. According to Jan Aart Scholte, from whom the concept of hyper-capitalism is taken, globalization has not only increased the profitability of older, well-established industries (such as textiles, garments, consumer electronics), but has brought new spheres of social life (care capital through maid trade, medical tourism, surrogate motherhood), new natural resources (genetic information, biotechnology), and new services (information, communication) under the sway of the capitalist logic of profit and loss. Aided by globalization, then, more and more aspects of how we live have acquired a capitalist logic.

In what can only be called a great ideological sleight of hand, the phenomena of globalization and hyper-capitalism are treated as if they are some fundamental laws of nature which must be obeyed, at whatever cost to the social fabric. Everywhere, one hears the assertion that it is 'globalization' that is forcing the public sector to sell off taxpayer-funded

17

assets to private businesses, and that it is 'globalization' that is forcing factories to be shut down at one place only to reopen at a location where wages are low and working conditions poor. Everyone, from democratically elected representatives of nation-states to powerful business interests, claims that they have no choice because there is simply no alternative to globalization.

This worship at the altar of globalization hides the reality of neo-liberal ideology. The fact is that contemporary global hyper-capitalism has been made possible by a drastic restructuring of nation-states from their role as promoters of social welfare to enablers of markets. This transformation did not happen as the natural result of space–time compression made possible by new communication technologies. Rather, it is a thoroughly political project involving powerful transnational institutions like the World Bank, the International Monetary Fund, the World Trade Organization, multinational corporations, and the national elites of different countries. What unites them is their shared faith in neo-liberal economics.

What is neo-liberalism and what does it have to do with globalization? The two are quite often merged, but they are conceptually distinct and can exist without each other. (That is to say that another kind of globalization that is not based upon neo-liberal economics is possible.)

The word neo-liberal is an abbreviation of 'neoclassical liberalism', a tradition which draws on several centuries of modern economic thought dating back to the writings of John Locke (1632–1704), Adam Smith (1723–90), and David Ricardo (1772–1823). Neo-liberalism builds upon the *laissez-faire* (French for 'let people do as they choose') tenets of classical liberalism which promises that unconstrained market forces will 'naturally' bring prosperity and peace to society. Part of the classical liberal vision of unconstrained markets included lifting the national barriers to trade, which they believed

18

interfered with efficient allocation of resources. Neo-liberals apply this eighteenth century thinking, which made sense when relatively small owner-managed enterprises, workers, and consumers were located in the same communities, to the vastly different twenty-first century hyper-capitalism when all local links between ownership, production, and consumption have been broken and reconstituted at a super-territorial level all across the globe.

Economic liberalism went into eclipse for a brief period of about forty years, from the 1930s to the 1970s. This was the period when Western economies, battered by the Great Depression, were open to trying out the ideas of John Maynard Keyenes (1883–1946) who recommended that governments 'prime the economic pump' by spending on public goods and giving direct support to the unemployed. In the US, the New Deal policies of Franklin D. Roosevelt were directly influenced by Keynes. Outside the Communist Bloc, Keyensian economics was the major inspiration for the welfarist economic policies in Britain, Sweden, Canada, and Australia.

By the 1970s, however, the state welfarist policies got bogged down with bureaucratic excesses and were exhausted of creative ideas. That is when economic liberalism came roaring back. Ideas of a new generation of free market economists, exemplified by Friedrich von Hayek (1899–1992) and Milton Friedman (1912–2006), came to dominate the economic mindset of politicians and policymakers. These revived free market doctrines were embraced by Margaret Thatcher in the UK and Ronald Reagan, followed by all other presidents, Republican and Democrats alike, in the US. Neo-liberalism soon became the dominant ideology (often referred to as the 'Washington Consensus') of global economic institutions like the International Monetary Fund and the World Bank which have shown a missionary zeal in spreading the gospel of markets to developing countries. All four of the fast growing economies of the so-called BRIC quartet—Brazil, Russia, India, and China—have embraced neo-liberal economic policies prescribed by global financial institutions.

What are these policy prescriptions? The core of neo-liberalism, like that of classical liberalism, is the belief that unconstrained market forces ('the invisible hand') will bring prosperity, democracy, and peace to all people, in all societies. The underlying principle is that the markets should lead, and societies should follow, without governments, labour unions, business cartels, or any other interest group trying to tinker with the imperative of making money. The rather devious genius of neo-liberalism is to wed this economic logic to core democratic ideals which people everywhere aspire for —the ideals of freedom from unchecked state power and individual freedoms of thought and speech. This market view of freedom ignores other equally valid aspirations for equal opportunity, justice, and fraternity which are often thwarted by the logic of profit making. It simultaneously celebrates individual freedom, and trivializes it by treating individual persons merely as economic agents who are only motivated by the pursuit of material gain.

What are the practical consequences of neo-liberalism, especially regarding globalization? Neo-liberalism argues for a borderless economy. It argues that the territorial borders of nation-states should not act as barriers against the free flow of goods, services, and capital investments. Even though import of cheaper goods and services could wipe out the local producers (as in the case of cheap corn imports from the US into Mexico, or cheaper IT and BPO services from India to the US), national economies are advised to allow these imports without any protective taxes because in the long run, so the thinking goes, free trade will 'weed out' inefficiencies and make the overall world economy more efficient. While businesses rake in the profits that come with such trade liberalization, the social costs of this 'weeding out' are passed on to workers and communities. In this scenario, democratically elected governments become the handmaidens of global capital: it becomes a part of their job description to work hard to remove tax barriers to imports and to facilitate exports so that hyper-capitalism can thrive.

This prescription for deregulation and tax cuts applyies not only to foreign trade but domestic as well. Because markets are seen as the natural guarantors of prosperity and freedom, governments—even those that are democratically elected—are seen as a necessary nuisance at best. By this logic, good governments are those that shrink themselves by contracting out taxpayers' supported public institutions to private businesses and other non-governmental organizations, including the so-called faith-based organizations.

While privatization, disinvestment, and deregulation are the pillars of neo-liberalism, the state is not made entirely irrelevant. Radical conservatives like Grover Norquist may dream of cutting the government 'to the size where we can drown it in the bathtub', but neo-liberalism is not against government per se. After all, ardent neo-conservatives in the US have no problems with the massive subsidies defence and agricultural sectors get, nor have they been particularly exercised about the many wars their government continues to wage which take an enormous bite out of public finances. What the neo-liberals want, to use Aijaz Ahmad's pithy phrase, is 'a state that is weak in relation to labour but strong on behalf of capital'.

The state's topmost priority, under the regime of neo-liberal globalization, is to facilitate the smooth running of the markets. In order for governments to become enablers of markets, they come to embrace the interests of the markets as the interests of the citizens and the nation itself. In the neo-liberal vision, national economy should be run as a business and the focus should be on improving the bottom line. This managerial model of democracy has found many admirers in India. Chandrababu Naidu, the Andhra Pradesh chief minister who wanted to turn Hyderabad into Cyberabad, and Narendra Modi, the chief minister of Gujarat accused of engineering the massacres of 2002, both like to call themselves CEOs of their states. The actual record of these 'CEOs' has not been good for the poor. Chandrababu Naidu's regime aided by the World Bank, for example, slashed as 'wasteful' public investment in agriculture from 8.5 per cent in 1980s to 1.4 per cent in 2001 and agricultural output fell by nearly 17 per cent. The falling public investment, growing commercialization of agriculture, and indebtedness resulted in 16,770 farmers committing suicide in 1997–2005, the time period when neo-liberalism was the reigning ideology of the state government. The state also led the country in distress sale of kidneys, mostly by indebted farmers.

What is more, neo-liberalism changes the texture of democracy. If the government is to become more like a for-profit corporation, citizens become more like consumers. Their relationship with the representatives of the state changes from that of citizens to that of clients or consumers of government services. As consumers, they can demand better and more efficient delivery of services, but they cannot have much of a say in what services should take priority. The new buzzwords of neo-liberal governance are 'empowerment' through 'public–private partnership' to 'solve problems' and to make 'better choices'. This model of 'consumer-citizen' is what the World Bank, the International Monetary Fund, and other crusaders for globalization are promoting around the world. As in the marketplace where the better heeled customers get better services, so in the neo-liberal public sphere the better off and more educated 'customers-citizens' manage to get more choices, while bypassing the poor whose options actually shrink because they lack the cultural capital to be included in many middle-class neighbourhood associations and other civil society organizations. Recent evidence gathered by John Harriss shows that in India, participation in civil society institutions is heavily skewed towards those with higher incomes and higher levels of education.

To sum up this section, neo-liberalism changes the texture of the state and civil society: it brings them both under the sway of hyper-capitalism. It assumes that accumulation of private profit is the highest social good that governments ought to promote and that the benefits of the markets will trickle down to all people. Having clarified what the current wave of economic 'reforms' means, it is time to see their evolution in India.

India's Path to Neo-liberalism

How did India move from its days of Nehruvian socialism to where it is today? The year 1991 is seen by many as the watershed year in India's economic fortunes. That is the year when Rajiv Gandhi, Indira Gandhi's son and one-term prime minister (1984–89), was assassinated by a suicide bomber. That is also the year when the Congress-led government took the first steps to open up the Indian economy. Since then, the country has followed the neo-liberal mantra of the four Ds–'deflate, devalue, denationalize, and deregulate'.

Independent India's economic history can be divided up into three periods: the period of founding, from Independence in 1947 to the Emergency in 1975; the period of experimentation, from the election of the Janata Party government in 1977 to the assassination of Rajiv Gandhi and the beginning of economic reforms in 1991; and the period of liberalization, from 1992 onwards up to the present.

Phase I: The Founding, 1947–1975

The first period (1947–75) was the period dominated by Jawaharlal Nehru's ideal of a planned economy in which the public sector was entrusted with the task of making India economically self-reliant in industry as well as in agriculture, while ensuring equitable growth and welfare of all segments of society. The three major areas which Indian planners focused on were: building industrial infrastructure so as not to be reliant upon imports; creating institutions of higher education which could produce the scientific and technical workforce needed for the economic take-off; and bringing about land reforms that would redistribute land to sharecroppers and landless agricultural workers. Often characterized as 'socialist', Nehruvian policies were a far cry from the top-down socialism of the Soviet Union and China. The softer, Fabian socialism of Nehru was not meant to destroy capitalism but rather to enable its take-off while trying to bring about a modicum of welfare and justice.

Regardless of what the critics say in hindsight, Nehru's industrial policy was not imposed on a reluctant capitalist class against their wishes or interests, nor was it meant to squelch private enterprise. On the contrary, it had the full support of the dominant coalition of India's major industrial houses, big farmers, professionals, civil servants, and other 'white-collar' workers: they understood that only the state had the wherewithal to create the required infrastructure for the economy to take off. Given the enormity of the problems confronting it, the Indian economy grew only at a relatively low rate of 3.5 per cent in this period. But by the end of the second and third Five-Year Plans (1956–61 and 1961–66), the import substitution model had succeeded in laying the essential foundations of India's industrial structure.

Since it has become fashionable to heap scorn on Nehruvian socialists and advocates of planned economy, it is important to acknowledge their achievements, which were many. To list just some of them: by the early 1970s, India had achieved near-total self-sufficiency in the standard capital goods required by domestic industry; India produced its own machine tools, chemical equipment, mechanical machinery, heavy and other electrical equipment, basic metals, and alloys. It had its own steel and power plants while developing its all-important railway network, the most extensive in the world. These achievements laid the groundwork for all that was to come later.

Throughout this period, from India's Independence to his death in 1964, Nehru, India's first prime minister, remained at the helm. After the short-lived government of Lal Bahadur Shastri, Nehru's daughter Indira Gandhi became the prime minister twice, first from 1966 until 1977 and then again, after the Emergency, from 1980 until her assassination in 1984.

The first (i.e., pre-Emergency) administration of Indira Gandhi is remembered largely for her left-of-centre Ten-Point Programme which promised to eliminate poverty (*garibi hatao*). The programme enforced wide-ranging policy changes, including nationalization of banks and insurance companies, ceiling on urban property, restrictions on monopolies, public distribution of foodgrains, land reform, improvements in productivity of agriculture (the Green Revolution), and other pro-poor but top-heavy policies. The justification for imposing greater state controls over economic enterprises was to ensure that banks and other financial institutions made resources available to small urban and rural enterprises.

These programmes were hugely popular among the poor, but Indira Gandhi faced opposition from within her own party. Even though well intentioned, the increasing state controls on the economy created conditions for nepotism, corruption, and rent-seeking which largely benefited the middle-class bureaucrats and clerks. The Indian economy had already reached a level of maturity when private capital needed to take the lead which Indira Gandhi's top-heavy reforms did not allow. Moreover, the Indian economy had to confront the oil crisis and a severe drought in the early 1970s. On top of it all, in 1975, the Allahabad High Court found Mrs Gandhi guilty of election fraud. She responded to these multiple crises by imposing the infamous Emergency.

This, in brief, is what was going on the economic and political fronts in India during the first phase which lasted for about 25 years after Independence.

It is illuminating at this point to look at the right-wing opposition to Nehru's state-managed capitalism. One came from the Hindu nationalist parties, the other from the Swatantra (or Freedom) Party. Many of the ideas of the Swatantra Party are coming back, now that the Indian politics and economy have shifted to the right of the centre.

For the most of this period, Hindu nationalist organizations remained in the shadow cast by the murder of Mahatma Gandhi by one of their own: Nathuram Godse. Leaders of the Rashtriya Swayamsevak Sangh (RSS) and the Hindu Mahasabha, the two veteran Hindu nationalist organizations, moreover, preferred not to participate in electoral politics because they cast themselves in the role of cultural revolutionaries, concerned more with reinforcing the Hindu foundations of Indian culture than with winning elections.

While they did not directly get involved in economic debates, Hindu nationalist thinkers did manage to produce trenchant criticisms of the Nehruvian planned economy. They opposed the socialist spirit of the Indian economy from two angles: the first from the perspective of 'integral humanism' based upon the primacy of community, and the second from the perspective of a full-blown free market capitalism, based upon the primacy of the individual above all. Intriguingly, Hindu ideologues would claim to find support for both of these contradictory ideologies in the sacred teachings of Hinduism and Hindu spirituality! Both of these ideologies are making a big comeback, with many new publishing houses, think tanks and their corporate supporters pushing for free markets within the purported civilizational superiority of Hinduism and its ideals of integral society.

The philosophy of integral humanism was most clearly enunciated in 1965 by Deendayal Upadhyaya, the first general secretary of the Jan Sangh, the forerunner of today's Bharatiya Janata Party (BJP). Integral humanism, along with Hindutva, is still the official philosophy of the BJP and new members are required to swear an oath that they support this philosophy. While integral humanists attacked the commanding heights assigned to the state by the Congress socialists as alien and un-Hindu, they did not embrace free market capitalism either. What they recommended was a 'third way' which was neither socialist nor capitalist but 'dharmic', with a distinct Gandhian touch of swadeshi or self-reliance.

According to Upadhyaya, it is Hindu India's inherent, inborn nature–or *chitti*, to use the appropriate Sanskrit word —to integrate individuals into the organic whole, or the group mind. Once so integrated, individuals do not need control from some external power like the state, nor do they fall prey to the selfish instincts of capitalists, for they are capable of limiting and controlling their desires and demands in the interest of the national community. What India needed was the cultivation of dharma, creation of men and women who would learn to see themselves as limbs of the body politic made up of the family, caste, guild, and the nation. Just as there can be no conflict between the limb and the body, there could be no conflict of interest between individuals born in different castes and classes and the rest of the society. This was to be India's very own 'third way' which reached beyond socialism and capitalism, both of which were declared to be alien to the Hindu ethos. Economic policy in India, like all other aspects of social life, was to be infused with Hindu religious and moral values.

Slowly but surely, Hindu nationalists began to present this philosophy of integral humanism in the language borrowed from Gandhian socialism which celebrated swadeshi or self-reliance. Gandhi's conception of swadeshi shared the essential core of integral humanist argument that economic policies adopted for national development must be guided by the cultural values of the Indian people, which were supposed to be communitarian, non-materialistic, or spiritual. In practical terms, it meant exaltation of the local and the national over foreign imports, a preference for small-scale, village-based industry over modern industrial production and an opposition to state ownership and control of economic activity. While this vision resonated with the memories of the swadeshi campaigns during the freedom struggle when people were exhorted to burn imported products in the streets, it failed to have much influence after Independence. Economic and industrial policy in this phase continued to favour big, state controlled public enterprises.

But swadeshi was not the only argument against Nehru's state-heavy socialism. In the late 1950s through the 1960s, Nehruvian economics was also challenged by the Swatantra Party which adopted the classical liberal position in defence of free markets with minimal government controls. Since such well-known people like Narayana Murthy and Gurcharan Das are trying to revive the old Swatantra Party, it will be useful here to take a closer look at its historical record.

The Swatantra Party was founded in 1959 by C. Rajagopalachari, a veteran of the freedom struggle, a one-time associate of Gandhi (whose daughter married Gandhi's son) and an avowed social conservative. The core group was made up of K.M. Munshi, who had been active in Hindu religious and cultural affairs and who founded the Bharatiya Vidya Bhavan; the economist Minoo Masani, who was one of the founders of the Congress Socialist Party before he became an ardent anti-socialist; the industrialist Sir Homy Modi, a very anglicized Parsi; along with a number of senior civil servants who had served in high positions under the British. (Incidentally, Sita Ram Goel, the recently deceased founder of India's leading right-wing publishing house, Voice of India, and well known for his radical anti-Islamic and anti-Christian views, was a member of the Swatantra Party. We will examine Goel's legacy in Chapter 4.) The party's membership also included traditional power-wielders like big landlords, and members of provincial royal families who stood to lose their thrones to the new republic. For all their avowed liberalism, the party also made electoral alliances with distinctly illiberal and obscurantist groups like the Ram Rajya Parishad, the Hindu Mahasabha and the Jan Sangh. Nehru, the *bête noire* of the Swatantra Party, described it as belonging to 'the middle ages...the party of lords, castles, and zamindars which is becoming more and more fascist in outlook'.

What united this motley group of well-educated liberals, provincial rajas and ranis, and big landlords was their staunch opposition to a Soviet-style planned economy which they feared was being introduced into India by the Congress Party under Nehru. The Swatantra Party promised 'prosperity through freedom', and its 21-point manifesto declared its commitment to 'maximal freedom for the individual and minimal interference from the state'. In practical terms, 'minimal interference from the state' meant an opposition to land reforms, opposition to public sector involvement in industrial production, and support for lower taxes, low government spending, right to own property, and limits on the power of the government. In the political realm, the party stood for the Gandhian principle of trusteeship of the rich and the well born who were exhorted to use their privilege to serve the poor. All of this added up to a classical free market agenda, with the state reduced to the role of a night-watchman, with no role in redistribution of wealth.

By themselves, of course, there was nothing wrong with these classical liberal doctrines when the Swatantra Party first espoused them—just as there is nothing wrong with them now when they are being revived. What we have learnt from the failure of state socialist experiments around the world is that without some mechanism for responding to market signals, and without some checks and balances, public sector institutions have a habit of becoming inefficient, corrupt, and overbearing. At the same time, the case of the Swatantra Party clearly shows the limits of economic liberalism divorced from the social and cultural realities of India. Swatantra shows that liberalism can end up in bed with the worst kind of reactionary traditionalism when the very real problems of caste/class, inequality, and exploitation are resolved not in material terms, but in the realm of spiritual values of duty, harmony, and trusteeship.

Swatantra was accused of harbouring communal, and even fascist tendencies in its own time. Looking back at it today, some scholars describe Swatantra Party leaders as 'sympathetic to Hindu nationalist ideology and active in Hindu religious and cultural institutions'. But this is a misreading of what the party actually stood for. According to Howard Erdman, the author of the best-known study of the Swatantra Party to date, the leaders of the party were neither abjectly reactionary nor militantly nationalistic... [it is an] error to call it a 'communal' party for it made no appeal to any communal or parochial interest...It is conciliatory

30

towards Pakistan and its leaders have been solicitous of the interests of Muslims…Swatantra is steadfastly secular and is committed to the observance of constitutional procedures.

It is true that C. Rajagopalachari and K.M. Munshi were devout Hindus and they introduced prayers and discourses on the Vedas and Bhagwat Gita at political meetings. But this public display of religiosity was not shared by other members of the party, most of whom were secular minded and respected the principle of separation between public and private realms. They did not define the nation in religious terms, setting Hindus against Muslims, as Hindu nationalists are wont to. On top of it, they did not support the Gandhian economic agenda of promoting handicrafts and traditional technologies and instead stood for freedom of enterprise in the modernized industrial and agricultural sector. It is fair to call them 'moderate' (as Erdman does) in their social and political convictions.

And yet, Swatantra made political alliances with some of the most obscurantist and reactionary parties of its time, including the Ram Rajya Parishad, the Hindu Mahasabha, and the Jan Sangh. Why did the moderate liberals ally themselves with such obviously illiberal groups?

The key to this puzzle lies in the fact that while the Swatantra liberals—much like neo-liberals of today—poured their bile on the evils and inefficiencies of state intervention in the economy, they did not pay even a fraction of the same attention to the illiberalism and injustice that is taken for granted in our cultural traditions. Because of their single-minded obsession with opposing state-led socialism, Swatantra liberals, as Erdman correctly points out,

> did not speak out against the many suffocating influences of the old order, or against the dangers of freedom which lie on the right. Largely for this reason, the attacks on traditionalism

> which is implicit in the party's fundamental principles, is
> muted to the point of inaudibility…As long Swatantra attacks
> only the left, it will represent a drastically truncated form of
> liberalism.

Far from speaking out against the 'suffocating influences of the old order', Swatantra practically courted Hindu traditionalist parties seeped in the old order. Why? Again, the reasons are important to understand for the sake of illuminating our present predicaments with neo-liberalism.

As Swatantra members themselves realized, their great faith in the free market did not resonate with the masses, most of whom were desperately poor and welcomed the helping hand of the state they had elected. In order to win the masses to their side, without providing real solutions to the multiple inequities they were suffering from, the Swatantra Party had no other option but to wrap itself in religion and adopt a warmed-over Gandhian talk of trusteeship. Unable or unwilling to take on the religious sources of injustice in India, Swatantra tried to resolve these injustices at the spiritual level. They argued that the poor may be poor but traditional Hindu society honour their spirituality. Individual enterprise, freed from the supposedly tyrannical government controls, would be guided by their high spiritual values and use their wealth for the common good. This was the defence of liberalism with an Indian face that the Swatantra Party peddled. The fact that these same spiritual values had served as ideological cover for hierarchy and injustice did not bother these apologists of free enterprise.

To continue with the story, the Swatantra Party made electoral alliances with the Jan Sangh during the 1960s and ran on its free market platform without much success. If anything, its partnership with a party of rajas ended up giving the Jan Sangh the reputation of being a party of haves against the have-nots. Partly as the result of its experience with Swatantra, the current leadership of the Sangh Parivar has learnt the art of covering its pro-globalization agenda in the Gandhian language of swadeshi.

Incidentally, the new incarnation of the Swatantra Party, the brand new Liberal Party of India, established in 2005, is faced with some of the same ideological dilemmas that confronted its forerunner. The label 'moderate' fits the new party which wants to 'rid India of socialism and bigotry', as its website proudly proclaims. The new Swatantraites, like their predecessors, don't have any obvious animus against Pakistan, Islam, or Muslims, and nor have they made any communal appeals. Even though their writings often make references to Hindu sacred books like the *Manusmriti* and *Arthashastra* in order to explain and bless the Indian spirit of enterprise for private gain, it is fair to say that their commitment to neo-liberal market reforms is motivated by a non-communal outlook. Later in this chapter, we will ask if the new Swatantraites can avoid allying themselves with the religious right.

No discussion of ideological trends in this early phase can be complete without at least a mention of Subramaniam Swamy, a one-man squad championing free markets along with Hindu revival. A Harvard-educated economist, Swamy (b. 1939) first joined the Jan Sangh in the 1960s but later quit to form the Janata Party and now directs a New Delhi think tank called the Centre for National Renaissance and writes regular columns for *The Organiser,* the weekly newspaper of the RSS.

Swamy's agenda has been—and still is—to hitch economic development with Hindu revival. Like his fellow travellers, he too took the obligatory dive into the Bhagvat Gita and the Vedas. But unlike those who found the Hindu genius to be integralist, Swamy declared the 'Hindu ethos to be individualistic' and more hospitable to free markets and a minimalist state. The minimal state of Swamy's dreams, however, is not so minimal that it would not actively support Hindu revival: on the contrary he urged the Indian state to give up the 'Western nihilist' idea of secularism and actively promote Hindu culture as the source of national unity and pride.

Swamy's great plans for free markets along with Hindu renaissance did not go anywhere when he first proposed them in the late 1960s–early 1970s. But Swamy appears to be undergoing something of a renaissance himself. His new *Fundamentals of Indian Renaissance* published in 2005 tries to revive his failed *Agenda of Hindu Renaissance* which was reportedly dismissed by Indira Gandhi in 1969 as 'devised by a Santa Claus'.

For all the bombast, the economic philosophy of the right, both in integral humanist and the Swatantra garb, remained politically marginalized through this phase of the founding of the Indian republic. What ended the Nehruvian era of self-reliant and inclusive economic growth was a combination of its own successes and failures. It is to the slow unravelling of the Nehruvian programme that we now turn.

Phase II: Experimentation, 1977–1991

This period began with the election, in 1977, of the first non-Congress coalition party, the Janata Party. This was followed by the return of Indira Gandhi as prime minister in 1980 until her assassination in 1984. Rajiv Gandhi, Indira Gandhi's son, ascended to political power until his assassination in 1991. The mother–son duo set in motion many reforms which sought to undo the stringent regulations that had been put in place in the first phase by Mrs Gandhi's government.

By all accounts, the short-lived Janata Party government was quite inconsequential on matters of economic reforms and is remembered mostly for its inefficiency and corruption.

The Janata Party was a coalition of non-communist political parties opposed to Indira Gandhi and the Emergency. The coalition included the Bharatiya Jan Sangh, the forerunner of the BJP, along with a number of other parties which had been a part of the movement for 'total revolution' started by the veteran socialist turned Gandhian, Jayaprakash Narayan, or JP, as he was called. It was the first time that an openly Hindu nationalist party like the Jan Sangh had come to power at the Centre, albeit in a coalition.

The Janata Party shared the Gandhian and Hindu traditionalist outlook of the Jan Sangh. It sought to reverse the emphasis on big industry in favour of small, village-based industries and village councils (or panchayats). But all said and done, the real effect on industrial policy was rather minimal. The only added nuance was a greater emphasis on protecting urban small-scale producers and farmers.

The real burden of rationalizing and loosening some of the excessively rigid and constraining regulation was left to someone who was responsible for putting them there in the first place, namely, Indira Gandhi, and following her assassination, her son, Rajiv Gandhi.

In 1980, Indira Gandhi was swept back into power. It became clear even to her that the economy was under-performing and controls on the private sector had gone too far. Indira Gandhi announced a new Industrial Policy in July 1980 which carried forward the piecemeal retreat from the highly restrictive regime that she had herself put in place during her first (pre-Emergency) term in office. These reforms removed some restrictions on imports, allowed private industry to add more production capacity, and allowed firms to get bigger without the fear of anti-monopoly laws.

After Indira Gandhi's assassination in 1984, her son, Rajiv Gandhi, continued with the reforms. Unencumbered by the socialist or Gandhian thinking of the earlier generation,

35

and more accepting of modern conveniences like personal automobiles and colour TV, Rajiv Gandhi promised to launch India into the 21st century by developing modern technology and by promoting managerial efficiency and economic competitiveness. This won him the allegiance of the urban middle classes who wanted access to Western the style consumption patterns. This elite-led deregulation of the 1980s further loosened restraints on the private sector, liberalized imports of consumer goods, and gave tax breaks to consumers so that they could afford automobiles and colour TVs which were assembled out of imported components. The result was a consumption boom led by the durable goods sector whose expansion surged from 8 to 22 per cent a year through the 1980s. Overall growth rose to 5.6 per cent, well above the notorious 'Hindu rate of growth' of 3.5 per cent in the previous years. External debt and payment on the interest on the debt grew to three times its size over the 1980s, from $23.8 billion to $62.3 billion. But this import-led consumption boom was not matched by a corresponding rise of exports, a situation which led to a serious deficit of foreign currency reserves.

During an election rally in 1991, Rajiv Gandhi was assassinated by a Sri Lankan Tamil suicide bomber protesting India's intervention in Sri Lanka on behalf of the Sinhalese. The piecemeal reforms initiated by the two Gandhis set the stage for a full-blown embracing of neo-liberal reforms which were put in place by P. Narasimha Rao who became prime minister in June 1991 when the Congress Party won the sympathy vote after the murder of Rajiv Gandhi.

Phase III: Neo-liberalism, 1991 Onwards

The year 1991 is to India's neo-liberals what 1989 is to Soviet Bloc countries: it marks the end of the bad old days. Gurcharan

Das, India's most erudite neo-liberal, thinks of the 'golden summer of 1991' as 'India's second independence...an economic revolution...more important than the political revolution that Jawaharlal Nehru initiated in 1947'. The business lobbies, most of the mainstream media, free-market economists, and India's upwardly mobile urban middle classes have nothing but words of celebration and thanksgiving for the neo-liberal reforms that the Indian government initiated in 1991. Narasimha Rao, the Congress prime minister (1991–96), and Manmohan Singh, his finance minister (and India's current prime minister), are hailed as revolutionary heroes who put India on a fast track to wealth and glory.

The 1991 reforms were a response to the trade deficit and depletion of foreign exchange reserves created by the elite-led consumption boom of the previous decade. This was compounded by the Gulf War in 1990 which raised the price of oil. Bad economic tidings led to capital flight, with many non-resident Indians withdrawing their savings out of Indian banks. That is when India went for a strings-attached, IMF–World Bank loan.

This loan became the pretext for a total overhaul of the state–economy relationship. As a condition for the loan, India was told to get the government out of the business of owning and running economic enterprises, curb government subsidies, make its economy more market friendly, remove import restrictions, allow more foreign investment, and cut red tape—the standard conditions of IMF–World Bank loans.

But it would be wrong to see the reforms as some sort of neo-imperialist imposition on poor, hapless India. The situation was more complicated. The Indian industry and policymakers were not averse to these reforms. In fact, they welcomed them as the needed tonic that would release the animal spirit of money-making and entrepreneurship of Indians. According to the Columbia University economist

Arvind Panagariya, who was working for the World Bank at the time, although the necessity to borrow from the IMF and World Bank had subjected the initial liberalization package to the conditionality of these institutions, the proposed reforms were 'essentially domestic in origin and reflected the consensus that had emerged among the Indian policymakers. Contrary to the assertions by many, the influence of the IMF and the World Bank was confined to the first set of actions. After the World Bank's structural adjustment loan (SAL) of December 1991, the Government of India was back in the saddle.'

The fact is that starting with Rajiv Gandhi's experiments with liberalization in the 1980s, Indian industry was anxious to break free from the kind of inward-looking and state-managed economic path India had been following. It was keen to break into export markets where it needed partnership with multinational corporations. Indian businesses were also keen to enter newer areas of the economy like telecommunications, financial services, stock trading, and such. Thus the corporate sector of the country was practically itching to get rid of state regulations that prevented it from getting bigger and spreading into the global arena, alone or through foreign tie-ups.

Narasimha Rao and his finance minister, Manmohan Singh, an Oxbridge-educated economist, turned the IMF–World Bank conditionality into an opportunity for a complete makeover. Manmohan Singh teamed up with P. Chidambaram, a Harvard MBA, and Montek Singh Ahluwalia, a renowned Oxford-trained economist. The three of them went on a spree of deregulation, sometimes taking only hours to dismantle complex regulations that had taken years to formulate. Within a span of two years, they managed to loosen restrictions on monopolies; open the public sector institutions in banking, airlines, electric power, petroleum, cellular phones, etc. to the private sector; and open the country for foreign investment, allowing 'automatic entry' and majority ownership in 34 industries. To top it, they cut taxes on businesses and corporations; reduced excise duties; opened the capital markets to international investors; and allowed Indian companies to borrow and invest in foreign money markets.

All these reforms brought the Indian economy largely in conformity with the market fundamentalism of the IMF and the World Bank. All elements of the neo-liberal gospel – free trade, unfettered investments, deregulation, and privatization of publicly owned enterprises—were embraced by Indian policymakers. Even though they kept paying lip service to the old socialist rhetoric of 'development with a human face' inherited from the Nehru era, Indian policymakers began to buy into new mantras that markets are good and governments are bad, and that there is no alternative to global markets. As we shall see below, this rosy assumption that a rising tide lifts all boats is not true anywhere, least of all in India where barriers to class mobility are exceptionally difficult to surmount.

Despite the boost to the economy, the Congress lost the elections in 1996 and after a series of short-term governments, Atal Bihari Vajpayee of the BJP, the leading partner in the coalition government of the National Democratic Alliance (NDA), became the prime minister on October 13, 1999.

For all its allegiance to swadeshi and the integral-humanist 'third way', the BJP-led NDA enthusiastically carried forth the neo-liberal reforms set in motion by the Congress government in 1991. When out of power, the BJP had distinguished between 'internal liberalization' (i.e., privatization) which it supported and 'external liberalization' (i.e. globalization) which it opposed in the name of protecting Indian businesses from foreign competition. But once in power, it gave up on protectionism and opened up important sectors of the economy including consumer goods, electricity generation, IT-sector, and insurance industry, while liberalizing intellectual property laws. Perhaps most important of all, the BJP government took the lead in privatization of education at all levels, including colleges and universities. As we examine in more detail below, opening higher education to the private sector—including the religious sector—has created the infrastructure for a deeper Hinduization of civil society.

The government had starting selling public enterprises in 1991 in order to reduce fiscal deficit. But gradually, disinvestment took on a life of its own. The BJP-led NDA government declared that disinvestment was no longer a choice but an imperative, and established a full-fledged Ministry of Disinvestment with Arun Shourie, a well-known journalist and Hindutva sympathizer, in charge. Overall, the NDA government made it easier for bigger chunks of more and more sectors of the economy to be sold to private businesses, Indian or foreign. Except for nuclear power, defence, and railways, everything else was declared 'non-strategic' and therefore eligible for privatization. And yet, for all the claims of 'India shining', the NDA lost the 2004 elections. A coalition government (United Progressive Alliance) led by the Congress took control. The party chose Manmohan Singh, the architect of neo-liberalism, as the new prime minister. Under the UPA, the country has continued with the economic policies it embraced in 1991 with mixed results—higher GDP growth, deepening inequities, and sliding human development when measured by the United Nation's Human Development Index (down to 132nd in 2009 from an already pitiful 127th).

The 2009 general election came in the midst of a worldwide crisis of capitalism, the kind not seen since the Great

Depression of 1929. The Americans, who for so long were treated as consumers of last resort who would buy goods and services from the rest of the world, started to drown in debt. As a result, the housing market crashed, taking down major multinational investment houses and banks, all of whom had invested in the US mortgage market. The ripple effects are being felt all across the world: workers are being laid off everywhere as the global consumer demand declines, bank loans freeze up, and new investments are not forthcoming. Every tenet of the neo-liberal dogma—that unfettered markets are good and government regulation is bad, or that globalization is good and national priorities are bad—is now being questioned.

The Indian economy is hardly immune from the crisis. The recent economic data is grim. The country's gross domestic product fell to 5.3 per cent during the last quarter of 2008, down from 8.9 per cent in the same time period in 2007. The economy lost half a million jobs in the final four months of 2008. Export sector jobs—from traditional exports of garments, diamonds, gems and jewellery to the modern IT and financial sector—have suffered deeper cuts. But the non-exporting sectors—real estate, construction, automobile industry, for example—have not been spared. According to a recent *New York Times* report, the only industry that is showing signs of growth is the private security sector which is hiring close to a million employees to keep the riff-raff out of shopping malls, corporate office parks, apartment blocks, and even public transportation in India's urban areas. The already deep class distinctions are expected to get deeper still.

And yet, the Congress-led UPA won the 2009 elections: it appears that the electorate voted for stability and whatever little the government did for the *aam aadmi* (ordinary man). the UPA's victory is expected to hasten even more radical pro-market reforms. Neo-liberalism is here to stay.

Growing inequality

When sociologists of religion try to understand the changing patterns of religious faith in a society, they tend to concentrate on the socio-economic profile of the population. They assume that when people grow up in conditions where their survival is not secure, they tend to be more religious. It makes sense, therefore, for us to begin our enquiry into the changing nature of Hindu religiosity under neo-liberalism by first looking at the changing distribution of wealth. Some, or even most, readers may already be familiar with the data and analysis provided below. But it will be useful to start with a panoramic view of the political economy before we narrow our focus to take a fine-grained picture of the religious landscape.

Nearly a quarter century into the so-called reforms, there isn't much of a trickle-down of wealth, nor a pull-up of the poor through growth of gainful employment. If anything, the growing prosperity of the middle-and upper-income groups depends upon the growing impoverishment of the rest. In the words of Amit Bhaduri, a well-known Indian economist, 'growing inequality is driving growth, and growth is fueling further inequality'.

Consider the following two sets of evidence:

- India is rising in the Forbes global ranking of billionaires, while sliding in the United Nation's global ranking of human welfare. In 2008, there were 53 dollar-billionaires (that is, those with rupees equivalent of 1,000,000,000 US dollars) in India, up from 40 in 2007 and nine in 2004. India is home to more billionaires today than any other Asian country, more than China and Japan. Then there are the millionaires: the Merrill Lynch/Cap Gemini report says that India's population of millionaires grew by 20 per cent in 2007 to 100,000. That rate of growth was more than twice the growth of millionaires in the US. A substantial chunk of this wealth has already found its way into secret tax havens abroad. Recent reports have revealed that out of the $2.2 trillion secretly stowed away in Swiss banks, $1.45 trillion belongs to Indians. India tops the list of five countries (including Russia, Britain, Ukraine and China) with largest secret accounts in Swiss banks.

But at a time when great fortunes are being amassed, India is backsliding on the Human Development Index, or HDI, which measures well-being along three dimensions of health, education, and income. According to the figures compiled by veteran journalist P. Sainath, from an already pathetic rank of 124 (out of 177 nations) in 2000, India fell to 127 in 2001, 128 in 2007, and 132 in 2008. These are dismal numbers, which put India not among the club of superpowers where it wants to belong, but among some of the most impoverished countries in the world: at 128, India was just behind Equatorial Guinea (127), and just ahead of Solomon Islands (129). Incidentally, India ranks far worse than its closest competitors. According to the 2007 *Human Development Report*, Brazil stood at 70, Russia at 67, and China had an HDI of 81 (an amazing improvement from 99 in 2000).

• While there have been many surveys to track poverty in India, they have gotten mired in methodological debates. But, to quote from one of the most respected studies by Angus Deaton and Jean Dreze, 'the broad picture emerging…is one of sustained poverty decline in most states and also in India as a whole'. But it appears that the poor only move from being 'extremely poor' and 'poor' to joining the sea of hard-working poor who make up the unorganized sector of the economy. Although above the official poverty line, this segment of the Indian population —as many as 836 million men, women, and children in 2004–05 – lives on only Rs 20 (or half a US dollar) per day, and without even a semblance of a social security net.

There are built-in reasons why India's economic growth has not— and will not—trickle down any time soon. Most of the growth is taking place in the IT-enabled services sector which requires the kind of cultural capital—fluency in English, familiarity with Western businesses and cultural norms —that is not readily available to the masses. Manufacturing —the sector which has traditionally absorbed non-college-educated, unskilled workers and put them on the path to middle-class wages—makes up only 16 per cent of India's GDP. (Comparable figure for China is 35 per cent.) This sector is experiencing a relatively jobless growth due to growing automation and the recent economic downturn.

These figures tell only a part of the story. India has witnessed a massive land-grab by the private sector, aided and abetted by the state in the name of development—a process that has been dubbed 'developmental terrorism'. Using the power of eminent domain, the central and state governments have been buying agricultural and tribal land and literally giving it away to the corporate sector to set up factories, mines, special economic zones, private for-profit hospitals, colleges, and universities—and as we shall see in the following chapters, temples, ashrams, and 'research institutes' that propagate traditional 'science' of astrology, yoga, and Ayurveda. Regrettably, the Communists have been as complicit in this land-grab as the more pro-liberalization parties: Nano, the much-hyped, low-cost car was originally planned to be manufactured in a factory built upon 997 acres of fertile farmland that was practically gifted to the Tata Group by the Communist Government of West Bengal. Violent protests by peasants and their supporters forced Tata

Motors to move the plant to the sate of Gujarat. Dispossession of the poor has become a necessary factor in the creation of riches.

The poor in the countryside, in small towns, and in the slums of big cities suffer not only from direct dispossession but from neglect and cutbacks in public sector employment. With the public sector shedding jobs, and the organized corporate sector more or less closed to them for the lack of high-tech skills and cultural capital, the vast majority eke out a living in the unorganized, or informal, sector. Government's own data collected by the National Commission for Enterprises in the Unorganized Sector (NCEUS) shows that out of India's total labour force of over 458 million in 2005, 86 per cent, or 395 million, were in the unorganized sector, either self-employed (shopowners, street vendors, hawkers, craftsmen), or working for wages as casual labourers, domestic servants/housemaids, farmhands, etc. Most of the job growth sparked by globalization has taken place in this segment of non-unionized, informal workers both in the organized and unorganized sector of the economy.

This vast army of informal workers has no welfare floor below which they are not allowed to fall, and no exploitation ceiling beyond which they cannot be squeezed. Their relationship with the employers is regulated not by legal contracts but by traditions, enforced by religion and custom. Their labour is extracted by what Barbara Harriss-White calls 'compulsions of assetlessness, clientelage, beck-and-call contracts, debt-mediated labour attachment [or servitude], but also through the social structure of gender, religion, caste...'

In the informal economy, the adverse effects of neo-liberalism are felt in an inverse proportion to one's standing in the socio-economic order: those who are lowest in the scale are most badly hit. Two of the most vulnerable and large segments of the Indian population—Dalits and Muslims—are a case in point: as many as 88 per cent of Dalits and 84 per cent of Muslims make a living in the informal or unorganized sector. Even the government admits that 'they have remained poor at a bare subsistence level without any job or social security, working in the most miserable, unhygienic, and unliveable conditions throughout this period of high economic growth since the early nineties'.

Yet, influential voices are emerging that celebrate market reforms as liberating for Dalits. Chandra Bhan Prasad, a columnist for *The Pioneer,* has taken the lead in encouraging Dalits to join, rather than resist, the new market economy. In 2002, Prasad and like-minded intellectuals and activists brought out their manifesto for Dalit capitalism called the Bhopal Declaration. It called upon the government and the captains of industry to 'democratize capitalism' by enabling Dalits to enter the market economy. To that end, the Bhopal Declaration calls for a public–private partnership to provide new marketable education for Dalits and for American-style affirmative action in the corporate sector. Proponents of Dalit capitalism point to the rising levels of consumption and wages among Dalits as a result of the tightening of labour markets in some parts of the country as evidence that capitalism is breaking the back of the caste system.

There is only one problem with this vision: it is a fairy tale. In India, capitalism is not dissolving the existing caste relations but rather using them to maintain a vast army of workers who can literally be at the beck and call of employers for pathetically poor wages and without any social security. While there might be some local tightening of labour markets which may help Dalits and other backward castes to improve their bargaining power, the fact remains that 'being a "Scheduled Caste" makes a person twice as likely to be a casual labourer in agriculture, and poor'.

In many ways, Muslims in India are faring much worse than even the Dalits. They are largely self-employed—only 13 per cent of the entire Muslim population has salaried jobs in public or private enterprises, with barely 5 per cent of public sector jobs going to Muslims. The recent Sachar Committee report found that globalization has hit the Muslim workers harder than other communities. Many of the traditional occupations of Muslims in industries such as silk, weaving, leather, and garment making have been hurt by cheaper imports from China. There are industries like gem cutting and brass work which are experiencing large growth in exports, but the benefits are mostly going to the Hindu owners of these enterprises.

To sum up: the rising tide is not lifting all boats!

Privatization of Education

The sale of public sector institutions to private investors was justified, at least in part, by the promise that once the state gets out of the business of running hotels and making and selling bread, television sets, and telephones, it will have more resources for social services like education and health. But that is not what has happened. On the contrary, education, especially higher education, has become one more area which the state is disinvesting from, leaving the field open to private enterprise often in partnership with the state.

The per centage of GDP the government spends on education and health care has remained almost constant, or declined, even as the revenues have grown. The most recent budget (2008–09) clearly displayed the 'tax less, and spend even less', spirit of neo-liberal philosophy. Even as the revenues grew by 15 per cent over the previous year, the budget for elementary education went up by only 7 per cent, barely enough to keep pace with inflation and falling below the 6 per cent of GDP promised by the UPA government. Even while the government coffers are awash with money, spending on education has hovered between 3 and 4 per cent of the GDP, with only half of it going to primary and secondary schools.

The despair-driven, *de facto* privatization of primary schools is well-known and much written about. Public schools have fallen into such disrepair that even slum dwellers prefer to send their children (especially sons) to English medium private schools. Private, for-profit schools catering to the children of the very poor for a fee have sprung up all over the country, even in small towns and remote villages. Critics point out that rather than improve the dismal conditions of public schools, the government—with the complicity of the middle classes who have been quietly but steadily seceding from public services – has decided to let them rot to death. Even the Right to Education Bill of 2008 has accepted the reality that the right to education means a 'right' to unequal and inferior education. The ideal of creating a common school system is all but dead.

Higher education is the new frontier for privatization. Today, any registered society, a public trust, or a company registered under the Companies Act of 1956, can set up an educational institution and then either get the state to simply pass a bill declaring it a university, or get the educational bureaucracy (the University Grants Commission [UGC]) to 'deem' it a university. Once it gets the coveted status of a university, it can set its own standards for admissions and fees, decide the content of the courses, and choose its teaching methods. Above all, once deemed, a teaching shop gets the right to confer degrees—and make money through fees and 'donations'. In theory, of course, some minimum standards set by the UGC have to be met, but that is not much of an impediment, especially when it comes to injecting religion into the curricula. Under the previous BJP administration, the UGC had already approved BA-and even MA-and Ph.D.-level courses in subjects like Vedic astrology and had pushed for courses in vastu shastra and karmakanda. (Despite its promises to desaffronize education, the UPA government has not been able to put an end to these obscurantist courses, in part because in 2004 the Supreme Court gave the green light to teaching astrology in colleges and universities.)

Later in the book, we will provide evidence to show that privatization is not just turning higher education into a business; it is opening it to the business of God and god-men as well. The regulatory changes that are allowing private, for-profit teaching shops to enter higher education are also paving the way for religious endowments, ashrams, gurus to move into the business of conferring degrees in priestcraft and astrology, and otherwise setting up modern institutions with a traditionalist bent. But first it is important to get a better understanding of the larger picture. Consider the following statistics:

- In 2000, India had only 21 completely privately owned (i.e., unaided by government), not-for-profit institutions that had been 'deemed', or declared, to be universities. The number jumped to 70 in 2005, and to 117 in 2007. Nearly all the new universities created after 1998 have been privately owned. Even though many are registered as philanthropic trusts and get tax-breaks for their 'non-profit' status, in reality they are nothing more than teaching shops which charge exorbitant sums of money disguised as 'donations' for entry, especially into engineering, medical, and business schools.
- The total number of private colleges, including professional engineering and medical colleges, shot up from 5748 in 1990 to 16,865 in 2003, a net increase of 11,117 new colleges in about a decade.
- In 2003, 86.4 per cent new engineers were products of

private colleges, as compared to only 15 per cent in 1960. Likewise, the share of private medical colleges went up from 6.8 per cent in 1960 to 40.9 per cent in 2003.

- There is a push to allow foreign educational institutions to offer degrees either independently or through collaboration with any already established institution in the country. The bill that would have allowed foreign universities to set up campuses in the country was drafted in March 2007, but has been stalled due to political opposition. In the meantime, at least 130 foreign educational institutions, mostly from the US and the UK, have forged partnerships with local, mostly unaccredited, private institutions. Many of these are fly-by-night operations, offering degrees which are not recognized in the countries of origin.

In principle, there is nothing wrong with allowing private sector entities to set up institutions of higher education. After all, world-renowned universities like Harvard, Yale, Stanford, MIT, and the University of Chicago are private institutions. In principle, one could also argue that the private sector should step in to meet the enormous unmet demand for higher education that clearly exists in the country. Even though India has one of the largest number of colleges and universities in the world, they barely provide for about 10 per cent of college-age students. (In contrast, China enrolls nearly 20 per cent of college-age youth and in the US, more than 80 per cent attend college.)

The problem with this reasoning is that it ignores the ground realities of India. Those who argue for privatization accept the World Bank's orthodoxy that the government should concentrate on primary and secondary education —which was seen as equality enhancing—and leave college and university education to the private sector. In 1997, the Government of India accepted this logic and declared education beyond primary level a 'non-merit' good. It argued that subsidies for higher education were unfair and favoured the rich who should be made to pay for college degrees with their own money.

But it is simply not the case that the benefits of public sector subsidies for higher education, meagre though they have been, have accrued only to the rich. If it were not for government subsidies, the first generation of college graduates among women and discriminated castes and tribes that we find in India today would not be there. As Devesh Kapur and Pratap Bhanu Mehta have pointed out:

> There is absolutely no doubt that marginalized groups have been given much greater access to education as a result of government subsidies. The ratio of male to female students in higher education dropped form 8.29:1 in the 1950s to almost 1.5:1 by the late 1980s and is continuing to drop...parents are more likely to incur private expenditure for sons rather than daughters...Another point of evidence against the proposition that education subsidies go largely to the privileged is the increase in enrollment of India's most marginalized social groups, namely Scheduled Castes (SC) and Scheduled Tribes (ST): the ratio of general to SC/ST students in professional education has dropped from almost 12:1 in the late fifties to 8:1 during the late eighties.

Despite the facts on the ground, support for commercialization of higher education has continued to grow. Under the BJP- led NDA government, higher education was practically offered on a silver platter to India's corporate tycoons. The government invited Mukesh Ambani and Kumar Mangalam Birla, scions of India's leading business families, for advice on the education policy. With the larger aim of producing 'knowledge workers' of the 21st century rather than industrial workers of yesteryears, Ambani and Birla recommended deregulation and privatization of all education, except for the humanities, liberal arts, and performing arts. Government's role in higher education was reduced to insuring the student loan industry which would enable students to pay the asking price for their degrees.

Commercialization of education is backed by legal rulings. In its 2002 judgment in the *TMA Pai Foundation v. State of Karnataka*, the Supreme Court gave its blessings to for-profit private colleges and universities. In a creative interpretation of the constitutional right (Article 30) of minority religious and linguistic communities to set up their own educational institutions in accordance with their own norms and values without being denied grants from the state, the Supreme Court decided that private educational institutions must have the same rights. In addition, the courts redefined profits as 'reasonable surplus' and allowed private colleges to set their own fee and admission criteria.

Privatization does not mean an end to saffronization of education. Injection of Hindu traditionalism into apparently modern curricula takes place through the perfectly innocuous sounding objective of imparting 'value education'. The private sector is not at all averse to the idea of value education, even in tertiary level science and engineering colleges. If anything, 'blending' the best of Western knowledge with Bharatiya (read Hindu) values has become a part of their sales pitch.

While it looks harmless, value education has been the favoured vehicle of traditionalists of all political parties to inject an uncritical adulation of India's Hindu heritage into school curricula. The BJP-led NDA government rewrote the national curriculum in 2000 which was rightly criticized for saffronizing school education. But the new 2005 National Curriculum Framework crafted by the secular UPA government has also given its blessings to introducing all kinds of obscurantisms in the guise of respecting the 'local knowledge' and 'innate wisdom' that students bring with them into the classroom. Using a postmodernist argument that there is no one truth, but just so many different versions of knowledge, the new curriculum advises teachers to teach both local knowledge and scientific principles and let the students create their own meanings out of both systems. There is nothing to prevent spiritual or religious knowledge from being accommodated within the various possible versions of knowledge, and thereby surreptitiously bringing religion into school instruction. Privatization in the realm of political economy, and relativism in the realm of ideas seem to go well together.

Opening education to the private sector while relaxing oversight on course content has created conditions for Hinduization of higher education. The kind of Hindu-centrism of culture that the BJP-led government could not accomplish through legislative means is now being accomplished through privatization of education. (The next two chapters will provide evidence to support this claim.)

Superpower Swadeshi: Selling Globalization

In the face of the deepening inequity and the growing sense of insecurity, the natural question is how is this model made palatable to the masses? How are political parties trying to sell disinvestment, privatization, and globalization to the people whose approval, after all, they have to seek every five years or so in state and national elections?

The issue of public consent became important only after reforms moved from the elite phase when the debate was still among academics and policymakers, into the mass phase (from the mid 1990s onwards) when ordinary people began to feel the impact of liberalization. For most of the mass phase of liberalization, the BJP-led NDA government was at the helm (1998–2004), followed by the Congress led UPA government.

Both parties have gradually redefined the old Gandhian ideal of swadeshi or self-reliance to mean *whatever will make India powerful on the world stage.* Gradually one hears less and less of swadeshi, and more and more of superpower-dom.

The superpower talk began to be heard more frequently after the nuclear tests the BJP government carried out in 1998. The tests were interpreted as giving a huge boost to India's prestige on the world stage. According to Rob Jenkins, the BJP promised to replicate the same boost in prestige in the economic sphere as well:

> In BJP's vision…globalization became the site in which India will take up her rightful place in the international community; just as this has been accomplished in the global security field with the nuclear tests in 1998, so will India's IT expertise and business acumen allow India to thrive in the global economic field as well.

A representative example of the rhetoric of superpower swadeshi is the following statement from Jaswant Singh, the finance minister under the NDA government:

> Look at what is happening in the knowledge industry…we are reaching out the world and registering our presence through globalization. Today the Indian entrepreneur is celebrated. Look at Tata buying Daewoo. Reliance buying Flag. Research is moving out. Pharma is moving out. Indian companies are moving out and getting globalized. *This is swadeshi.* (Emphasis added)

By now, all parties use the promise of superpower status in their electoral pitches. Even the Swadeshi Jagran Manch, the Sangh Parivar's watchdog against foreign capital, has bought into this vision. S. Gurumurthy, the leader of the

Swadeshi Jagran Manch, for long a fiery critic of foreign multinationals, now supports 'calibrated globalization [as] the vehicle for acquiring global economic strength', while sitting on the board of directors of Indian First Foundation, a think tank that pushes for globalization from a Hindutva point of view.

But there is opposition to privatization and globalization from within the Hindutva ranks, especially from the labour union aligned with the RSS (Bharatiya Mazdoor Sangh [BMS]) and from small manufacturers who are not able to compete against cheaper imports (mostly from China). There is also considerable, and often violent, opposition to Western cultural imports (Valentine's Day celebrations, beauty pageants, and pubs, for example) by the more militant sections of the Sangh Parivar. The BJP tacitly supports those who commit these acts of vandalism, but at the same time, it takes pains to distance itself from them in public so as not to offend its growing constituency among the middle classes.

There are two other elements of ideological discourse which are more unapologetic in their defence of free markets. The first comes from those who share the communalist agenda of the Sangh Parivar, while supporting an individualistic interpretation of Hinduism. Prominent and influential among them include Subramaniam Swamy, a maverick politician-economist we encountered in an earlier section, and Arun Shourie, a well-known public figure who served as the disinvestment minister for the NDA. One can also include here Narendra Modi, the chief minister of Gujarat, who has become the darling of industrialists and businessmen from the world over. Those who share this orientation can be called Hindutva neo-liberals.

The second group is made up of those trying to stake out a secular (or at least non-Hindutva) right-wing party which would eschew the divisive anti-Muslim and anti-Christian agenda of the BJP and the RSS and popularize classical liberal positions on individual rights and freedoms, small government and religion–state separation—a sort of modern-day Swatantra Party. Those who share this orientation can be safely described as non-Hindutva neo-liberals.

Hindutva neo-liberals are the closest ideological cousins of American religious neo-conservatives—the so-called 'theocons' – who justify their fervent American nationalism and their ardent admiration of capitalism in a theological world view derived from the natural law tradition of Roman Catholicism. Unlike the mainline Protestant denominations who accept (at least in principle) the fundamental American creed of church-state separation, American theocons see the very idea of a secular society as an abomination and the primary source of the cultural pathologies of American society. Theocons, who have provided the philosophical justification for George W. Bush's so-called 'faith-based initiatives', insist that Christian faith is the precondition for the American nation and a prerequisite for the functioning of capitalist free markets.

The idea of Hinduism as the precondition for the Indian nation and a prerequisite for the proper functioning of Indian capitalism is the ideology of the Indian theocons, or Hindutva neo-liberals. The ideas of Subramaniam Swamy are illustrative of this position. When Swamy proposed the marriage of Hindu renaissance and *laissez-faire* capitalism in the 1970s, he was laughed off. But the same ideas, repackaged in various columns and blogs, are finding new audiences at home and among the NRI community abroad.

Swamy promises that India will become a global superpower by 2025 provided Indians develop the political will to dismantle all aspects of Nehruvian socialism and secularism, reduce the state to merely providing the infrastructure and the policies for private sector to flourish at the rate of 10 per cent GDP growth per year, and align their interests with the strategic interests of the US and Israel. But while necessary, all these economic and foreign policy reforms are not sufficient. What is needed is a 're-throning' of Sanskritic Hinduism in the hearts and minds of the masses (Muslims and Christians included), schools, government, and business enterprises of Hindustan (his preferred name for India). Economic superpower-dom will only come if it is accompanied with a Hindu renaissance:

> India becoming a global economic power is not enough. To get her due place in the world order, India must become thoroughly united with a virile mindset without self doubt and undergo a [Hindu] renaissance to cleanse the dirt and unwanted baggage acquired over the past thousand years.

Interestingly, while Swamy and his fellow Hindutva neo-liberals want the state to get out of the way of private enterprise, they want the state to use public resources to actively promote a renaissance of Hinduism. In other words, the state has to have a minimal role in economic affairs, but maximal role in propagation of Hinduism. The state is exhorted to teach the 'correct' reading of history which makes India the homeland of the Aryans and to bring science and Hindu spiritualism together in classrooms in order to promote an Indic model of education. All Indians, regardless of their own religious beliefs and traditions, are asked to accept this 'scientific spiritualism' as a part of their own ancestry. (Here again, the parallels with the religious right in the US are quite striking. Conservative Evangelical and Catholic groups have shown no compunctions in using the power of the Bush White House to enact socially conservative laws on matters of reproductive rights, stem cell research, and faith-based initiatives, while fully supporting the massive cutbacks in government support for public welfare.)

Let us turn now to the non-Hindutva neo-liberals. After their disappointment with the BJP's complicity in the anti-Muslim pogrom in Gujarat in 2002, many among the free market enthusiasts began to seriously think of reviving the old Swatantra Party. Two of India's biggest information technology tycoons have expressed their support for such a project. Jaithirth (Jerry) Rao, the founder CEO of Mphasis, a Bangalore-based IT and outsourcing firm, has been arguing for the creation of a new party on the lines of Swatantra that will not hide behind populist nostrums, but offer a *khullam-khulla* (open and unapologetic) defence of free markets. Narayana Murthy, the founder-CEO of Infosys, India's best-known software company, is reported to be 'willing to put up as much as four billion rupees of his own money' to revive the old Swatantra Party and run for elections on its platform. Gurcharan Das, who has emerged as a very influential voice among neo-liberals, has urged the formation of a new party that will:

> put economics above political matters, and trust markets rather than bureaucrats. It will do what no party has done so far—it will sell economic, social, and administrative reforms to the people...Finally it will work to confine religion to the private space, keeping it away from the public space.

The admirers of Swatantra are well aware that the chances of such a party actually winning elections are quite slim. That is why they seem to be ready to settle for the second best option—to start a movement which, in partnership with think tanks and NGOs, will take on the task of defending free market, pro-growth solutions in the public sphere. One can see the beginnings of such a movement in the emergence of think tanks like the Delhi-based Centre for Civil Society, the formation of *The Indian National Interest*, a consortium of bloggers which brings out a monthly magazine, *Pragati,* and the increasing visibility of neo-liberal positions in editorial and opinion pages of English language newspapers. Only time will tell what real impact these efforts will have on electoral politics in the country.

But the neo-Swatantraites seem to be making the same errors that led the old Swatantra into the arms of the Hindu right. Like their predecessors, neo-Swatantraites simply have only the mantra of trickle down to offer to those at the receiving end of the deeply entrenched inequalities in India. They, like their predecessors, concentrate their fire on the sins of government intervention while ignoring and soft-pedalling the religious sources of hierarchical ways of thinking that are deeply ingrained in Indian culture. Take, for example, their willingness to work with the BJP when it was in power before the BJP's complicity in what happened in Godhra finally disillusioned them. The BJP by no means, subscribes to the kind of philosophical liberalism based upon respect for the rights-bearing individual. The BJP's conception of a minimal state is premised on the fundamental correctness of a self-regulating caste society. While to their credit, neo-liberals have denounced the venomous communalism of the BJP and the Sangh Parivar, they have not taken the trouble to engage with the illiberal world view of integral humanism (which is the worldview of a caste society) which still constitutes the common sense of the Indian society. As long as Indian liberals do not actively challenge the illiberal world view of Hindu traditionalism, they run the risk of co-opting and getting co-opted by the Hindutva neo-liberals. Unless they actively take on the challenge of creating a new secular culture, their talk of confining religion to the public space will remain hollow.

Conclusion

This chapter is an overview of the political-economic context that India finds itself at the beginning of the 21st century. It traces the history of how the Indian elite stopped worrying about Nehru–Gandhi ideas of national self-reliance and came to love the global markets.

While fully acknowledging that the Indian economy needed reform of the excessively interventionist state, this chapter exposes the dark side of India's so-called economic miracle. It lays bare the structural features of the Indian economy which shut out the vast majority of workers from the gains of the new economy. It also looks at the growing commercialization of education, especially higher education, which is a key to acquiring the cultural capital needed to participate in the new economy. Last but hardly the least, this chapter highlights the growth of national pride which often expresses itself in dreams of superpower status.

It was crucial to dwell on this new political economy in order to understand better the changes that are going on in the religious landscape of India. It is to these changes in popular Hindu religiosity that we now turn.

2

The Rush Hour of the Gods: Globalization and Middle-class Religiosity

The world today is as furiously religious as it ever was...
Experiments with secularized religions have generally failed;
religious movements with beliefs and practices dripping with
reactionary supernaturalism have widely succeeded.

Peter Berger

Indians have never been, and will never be "other worldly".
Their spiritualism, though lofty in its metaphysics, is mostly a
means to harness divine support for power and pelf.

Pavan Varma

Those looking for evidence to back Peter Berger's verdict
cited above that 'the world today is as furiously religious
as it ever was...[and that] beliefs and practices dripping
with reactionary supernaturalism have widely succeeded',
can do no better than to take a closer look at the religious
landscape of India, the crouching tiger of the 21st century
global capitalism.

India today is teeming with millions of educated, relatively
well-to-do men and women who enthusiastically participate
in global networks of science and technology. The Indian
economy is betting its fortunes, at least in part, on advanced
research in biotechnology and te drug industry, whose
very existence is a testament to a thoroughly materialistic
understanding of the natural world. And yet, a vast majority
of these middle-class beneficiaries of modern science and
technology continue to believe in supernatural powers
supposedly embodied in idols, divine men and women,

stars and planets, rivers, trees, and sacred animals. By all indications, they treat supernatural beings and powers with utmost earnestness and reverence and go to great lengths to please them in the hope of achieving their desires. Hindus are not the only ones who are becoming more religious —data shows that all the many religious communities of India are showing signs of growing religiosity. But since this book is about Hindus who make up the majority, we will be looking mostly at how the expressions of Hindu religiosity are changing.

That a great many Indians of all religious faiths are taking their gods with them into the new economy is hardly surprising. In this, Indians are no different from people in other fast growing economies like Brazil, China, and Russia: all of these countries are experiencing an explosion of religiosity. Besides, there are industrially advanced countries like the US which have always been highly religious. Contrary to classical theories of secularization, scientific, technological, and economic development does not invariably lead to a decline of religiosity. (We will look at these theories of secularization in the last chapter of this book and see if they help us explain the Indian experience of juggling with religion as it modernizes.)

However, what is noteworthy about the new religiosity of middle-class Indians is how openly ritualistic, ostentatious, and nationalistic it is. Unlike the previous generations that grew up on a mixture of Nehruvian exhortations for cultivating scientific thinking and the neo-Vedantic preference for a more cerebral, philosophical Hinduism, the new Hindu elite and middle classes revel in ritualism, idolworship, fasts, pilgrimages, and other routines of popular, theistic Hinduism, sometimes mixed with new age spirituality. It is not that these more ritualistic expressions of popular Hinduism were entirely absent from the cultural milieu of the educated, middle to upper classes of the generations that came of age in the earlier, more 'socialist' and secular era. What has changed is that the ritualistic aspects have moved from the privacy of the home and family, to the public sphere, the domain of pride and prejudice, politics, and profits. What has also changed is that the educated elite don't feel that they have to defend their practices and beliefs against secularist finger-wagging (which has almost completely disappeared anyway). There is a new, unapologetic, and open embrace of religiosity in India today which wasn't there in, say, the first half of our sixty plus years as a republic.

Overall, it seems fair to say that economic prosperity is bringing with it a new 'rush hour of the gods' in India. The expression 'rush hour of the gods' was first used by H. Neill MacFarland back in 1967, in a book bearing this title, to describe the proliferation of new expressions of religiosity in Japan in the immediate aftermath of the Second World War. It was a time when 'new religions rose like mushrooms after a rainfall', attracting millions of Japanese who were left battered after the war. The term 'rush hour' was supposed to signify the 'frenetic quality' of the mass-based, media-savvy popular religious movements that promised fulfilment of worldly goals through spiritual means to ordinary people.

Today's India is obviously very different from post-war Japan. The Japanese rush hour, moreover, referred more to new religious cults rather than revival or reinvention of the traditional Shinto or Buddhist faith of the Japanese. Yet, one can legitimately speak of a rush hour of the gods in India, for the new religiosity displays that rather frenzied search for spiritual remedies for material concerns that characterized the Japanese case. Just like the Japanese religious movements were a response to turbulent and traumatic social change, the new Indian religiosity is in part a response to India's headlong rush into the global economy with all the attendant social and cultural dislocations. Moreover, the new middle-class religiosity in India bears distinct undercurrents of the kind of muscular cultural nationalism that the Japanese displayed before the Second World War that left them defeated, and in despair.

There is no doubt that growing religiosity is, at least in part, a response to new socio-psychological needs created by neo-liberalism and globalization. But this turn to gods and faith was not inevitable, or unavoidable. It is not an unalterable law that all societies undergoing rapid change have to become more religious, for there are societies (especially in Europe) that cope with change in relatively secular ways. Nor is it the case that Indians are innately more religious than any other people, for what often passes as religion in India is a cover for 'power and pelf', to use Pavan Varma's words cited above.

Far from being inevitable, public expressions of Hindu religiosity are growing because they are being facilitated by the Indian state and corporate interests, often in a close partnership. Despite the periodic panics about 'Hinduism in danger', and despite the often heard complaint that the Hindus face reverse discrimination in their own country, Hinduism is doing very well. The Indian state and its functionaries operate on the unstated assumption that Hinduism is not merely one religion among other religions of the Indian people, but rather the national ethos, or the way of life, that all Indians must learn to appreciate, if not actually live by. As a result, politicians and policymakers of all political persuasions think nothing of spending taxpayers' money and deploying public infrastructure for promoting Hinduism in the guise of promoting Indian culture at home and abroad. In recent years, direct state and corporate sponsorship of expressly religious elements of Hinduism (as opposed to artistic and cultural aspects) has become more blatant, as is evident from provision of public funding for yagnas, kathas, and yoga camps; matching grants for organizing religious festivals and pilgrimages; promotion of temple tourism and pilgrimage circuits; providing land and state-financed infrastructure for temples, ashrams and priest training schools; providing funds, physical infrastructure, and official credentials for training in Vedic astrology, vastu, and other elements of Hindu priestcraft; and in some states, even directly paying the salaries of temple priests. In addition, many of India's well-known family- owned business and industrial houses have a long history of contributing handsomely to building new temples and ashrams, and sponsoring religious events. In the absence of strong enough countervailing institutions and agencies that can offer secular alternatives to these well-funded initiatives, the public sphere in modern India has remained thoroughly intertwined with religious symbols and rituals of the majority religion.

We will unravel the workings of the state–temple–corporate partnership as we move along in this book. But this chapter has a rather modest aim: to describe the changing trends in popular everyday Hinduism. Too often these days, it is the radical religious-political or fundamentalist movements that get the bulk of attention, while the faith of ordinary believers who are not active participants of such movements remains unexamined. The chapter will try to fill the lacuna and focus on the religiosity of the emerging middle classes in India. Why the middle classes? They are the major beneficiaries of the neo-liberal reforms discussed in the previous chapter, and they are setting a new tone for the rest of the country when it comes to cultural trends and patterns of consumption. How their relationship with God and organized religion is changing as their socio-economic status is changing can tell us a great deal about the religious landscape of the rest of the country.

The Indian Middle Class: A Snapshot

Nearly a quarter century of neo-liberal economic policies have swelled the ranks—and bank balances—of a new middle class made up of white-collar workers in the new Internet enabled global service industry (IT business office processing [BOP]), banking, accounting, insurance, hotels, tourism, etc.) Although numerically still much smaller than the old or traditional middle class of shopkeepers, businessmen, government officials, teachers, journalists, and landowning farmers, the new middle class is much admired for putting India on the global map as an emerging world power.

In one sense, India does not have a middle class, new or old. It is simply misleading to call 200 million or so buyers of Western-style consumer durables 'middle class' because they do not represent the statistical middle of the population. They are instead what Achin Vanaik calls 'an elite of mass proportion'—the top 20–30 per cent of the population surrounded by a sea of utter poverty.

How big is this so-called middle class? Estimates vary. But the two most cited surveys put the numbers anywhere between 60 million and 300 million. According to the Indian National Council of Applied Economic Research (NCAER), the term 'middle class' applies to those earning between Rs 200,000 and Rs 1,000,000 annually. By this definition, about 6 per cent of 1 billion Indians—about 60 million people—were middle class in the year 2000–01, while close to 22 per cent 'aspiring classes' were expected to catch up in a decade or so. But if middle class-ness is measured by ownership of middle-class goods—telephones, motor vehicles (cars or two-wheelers), and colour TV—close to one-fifth of India was already middle class in 2007, as the State of the Nation Survey by CNN-IBN revealed.

Over and above income and assets, class is a matter of taste and style. The new Indian middle classes hold Europe, the US

States, Japan, and Australia as the benchmark for their taste in consumer goods and fashions. The very wealthy and the upper middle classes already have access to these lifestyles, while the lower middle classes aspire to get there. The older, more traditional segment of the middle classes, made up of government bureaucrats, public sector employees, family businesses, landed elite, on the other hand, is somewhat more ambivalent about Western fashions.

In matters of political beliefs and cultural values, the middle classes have decidedly said 'No' to the socialist and rationalist elements of the Nehruvian legacy. But they have yet to formulate an alternative vision of a good society. The result is a somewhat confused and contradictory mishmash of professed ideals and actual values and deeds.

Going by the recent Pew Global Attitudes Survey, the new middle class in India is overwhelmingly pro free market: a solid 89 per cent of Indian respondents supported free trade, 73 per cent welcomed foreign companies, and a solid 76 per cent were in favour of free markets 'even though some people are rich and some are poor'. (Comparable figures for the US, the bastion of unrestrained capitalism, are 59, 45, and 70 per cent respectively.)

These pro-market views, however, are not matched by a strong sense of citizenship and social responsibility. The idea that their own prosperity is linked to the well-being of the rest of society is accepted in theory, but belied in practice every day. Indian elite and middle classes display an exceptionally high degree of tolerance for the inhuman levels of poverty and deprivation all around them, a trait that could well derive from the Hindu conception of karmic justice and the individualistic conception of salvation or moksha in Hinduism. To be sure, when asked, an overwhelming proportion—92 per cent in the Pew poll—say they want the state to step in and help the poor. But in reality, Indian upper and middle classes have always preferred privatized services in schools, hospitals, transportation, garbage collection, and, down the list, over public goods that the poor can also benefit from. Economists have shown that one sign of the overall apathy towards public goods is the relatively low contribution taxes made towards the total government revenue in India, even when compared to poorer neighbours like Pakistan and Sri Lanka. As Chakravarti Ram-Prasad observed recently:

> [The haves in India]...do not, on the whole, extend a sense of solidarity to the poor; they often do not acknowledge the role of the state in their own rise or its capacity to solve any of the country's problems; and they are in general, politically apathetic.

The irony is that the majority of the fresh entrants to the new economy—software engineers, doctors, biologists, MBAs, and others—owe their success in large part to the highly subsidized higher education made available by the same Nehruvian public sector undertakings that they now condemn. The new rich, in other words, are perfectly willing to kick the ladder they have clambered up on to get to where they are.

The new middle classes are ready to jettison another plank of the Nehruvian project—namely, secularism. An overwhelming majority—92 per cent in the Pew Global Attitudes survey mentioned earlier—claims that religion is very important to them. What is more, an overwhelming majority (90 per cent) claim that they want to keep God out of government. But their actions do not match their words: secularism as separation of state and the temple has never had much currency in India. The educated and privileged segments of Indian society have never shown even the faintest sign of resistance to the close involvement of elected leaders and government functionaries, *in their official capacity*, sponsoring and celebrating religious rituals in public. There is no sign of public protest against using government funds to support denominational schools, pilgrimages, yoga camps, yagnas, and kathas. The only time anyone gets agitated about state support for religion is when the religion in question is someone else's religion, especially the supposedly 'non-Indian' religions like Islam and Christianity. The many direct and indirect subsidies to the faith of the majority are accepted—and expected—as business-as-usual. Given its comfort with open expressions of Hinduism in the public sphere, it is not surprising that the middle-class share of votes for the BJP and its NDA allies has been growing through the 1990s, while its support for the Congress has been declining. Analysis of election data shows that both in 1998 and in 1999, the combined middle-class vote received by the BJP and its allies was more than what the Congress received from the same class.

Another cultural trait of Indian middle classes that is relevant to understanding their religiosity is their view of modernity and science. By and large, Indian middle classes see themselves as modern in the sense of having seen through and rejected blind faith. In this milieu, you are expected to at least appear to be scientifically correct, and reject the superstitions of the unlettered and the mumbo-jumbo of priests. But the scientific correctness of the new middle classes turns out to be the exact opposite of what the advocates of rationalism —or 'scientific temper' as it is called in India—have in mind. Rather than cultivate a habit of critical thinking which subjects metaphysical assumptions of inherited traditions to a scientific challenge, educated Indians have shown a huge appetite for the pseudo-scientism being taught by neo-Hindu philosophers, modern gurus, and the peddlers of new age spiritualism. All the metaphysical concepts of traditional Hinduism—the existence of an all-pervasive, disembodied consciousness variously called atman, shakti, or prana; survival of the soul after death; reincarnation of the eternal soul in a new body; the existence of humours and innate essences in nature, or gunas; efficacy of yagnas in aligning human affairs with laws of nature; correspondences between the macrocosm (stars, planets, metals, directions, etc.), and the microcosm of human life—are accepted *as if* they are backed by scientific evidence. This kind of Vedic/Hindu scientism seems to have a wide appeal for those who consider themselves to be educated and modern.

Re-ritualization of the 'Great Tradition'

The available survey data supports the general impression that globalization is proving to be good for the gods in India.

- According to the 2007 State of the Nation Survey conducted by the Centre for the Study of Developing Societies (CSDS) for IBN-CNN–*Hindustan Times*, 'Among Indians, the level of religiosity has gone up considerably during the last five years. While 30 per cent said they had become more religious during the last five years, only 5 per cent mentioned in negative.'
- The same survey poll also found that education and exposure to modern urban life seems to make Indians *more,* not less religious: 'urban educated Indians are more religious than their rural and illiterate counterparts... religiosity has increased more in small towns and cities than in villages.'
- Hindus are not the only ones becoming more religious. The 2007 State of the Nation Survey shows that 38 per cent of Indian Muslims, 47 per cent of Christians, and 33 per cent of Sikhs, as compared to 27 per cent Hindus, claim to have become more religious in the last five years.
- Based upon the National Election Survey of 2004, the CSDS

team reported the following: 'We asked our respondents if their involvement with religious activity had increased in terms of attending religious functions, regular participation in prayers, temple going, etc. Over one-third respondents said that religiosity had increased among their family members…Among the educated, particularly among those educated above secondary level, the proportion of highly religious is higher. Among upper castes (27 per cent) and peasant proprietary castes (25 per cent) the highly religious are in high proportions (24 per cent). Both among Hindus and Muslims, the upper class persons are more religious than the poor (26 per cent Muslim rich and 25 per cent Hindu rich are highly religious.) So religiosity may be a pastime of the high and the rich!'

- The number of registered religious buildings in Delhi grew from a mere 560 in 1980 to 2000 in 1987, with similar trends reported from other parts of the country.
- In his much-acclaimed book, *Being Indian* (2004), Pavan Varma reports that around the turn of the millennium, the country had 2.5 million places of worship, but only 1.5 million schools and barely 75,000 hospitals. He bases this observation on the data from the 2001 census.
- Another measurable indicator of rising religiosity is the tremendous rise in pilgrimages. According to a recent study by the NCAER, 'religious trips account for more 50 per cent of all package tours, much higher than leisure tour packages at 28 per cent'. The most recent figures show that in 2004, more than 23 million people visited the Balaji temple at Tirupati, while 17.25 million trekked to the mountain shrine of Vaishno Devi.

The phenomenon of rising religiosity in times of rapid technological modernization and economic growth is neither particularly new nor uniquely Indian: religions everywhere learn to adapt to, and coexist with, the infrastructure of modernity. But Indians are well known for being harmonious schizophrenics who live in many different worlds at the same time. Most educated Indians seem to switch effortlessly from the profane to the sacred, from the lab to the temple and back, without being troubled by the contradictions between the operative beliefs in the two spheres. As a scientist from the Indian Institute of Science described the situation some years ago, 'many of us are double people. As scientists we are rational. But when we leave the laboratory and go home, we behave differently.'

This is the phenomenon of compartmentalization made famous in the Indian context by Milton Singer in his influential 1972 book, *When a Great Tradition Modernizes*. Singer admired the country's unique 'cultural metabolism' that allowed Indians to keep religion and science / industry in two separate boxes, each with its own norms and its own objectives. Indians are supposed to be exceptionally good at compartmentalizing, thanks to what Alan Roland calls their 'radar sensibility' which makes them extraordinarily sensitive to what is expected of them in different contexts. Growing up in a society where different jatis have their own gods and their own cultural norms, the Indian way of thinking is supposed to be far more context sensitive and attuned to the particulars of any given situation than the universalizing tendencies of Judaeo-Christian religions and modern science. For many educated Indians, science classrooms and laboratories make up just one more particular context with its own peculiar rules and assumptions, which is supposed to coexist with other contexts with their equally valid rules and assumptions. Singer and his generation of India watchers were awestruck by modern Indians' ability to take whatever they liked from the modern scientific world, and retrofit it into their 'Great Tradition', without disturbing the latter's core axioms. Compartmentalization, followed by selective hybridization, was the key to India's 'modernization without secularization'—a development that Singer and other self-identified 'critical traditionalists' greatly admired.

So this phenomenon of keeping modern ideas and religious traditions in two separate compartments and mixing them as and when needed to basically validate and uphold the superiority of tradition is not new. What is new is how the contents of the compartment marked the 'Great Tradition' of Hinduism are being re-ritualized and re-enchanted.

The earlier generation of Indian elites was keen on redefining the essence of Hinduism in neo-Vedantic terms which de-emphasized rituals and temple worship in favour of a 'rational' mysticism centred on philosophical reflection and meditative contemplation of the impersonal Brahman. The rituals, the pujas, the pilgrimages, etc., were mostly left for the domestic sphere of wives and daughters and generally reduced in the time and energy they demanded. In Singer's words:

> [the captains of industry in Madras circa 1960 tended to]... downgrade the ritual observations, with a concurrent upgrading of devotional faith and a reformulation of philosophical and ethical tenets [of karma, dharma, and moksha]... for them, the 'essentials of Hinduism' consist in a set of beliefs and a code of ethical conduct than in a set of ritual observances...

This tendency to downgrade the popular, or *laukik*, in favour of the scriptural, or *shastric*, is a legacy of the Hindu renaissance that started in the 18th century but continued well into the 20th. Encouraged by the British and German Orientalists' discovery and translations of the Rig Veda, the Upanishads, the Bhagvat Gita, and other Sanskrit texts, Hindu reformers began to use the scriptural texts as the standard for judging the worth and validity of folk rituals and beliefs. In addition, spiritualist currents in the West served as inspiration for neo-Hindu thinkers and reformers like Swami Vivekananda who declared yoga and meditation as the essence of Hinduism. Finally, there were the powerful voices of secular humanists and rationalists like Jawaharlal Nehru, B.R. Ambedkar, Periyar, M.N. Roy, Bhagat Singh, and others who called for a critical stance towards supernaturalism and mystical knowledge.

This de-ritualized, slimmed-down, philosophized, or secular-humanist version of Hinduism that appealed to the earlier generation of elites does not seem to satisfy the religious cravings of contemporary middle and upper classes. They are instead looking for jagrit (or awake) gods who respond to their prayers and who fulfil their wishes —the kind of gods who are personal, caring, and loving. The textual or philosophical aspects of Sanskritic Hinduism have by no means diminished in cultural prestige: they continue to serve as the backdrop of 'Vedic sciences' and new age spiritualism, and continue to attract a loyal following of spiritual seekers from India and abroad. But what is changing is simply that it is becoming fashionable to be religious in the theistic (saguna bhakti) tradition of popular Hinduism and to be seen as being religious in this manner. The new elites are shedding their earlier reticence about openly participating in religious rituals in temples and in public ceremonies like kathas, jagratas, and yagnas. If anything, the ritual dimension is becoming more public and more ostentatious.

India is simply too vast, varied, and complex for any one author, however industrious, to provide an exhaustive survey of changing religious practices all over the country. But the representative examples provided below will show a complex religious landscape where new rituals and even new gods are being invented, old gods are getting a facelift, and new gurus are mixing up spiritualism with capitalism, consumerism, and often with blatant Hindu chauvinism.

Invention of Traditions

All societies have traditions, a set of myths, symbols, and practices passed down from generation to generation, which provide a certain degree of comfort that comes from familiarity. Societies undergoing rapid change, however, do not have the luxury of enjoying the psychological comfort that real traditions can provide because the social patterns for which the tradition made sense no longer exist. These societies end up inventing 'traditions', quite like museum shops manufacture 'antiques'. Invented traditions are new symbols and rituals grafted on to the old ones, or are crafted afresh out of the store of ancient materials stored in the cultural memory of a society. But what is unique about all invented traditions, according to Eric Hobsbawm and Terence Ranger, is that not only the symbols and the rituals have to be invented afresh, but a 'historic continuity has to be invented' for them. In order to function as traditions, the invented symbols and practices have to establish a lineage with the older tradition. Something like this seems to be happening in the creation of new gods and new religious rituals in India today.

Christopher Fuller's 2003 monograph, *Renewal of Priesthood*, is a good place to start our investigation of how temples are inventing new traditions to cater to the worshippers with a growing disposable income.

Fuller describes the installation of 'golden cars' in the famous Meenakshi temple in Madurai which the devotees can rent—for a fairly hefty fee—for ceremonial processions in the temple. These 'cars' are gold-and-silver plated chariot-like structures in which the idol of the goddess Meenakshi is taken around the temple perimeter in a procession led by priests, musicians, elephants, etc., all expenses paid for by the sponsoring party. The golden car at the Meenakshi temple has been a great hit: it used to be sponsored on alternate days in 1994–95, but by 2001 it was being taken out in a procession every day. The state government's latest figures show that twenty five temples across the state have installed golden cars and ten more are working on it.

Two other invented rituals are drawing huge crowds. The first involves re-enactment of the divine Meenakshi–Sundareshwara wedding. At the fabled Meenakshi temple in Madurai, devotees can sponsor, for a fee, a re-enactment of the wedding of the goddess Meenakshi with Sundareshwara, a form of Lord Shiva. They can, for an additional fee, also worship the newly installed image of another god, Kalyanasundara. For yet another fee, devotees can also buy the privilege of placing a diamond crown and golden body plates on the idol of Meenakshi. These rituals largely attract women devotees, for they are supposed to help young women find husbands. These newly invented rituals were being requested at least ten times per month in 1994–95. Five years later, the wedding ritual had become so popular that two or three parties had to share one ritual by co-sponsoring it.

There was some concern among politicians and temple priests that these pay-for-prayer schemes might turn off the faithful and cause resentment among those who cannot afford them. But these schemes—especially the golden cars, the wedding re-enactment, and the placing of the diamond crown—have been hugely popular perhaps because they provide the better-offs with new opportunities to distinguish themselves from the less fortunate through more splendid and more ostentatious expression of devotion. The exclusivity of the new rituals apparently adds to their attraction.

In Tamil Nadu—a state for which such data exists—the demand for Sanskrit-and English-speaking priests with expertise in Agamic rituals, preferably with a degree from priest training schools, is outstripping the supply. This is a fairly good indicator of rising religiosity. Starting around 1980, temple priests began to be hired for performing Ganpati homa rituals for homes, shops, and other workplaces, including ultra-modern industries that are opening up in the state of Tamil Nadu. Ganpati homa consists of worship of Ganesh, together with a fire sacrifice carried out by a group of priests and chanters. The service lasts a couple of hours and is generally performed on an astrologically auspicious day and time. Other popular rituals include homas for Lakshmi, the goddess of wealth. Astrologers often recommend the so-called navagraha homa to propitiate the malevolent Saturn, providing more work for the priests.

Another ritual that is gaining ground among politicians and businesses is the elaborate religious ceremony of kumbhabhisheka (or consecration) for temple renovations. Political parties compete against each other to fund temple renovations, while business houses make generous contributions. Jayalalitha, who served as the chief minister of Tamil Nadu from 1991 to 1996 and again from 2001 until 2006, took credit for personally raising millions of rupees for renovating hundreds of temples. Jayalalitha ran the state as if Brahminical Hinduism was the official religion of the state.

This practice of elected government officials participating in worship ceremonies for consecration of new temples is not limited to Tamil Nadu but takes place all over the country. It is commonplace for elected officials, from presidents and prime ministers to the members of state legislative assemblies, to participate in religious ceremonies for consecration of temples, birthdays of gurus, and other special occasions of religious significance. Without consciously intending to, secular India's elected rulers seem to be re-enacting the pre-modern Hindu political system in which it was the duty of the king to sponsor temples and protect dharma.

All temple building and kumbhabhishekas are not political, however. Joanne Punzo Waghorne describes a great surge of consecrations of new temples in the middle-class colonies of Chennai. Temples have become sites for 'educated people, intellectual people, to retain the old values', as a devotee explained to Waghorne. This attachment to tradition, however, does not rule out innovation within it. Waghorne describes the installation ceremony of a unique idol in the Madhya Kailash temple in Adyar, an affluent colony close to the campus of the Indian Institute of Technology in Chennai and patronized by the faculty, staff, and students. The idol represents a brand new hybrid god, half Ganesha, with his familiar elephant head, and half Hanuman, with his familiar ape-like features. The consecration ritual was equally innovative: unlike the traditional ceremony, the devotees consecrated the idol themselves without the help of the priests. The devotees saw it as an affirmation of democracy and equality.

At a more trivial level, many old religious observances are finding new, more modern, and consumerist uses. For example, Akshay Trithiya, a day in early May considered astrologically auspicious for marriages and other new ventures, is now being celebrated as auspicious for buying gold. Traditionally, Akshay Trithiya was linked to child marriages. Even today, in many villages and small towns, young boys and girls are married off on this day because the alignment of the sun and the moon is supposed to bring exceptionally good karma for the parents. Among the more educated and urban people, however, the presumed auspiciousness of this day is getting a corporate makeover: The World Gold Council has declared Akshay Trithiya as auspicious for buying gold coins and ornaments. Thanks to relentless advertisement and special sales, phenomenal amounts of gold is bought and sold on this day every year. According to media reports, in the year 2006–07, 'a very conservative estimate' puts gold purchases on that day at 38 tons, compared with a daily average sale of 2 tons. Thus, the world view that reads human significance in the stars is not only surviving, it is finding new uses for the era of hyper-consumerism that is dawning on India.

And then there is the growing popularity of redesigned fire sacrifices, yagnas, or homas. A simply domestic homa or yagna was made the centrepiece of religious ceremony by the Arya Samaj in the nineteenth century. Over the last two decades or so, yagnas have become fashionable in a wide variety of religious organizations, selling everything from 'scientific spirituality' to prayers for rains and protection from diseases. Not surprisingly, politicians and political parties have caught on and these 'ancient' Vedic ceremonies have become political spectacles for electioneering or, worse, communal agitations.

The growing popularity of public-political yagnas is not really a revival, because they have always been a part of modern India's public sphere. There are newspaper accounts of spectacular Vedic yagnas with 'thousands of pandits reciting millions of Vedic mantras for weeks and weeks' in February 1962 when the country was in a panic over astagraha, a particular conjunction of earth, sun, moon, and five planets. In 1970, there were even reports of the Jan Sangh (the predecessor of the BJP) organizing a Vedic sacrifice with the intent of killing Indira Gandhi through spells. But it turned out that the priest who was hired to carry out his deadly yagna himself died through electrocution while performing the ritual! Even though public yagnas are not entirely new, they have definitely become far more frequent, popular, and politicized.

A case in point is the worldwide popularity of the Gayatri Parivar, a Haridwar-based organization which teaches 'scientific spirituality' through the recitation of the Gayatri mantra, accompanied by collective performance of yagnas, often on a truly massive scale involving many thousands making oblations to 1008 fires simultaneously. Started by Shriram Sharma in 1953 and now headed by his son-in-law, Pranav Pandya, a medical doctor, the Parivar now runs a research institute and a deemed university in Haridwar, meditation and research centres in Mathura and Noida, and has branches in the US, Britain, Australia, and New Zealand and claims more than 70 million members worldwide. The members are largely professionals like doctors, engineers, lawyers, and corporate CEOs in India and abroad.

The crafty genius of the Gayatri Parivar lies in redesigning ancient Vedic mantras and rituals—like the famous asvwamedha yagna—for the twenty first century by smuggling in scientific-sounding language. Take, for example, the Parivar's definition of yagna—which it calls 'yagyopathy'—reproduced here from its website:

> Yagna, a scientific method aimed at the finest utilization of the subtle properties of sacrificed matter with the help of thermal energy of fire and the sonic vibrations of the mantras...Slow combustion, sublimation and most prominently, transformation into vapour phase of the sacrificed herbal and plant medicinal and nutritious substances takes place in the yagya-fire. Inhalation therapy and environmental purification are the paramount applications of yagna apart from the enormous sublime impact and auspicious spiritual effects called with reverence in the Shastric literature.

In other words, yagnas are really about vaporizing and inhaling the beneficial chemicals from the burnt offerings.

Similarly, the Gayatri mantra's 'astonishing power' becomes a matter of 'sonic vibrations' and 'energy-fields in the subtle sphere'. As Dr Pranav Pandya, the spiritual head of the Gayatri Parivar explains, the Gayatri mantra is supposed to have supernatural properties because the 'ultrasonic wave patterns' of the 24 syllables of the mantra are supposed to 'positively affect the subtle centres of human body'. What is more, just reciting the mantra is supposed to connect you to the 'energy field' created by millions upon millions of pious people who have been chanting this mantra since Vedic times.

The Gayatri Parivar has made this energy-based metaphysic concrete in its very popular, horse-free recreation of the famous horse sacrifice or asvamedha yagna. In its unique and original interpretation of this ancient and rather gory ritual in which a sanctified horse was killed, the Gayatri Parivar has declared that the asva, or horse, in asvamedha actually means 'demon animals of evil tendencies' within your heart and soul which the yagna, accompanied by chants of the Gayatri mantra, is supposed to tame. This novel interpretation is combined with another rather democratic innovation: as many as 1008 yagna fires are burned simultaneously and hundreds and thousands of people, regardless of caste and class, are invited to pour ghee, herbs, grains, and other sanctified material into the fires while chanting the Gayatri mantra. Considering that the Gayatri mantra was meant to be imparted only to the twice-born boys at the time of the upanayana (initiation) ceremony, using it on a mass scale without consideration of caste and gender is undoubtedly democratic in its spirit. While the yagna is going on, priests are at hand for performing life-cycle rituals like namkaran (naming ceremony) and even marriages. The collective chanting and vaporizing of ghee, herbs, and grains is supposed to release massive amounts of 'spiritual energy' which gets stored in the 'energy field' that can be accessed by others later.

These mass yagnas are spreading from the north into the rest of the country. The temple town of Tirupati hosted an asvamedha, as did the state of West Bengal. The Gayatri Parivar's centrepiece, the asvamedha, is also spreading into other countries with significant NRI communities: the yagna has been performed in Chicago and Los Angeles in the US, and more recently in New Zealand.

Who participates in these mammoth rituals? The Gayatri Parivar attracts the professional middle classes and the well-to-do NRI community. Along with its central theme of popularizing the Gayatri mantra and yagnas, the Parivar also offers courses in 'moral upliftment and stress management' to government and private sector professionals. The Gayatri Parivar's clients include well-known public sector enterprises like Bharat Heavy Electricals, inuted the National Thermal Power Corporation, Sales tax department, labour department, Department of Education, and a number of national banks.

The Gayatri Parivar's utterly novel and scientific interpretation of the Gayatri mantra and the horse yagna is clearly an invented tradition. It invents a whole new way of explaining the significance of a ritual with an ancient lineage in a language borrowed from modern science.

The other notable re designing of Vedic rituals is happening in Maharashtra, where the more complex rauta ritual is being revived. In 1992, Timothy Lubin, an American scholar of Hinduism, observed—and inadvertently became the chief guest of!—a month—long Vedic ritual performed by a holy man, Ranganath Selukar Maharaj, in a small town called Gangakhed in rural Maharashtra. The yagna was an expensive and complex affair, involving 17 priests working together and performing an assortment of complex ceremonies prescribed by classical Sanskrit ritual rulebooks or sutras. These rituals have become something of an institution in Maharashtra where Selukar has been hosting them every year since 1980. In recent years, Selukar and his followers have held similar yagnas in Pune, Delhi, and Haridwar as well. Selukar hosted a year-long yagna from April 1999 to May 2000. These yagnas seem to attract the educated and relatively well to do in small towns and rural areas, mostly shopkeepers, clerks, teachers, and landowning farmers.

Even though these yagnas are themselves not explicitly communal, Selukar belongs to the Ananda Sampraday of the Dattatreya sect which, for historical reasons, has had adversarial relations with Muslims. A very brief summary of these historical antagonisms may be useful here. Dattatreya is considered an avatar of Vishnu, along with portions of Shiva and Brahma, popular in Maharashtra, Karnataka, and Gujarat. The worshippers of Dattatreya admit five forms of Vishnu-Datta. Two of these forms are historical Maratha foes of Muslims: Ramdas Swami (1606–82) is claimed by his followers to be the guru of Shivaji, the Maratha warrior king who successfully defied Mughal rule to establish an independent Maratha kingdom in the Deccan; and Ranganath Swami (1612–84), the founder of the Anand Sampraday who also has a reputation for militant advocacy of the Hindu cause against the Mughal rule. Selukar himself comes from a family who fought for the freedom of Marathwada from the Nizam of Hyderabad around the time of freedom. These communal undercurrents are coming to surface in Karnataka where, as we will see below, the Vishwa Hindu Parishad (VHP), the Bajrang Dal and the BJP are demanding a Sufi shrine to be turned into a temple to Dattatreya.

The growing popularity of elaborate yagnas in the private and public sphere is matched by political uses of these rituals.

Elaborate fire rituals have become popular tools for appealing to Hindu voters and for mass mobilizations for communal and political causes.

Yagnas with elected representatives acting as the jajman, or the sponsor, have become so routine that hardly anyone objects any more to the open sponsorship of a majority religion by elected representatives of a secular state. A culture of political darshan is emerging in the country in which public displays of spiritualism have come to constitute a new form of statecraft. When the BJP–JD government in Karnataka wanted to showcase its 'pro-poor' initiatives even as it was giving subsidies to private enterprises, it organized a massive public yagna. Even more blatant was the utterly opportunistic use of yagnas and pujas at taxpayers' expense by Digvijay Singh, the Congress chief minister of Madhya Pradesh (1993 to 2003). When locked in a fierce election battle in 2003 against Uma Bharati, the firebrand Hindutva leader, Digvijay Singh, thought nothing of ordering his 50 cabinet ministers to hold yagnas and Bhagvat Gita recitations in their constituencies, followed by pujas during the ten day Ram Navmi festival. Not to be left behind, Bhairon Singh Shekhawat, vice president of India (2002 to 2007), is known to have a fondness for yagnas. He is reported to have participated in many high-profile yagnas for rain and for general advancement of Vedic culture in his capacity as the vice president.

Because the rituals of yagnas are familiar and because a whole lot of people, from the highly educated to the unlettered, are drawn to them out of their faith, they have become a handy tool for political mobilizations. Take, for example, the VHP–Bajrang Dal agitation to 'liberate' the Guru Dattatreya Baba Bundan Dargah, a Sufi–Hindu place of worship in Chikmagalur, Karnataka. For centuries, this shrine has been a place of common worship for both Hindus and Muslims. But for the last decade or so, the Sangh Parivar has been trying to do an Ayodhya in Karnataka: it claims that the shrine is built on the very same spot where Lord Dattatreya did his penance. The VHP and the Bajrang Dal have been demanding that the shrine be handed over to Hindus and idols of Dattatreya be installed. Perhaps through the influence of Selukar on the Dattatreya sect, massive yagnas, attended by thousands of saffron-clad men and women, have been the major mode of mass mobilization in this trouble spot in Karnataka.

In the run-up to the 2009 Lok Sabha elections, yagnas have replaced yatras as the preferred mode of mobilization for the Hindu right. In the communally sensitive state of Karnataka, for example, the VHP organized a hundred yagnas in temples all across the state where 'those gathered will be administered oaths to fight for Hindu religion'. In Orissa, where thousands of Christians have been displaced by violent attacks by Hindus in December 2008, Ashok Sahu, the BJP candidate for the Lok Sabha elections, is 'conducting mahayagnas in all the villages he visits, forcing the Kondh tribals to observe rituals they have never performed before'.

Even the Left social movements, including even the Communists, are not beyond using religious rituals for political use. In one of the most shameful examples of political exploitation of religion, top-ranking representatives of the Left Front government of West Bengal, including the district magistrate, police superintendent, and the director of the state's industrial development corporation, participated in a bhoomi puja ceremony for blessing the land that had been forcibly acquired and leased to the Tatas.

Political parties of all stripes find public display of 'spiritualism' useful, and both indulge in them to suit their own purposes. The net loser is often the public exchequer, for many of these religious ceremonies are funded at least in part by state and local governments. But an even bigger loser is the public sphere which continues to get more mired than ever in public displays of religiosity.

Obviously not all of those who participate in public yagnas have any political axe to grind, and not all yagnas have communal overtones. Just because the BJP and the VHP use yagnas as a tool for communalization does not mean that all yagnas are communal, or that the good, honest believers who volunteer their time and money to groups like the Gayatri Parivar support Hindutva causes. Likewise, those who throng to Selukar's elaborate performances will not necessarily agree with the VHP–Bajrang Dal agitation over the shrine in Karnataka. Religious behaviour does not line up so cleanly either with class interests or with political views. But by so uncritically accepting the fantastic interpretations of modern gurus, and by not taking a stand against the open use of religious rituals by the representatives of the state, the educated classes have allowed these rituals to saturate the public sphere. Indeed, participation by the elite classes, many with advanced degrees in most advanced sciences, only adds to the legitimacy of these rituals.

Gentrifying the Gods

Not only are new rituals being fashioned out of the old, but gods and goddesses are getting a makeover as well. Local gods and goddesses, which until recently were associated with the more plebeian masses, are finding new homes in swanky new suburbs with malls and multiplexes. In the southern part of the country, village goddesses or Ammas, that once protected the health of the people and the fertility of the soil, are being adopted by the middle classes—a process that has been dubbed 'gentrification of gods'. In the northern part of the country, there has been a tremendous growth in pilgrimage to Mata temples, or shakti peeths (sacred spots where various parts of the body of the goddess Sati are supposed to have fallen).

A recent study of roadside temples by U. Kalpagam in the city of Chennai brings out the dynamics of gentrification of Mariamman, the southern version of Shitala Mata, the small-pox goddess. The history of one particular roadside temple, the Sri Nagakanniamman temple in the Mylapore–Mandaveli area of South Chennai, is illustrative. Nearly 30 years ago, a flower seller, a woman by the name of Kanniamma, put a stone under the sacred peepul tree to create a small shrine for the goddess. Over the years, the stone has grown into a multi-temple complex which is an 'amalgam of tribal, Dalit, and Vedic gods and goddesses', with Amma's shrine coexisting with a shrine for Hanuman and shrines for Ganesha and Ayyappan. The day-to-day affairs of the temple are managed by a neighbourhood association made up of local businessmen, shopkeepers, and residents. Through this process of gentrification, the gods of Dalits and backward castes are brought within a style of worship acceptable to the educated middle classes, which includes hiring Brahmin priests, making only vegetarian offerings, and conducting Vedic and Agamic consecration ceremonies.

A very similar process of gentrification is going on in the middle-class Mylapore neighbourhood of Chennai. Joanne Waghorne describes the renovation, sanctification, and re-consecration of the famous Kolavizhi Amman temple with Vedic rites by Brahmin priests. Like the gentrification of the Amman shrine above, in this case, too, there was an old 'Mundakakkanni Amman who sat under a holy tree for two centuries in a simple stone body', and who now has a 'solid silver face, covering her conical stone body. Her tree and thatched hut [have been] incorporated into a brightly painted mandapa, walled and marked by two ornate gopuras'. The village goddess, who used to protect the fertility of the land in villages, is moving to chic new suburbs. To quote Joanne Waghorne:

> Many old seats of feminine power of goddesses attracted ardent new patrons among the middle classes...Open adherence to such forms of worship and such deities in south India once marked the religious divide between the 'educated' and 'uneducated'...yet in the 1990s, she appears to unify a new middle class world. The former village shakti pithas flourish in neighbourhoods where the middle classes have built their own homes.

The process of gentrification has clear elements of Sanskritization—Agamic mantras and vegetarian offerings, for example—by which the village goddess is made more acceptable to the religious sensibilities of the middle-class urbanites. Yet, there are also glimmers of a new, more democratic culture in which the differences between the elite and non-elite gods, classes, and castes are not strictly adhered to in temple rituals and festivals.

The fast growing cult of Adi Para Shakti at Melmaruvatur, close to Chennai, is another case of an upwardly mobile village goddess described in great detail by Vasudha Narayanan, a well-known scholar of contemporary Hinduism. This temple complex is visited by tens of thousands of pilgrims all clad in red, who believe that the mother goddess has incarnated herself into the body of the temple's male oracle, Bangaru Adigalar, who they call 'mother' or Amma. Speaking through her incarnation/oracle, the goddess addresses contemporary issues of caste, ecology, and world peace. Women devotees run many of its spiritual fellowships and associations; taboos against menstruating women and widows are not observed; and all distinctions of caste are set aside as all worshippers wear red (meant to signify the colour of blood common to all humanity) and address each other as 'shakti', implying all have divinity within them. The goddess is 'conscious of social and global problems', and frequently directs her oracle to conduct elaborate yagnas and other religious rituals for 'drought-stricken areas, for increasing natural resources, and for world peace'. Starting with a miracle of a neem tree in 1966, the temple has grown into a major pilgrim complex complete with prayer halls, ashrams, schools, and hospitals.

Another phenomenon worthy of note is the reincarnation of old gods and goddesses in new forms. Mariamman, who was once venerated as the goddess of smallpox, has been reinvented as the AIDS-Amman, or the 'mother who will cure AIDS', in the state of Karnataka. This new goddess is an invention of H.N. Girish, a high school science teacher who invented the goddess presumably to teach people about the causes and precautions against HIV-AIDS. (What does a goddess have to do with the AIDS virus is not a question that this particular science teacher cared to ask!) It has been argued by those sympathetic to mobilizing religious beliefs for secular purposes that this goddess will serve only educational purposes. But reports from the field belie the expectation that a goddess can be so easily divested of her supernatural and sacred dimension, or a temple so easily turned into a science classroom. Those who come to the temple are not looking for medical information. Rather, they come to beseech the goddess for protection and good health.

While the AIDS-Amman temple is a simple affair and does not seem to be drawing too many visitors, many gentrification projects are carried out at a truly stupendous scale and involve huge contributions from big businesses. A case in point is the gentrification of the Mariamman temple in the small urban centre of Pudukkottai through the largesse of TVS Motors. The TVS Group is a major benefactor of the Indian Culture and Heritage Trust, which is undertaking major temple renovations in Tamil Nadu. The TVS family, who are Iyengar Brahmins, see themselves as restorers of the tradition in the face of growing materialism and that perhaps explains their interest in temple restorations in the state.

The contemporary boom in the construction and renovation of Hanuman shrines has also been attributed to middle-class patronage. Philip Lutgendorf, who has studied the growing popularity of Hanuman across the nation, reports that there are 'more shrines to Hanuman than to his exalted master (Ram)'. Hanuman has not only become wildly popular, but there is also a rush to install ever bigger idols of the monkey god, including the gigantic 70 foot Hanuman gracing the ashram of Sai Baba in Puttparthi in Andhra Pradesh. Sai Baba's Hanuman, however, now stands dwarfed by two even bigger Hanumans in Delhi measuring 91 and 108 feet.

Signs of the growing popularity of Hanuman are easy to spot. The long winding lines of devotees outside the Hanuman temple in Connaught Place, the upscale downtown of New Delhi, gives a pretty good idea of Hanuman's popularity among the relatively well heeled. Keeping in mind the pressures of time, the Connaught Place temple has become a one-stop, full-service temple where devotees can pray to other popular divinities—Durga and Lakshmi, and the wish granting Santoshi Ma being the most popular, along with the perennial favourite, Ganesha. Given that Hanuman is traditionally considered a men's deity (because of his celibacy and physical strength), it is quite remarkable that his popularity is growing among women. According to Lutgendorf, women think of him as a god who is responsive to their wishes for sons and the material welfare of their families. The appeal of Hanuman cuts across gender as well as class. Another Hanuman temple in a less affluent area close to the cremation grounds draws equally large crowds of the less well-off devotees from the suburbs of Delhi and even the neighbouring states.

The natural question is why? What is fuelling this middle-class devotion to less elite gods? Devotees themselves provide a pretty cogent explanation: they see these local gods as being far more intimately familiar with the needs and desires of ordinary people than the 'great gods' who live up there in the celestial sphere. As Chris Fuller puts it:

> There is no doubt that the great deities, especially Vishnu and Shiva, are generally held to be unresponsive and even angered by futile efforts to persuade them to act in specific ways. Many little deities, by contrast, are thought to be open to the more or less direct bargaining about what they will do if such and such offering is made during worship.

In a similar vein, deities like Hanuman are described as 'made to order middle class gods' because they serve as middle-men, or messengers, between the worldly affairs of men and women and the celestial beings. As they confront old and new afflictions (sankat) in their lives, the middle classes are drawn to gods who can serve as 'middlemen who can expedite access to the required persons and sources'—someone, in other words, who can put in a sifarish (a recommendation) on their behalf to the higher-up gods.

Rather than retiring their gods, as the secularization theory expected, Hindus are remaking their gods as they modernize. The local deities who were once considered guardians of the village, and who protected against scourges like smallpox and other illnesses, are now being beseeched for blessings for success and sanctity in an increasingly competitive, urban environment.

New Gurus

There has always been a great affinity between the well-heeled Indians and miracle working gurus, many of them self-proclaimed avatars of God. All the well-known modern gurus fish for followers in the same fish bowl of upwardly mobile Indians, non-resident Indians, and Western seekers. It is only to be expected that as Indian middle classes come to acquire the lifestyle of their NRI and Western counterparts, they will come to share their taste in new age-ish spirituality —only more so, as so much of the new age in the West has borrowed heavily from Hindu and Buddhist traditions in the first place.

The modern gurus, who are practically CEOs of huge business empires, know that they operate in a highly competitive spiritualism market and try to differentiate their products and services accordingly. Spiritual seekers, too, shop around for just the right guru, often trying out many before settling on one. Depending upon their bent of mind and their spiritual needs, they go for one of the three main types of gurus: type I, the miracle making gurus; type II, the philosophical gurus who specialize in expounding on Vedic wisdom; and type III, the yoga–meditation–alternative-medicine gurus who may or may not combine yogic postures and breathing techniques with new age techniques of astrology/tarot, vastu/feng shui, reiki, pranic healing, aromatherapy, etc. The three categories are not watertight: gurus offering miracles will also offer philosophical discourses and new age techniques; those into Vedic heritage will not shy away from astrology, yagnas, and stories of miracles of their own gurus; while those offering yoga and alternative medicine will also offer reiki, acupuncture, biorhythms, colon irrigation, and the like. For their part, spiritual seekers also mix and match their gurus, and sometimes they move from one type to another, depending upon the need. On top of it, doing meditation in an ashram does not prevent anyone from visiting a temple or attending a yagna. India's religious supermarket is spiritual seekers' dream come true: it gives them an enormous choice of ways of exploring and expressing their religiosity.

While Satya Sai Baba is the very archetype of the miracle working guru, he faces fierce competition from Mata Amritanandamayi, the famous 'hugging guru'. Unlike Sai Baba who actually materializes physical objects through his supernatural powers (or is it magic?), Amritanandamayi encourages her followers to *think* she is making everyday miracles happen on their behalf. Either way, miracles—extraordinary happenings that defy all known laws of nature—are of huge importance to those who seek deity-saints. Miracles serve as the visiting card of God in the human body of the guru. Indeed tangible, physically observable miracles—and not just a promise of spiritual transformation—serve as the evidence which seems to prove the godliness of their chosen. As a result, the devotees end up convinced that their faith is rational, because they have actually *seen* the miracle with their own eyes.

Mata Amritanandamayi, or Amma as she is called by her followers, is a self-proclaimed avatar, an incarnation of shakti, or female divine energy. Her fame rests on the power of her embrace: devotees describe great spiritual, emotional, and material benefits from being embraced by Amma. But on special occasions, Amma 'sheds her human form', dons the regalia of a goddess, and reveals her 'divine aspects' to her devotees. Devotees come for the motherly embrace, but often stay for the miracles which seem to cement their faith.

The devotees see Amma as a 'divine stage manager' who takes care of their well-being and safety, while liberating them from their bad karma accumulated from indulging in Western-style consumerism. Indeed, Amma actively encourages them to trust her as a helpless infant trusts her mother. She urges her followers:

> [to cultivate] an attitude of complete surrender, profound love for the deity [i.e., herself, because she is supposed to be 'identical' with Krishna, Devi and Brahman] and extreme humility. She urges them to achieve an emotional state of helplessness, where they cry out in utter longing and despair, and plaintively seek divine help to see them through the travails of this life…

Amma's followers take this advice seriously. They ascribe every little lucky break they get—finding a gas station when the car is running low on gas, for example, or making a train reservation—to their guru's grace. But how is this relationship of dependence and the illusion of miracles created and sustained? The simple answer is through old-fashioned supernaturalism, complete with pujas and astrology. Amritanandamayi teaches the traditional Hindu philosophy of karma and rebirth and explains the travails of her followers as a result of the karmic burden they have accumulated from previous births and from excessive consumerism and the excessive reliance on reason and intellect that comes with modernity. She offers them a menu of ritual prayers and observances which promise to burn off all the negative karmic residues. Her embrace itself is supposed to transfer her karma-destroying 'energy' to the devotees. But beyond the hug, she prescribes a whole number of pujas, the most popular of them being the grahadosha nivarana puja, intended to counter the influence of malevolent planets on one's horoscope. For those who may not care for pujas, Mata Anandamayi prescribes mantra chanting and meditation. There is something for everyone, without anything fixed for everyone.

Regardless of the competition, India's best-known living God–Satya Sai Baba–continues to have a devoted following. Miracles, wrapped up in deeply conservative and nationalistic Hinduism, make up the bulk of the substance of Satya Sai Baba's teaching. To the faithful, however, Sai Baba's magic is evidence of his divinity. Through his magic, Sai Baba both sanctifies consumerism and, at the same time, brings it under the moral guidance of the spiritually superior Hinduism.

While many are content to accept miracle working gurus, others in the same socio-economic class hanker for more philosophy and less magic. Those with a more philosophical bent may still consult their astrologers and their vastu shastris, do their obeisance to miracle making god-men/women and may even host an occasional yagna or go on a pilgrimage. But all that doesn't satisfy them entirely and they want more philosophical depth to their spiritual experiences. For these believers, there are the type II gurus, the ones who can talk about the intricacies of the Vedas, Vedanta, and Bhagvat Gita in an idiom that the seekers are comfortable with.

Swami Dayananda Saraswati—not *the* Dayananda Saraswati, the founder of the Arya Samaj, but the founder of the more recent Hindu mission headquartered in the US—is the very model of a type II guru. Swami Dayananda Saraswati started out as a missionary of the Chinmaya Mission, but later took off on his own. He runs a gurukul called Arsha Vidya in the rolling hills of Saylorsburg, Pennsylvania, USA, which advertises itself as a centre for 'traditional study of Advaita Vedanta, Sanskrit, Yoga, Ayurveda, Astrology, and other classical Indian disciplines'. Arsha Vidya has established two branches in India, one in Coimbatore and the other in Rishikesh. With a growing cohort of disciples associated with his American and Indian operations, Swami Dayananda Saraswati has emerged as an influential preacher of ancient wisdom both in India and the US.

Swami Dayananda has a substantial following among the industrialists of Chennai. The Swami and the representatives of his Indian mission speak before packed halls of well-to-do business folks and professionals. Chris Fuller and John Harriss, two British sociologists, followed the guru and had intensive conversations with his followers in order to understand the attraction. What they found is a very good description of the widespread appeal of the so-called 'karma capitalism' to the captains of capitalist enterprises in India and abroad.

What attracted the Chennai capitalists to the guru the most was his demeanour: a pious and learned man, well versed in the scriptures, and yet fully at ease in the modern boardrooms. His teachings, especially his interpretations of the Bhagvad Gita, resonate well with their own belief in selfmade men and women. Dayananda interprets the Vedic heritage to mean that success or failure are not social but individual problems, and that individuals alone, through their own karma, can achieve moksha in this life, here and now, by freeing themselves from a sense of inadequacy. He interprets the teachings of Lord Krishna in the Gita to mean that desires are a 'manifestation of divinity' which should not be renounced but brought under control. Dayananda thus turns the Bhagvad Gita into a 'plan for living' which sanctifies desire for this-worldly success and riches. Incidentally, Swami Dayananda is but one of the many Indian gurus who have taken Indian philosophy to business schools and corporate boardrooms abroad, a trend that has been dubbed 'karma capitalism'.

Another feature that seems to attract businessmen to gurus like Dayananda is their insistence on a consonance between modern science and ancient Hindu wisdom. Hinduism, in this perspective which is repeated endlessly by each and every modern guru, is as scientific and as universally valid within its own axioms as Newtonian physics is within its own parameters. The presumed scientificity of Hinduism is a source of much pride for modern Hindus as it sets their faith apart from that of the religions of the book which appear more dogmatic.

Finally, there is the message of return to traditions in order to become fully modern that resonates powerfully with those who want to beat the West without themselves becoming westernized. Dayananda insists that by becoming more truly and more fully Hindu, Indians can best tackle the problems of the modern world: tradition is modernity and to go forward, Indians must face backward. That conservative message is very attractive to many upper-class Indians who have never been at the receiving end of the kind of restrictions tradition can impose.

But it is neither the miracle making, reason defying type I, nor the Veda expounding type II, but the yoga–meditation type III gurus who have taken the country by storm in recent years. Sri Sri Ravi Shankar and Swami Ramdev top the list of type III gurus.

Sri Sri Ravi Shankar has built a global spirituality programme which goes by the happy name of Art of Living, popularly known as AOL. The core of Art of Living is sudarshan kriya, a technique for rapid and rhythmic breathing which is supposed to bring the breather in contact with his/her spiritual self which, following the Vedantic axiom, is simultaneously the cosmic self. This contact with the cosmic self (or cosmic energy as it is also called) is supposed to ensure success in worldly ventures while bringing mental peace. The Art of Living claims 20 million members and a teaching staff of 5000 in 140 countries around the world. It is a highly profitable enterprise with a yearly income running into tens of millions of dollars, most of it from the fees it charges for teaching the breathing technique to people with high incomes and stressful jobs in India and abroad. Corporations like Oracle, Sun Microsystems, and Cisco Systems hire AOL teachers to conduct seminars at $150 per person. Fees in India range from Rs 1500 for a basic course to Rs 2,00 for an advanced course.

This focus on turning the body into a conduit to the Cosmic Self is pretty much in the tradition of transcendental meditation of Mahesh Yogi and his famous disciple, Deepak Chopra. (Ravi Shankar and Deepak Chopra are guru bhais: both received their training under Mahesh Yogi.) Together, they represent the cutting edge of the new age phenomenon in India. They have managed to reinterpret Patanjali's Yoga Sutras, Vedanta, and the Bhagvat Gita as manuals of material success in the modern world. (Deepak Chopra even calls his interpretation of the Yoga Sutras *Seven Spiritual Laws of Success*.) Cultivation of inner spirituality becomes the means for attaining and enjoying the best of the material world.

What sets AOL apart is its popularity with generation next: reportedly 60 to 70 per cent of its members are below 30 years of age, and most them work in the IT industry. Part of the attraction is simply stress relief: the disciples report that Sri Sri's approach to yogic breathing eases tension and relieves the pressures of their tension-filled professional lives. The 'rock satsangs' in a Bangalore ashram are very popular as well and draw a crowd of nearly 3000 people every evening after work where they sing along with and dance to devotional songs. Another reason that followers themselves offer for their attraction to AOL is that it places very few demands on them: 'There is no reading of scriptures. It's very practical,' as one follower explained. The only question is, as another member put it, 'are you happy?'

Finally, mention must be made of the enormous popularity of Swami Ramdev, the yoga teacher and Ayurvedic doctor. His yoga camps draw tens of thousands who pay to attend his lecture-demonstrations and millions more watch him on TV. In his many discourses on TV, he offers 'complete cure' in 'weeks, if not in days', of 'diseases from A to Z', from 'common cold to cancers', including cholera, diabetes, glaucoma, heart disease, kidney disease, leprosy, liver disease, so on and so forth. There is practically nothing that his method of Divya Yoga, alone, or in combination with his own Ayurvedic formulations, cannot cure. He claims that all his 'miraculous' cures are not merely 'confirmed by science', but are claimed to be 'science in its purest form'. When examined objectively, the quality of his medicines and the claims he makes for yogic cures are highly dubious. But that has not deterred him from developing a huge following in big cities and small towns in India. He is now in the process of establishing a presence among the NRI communities in Britain and the US.

Regardless of their styles, the prominent gurus of all three types have one thing in common: their soft Hindutva. While using the language of universalism, tolerance, good health, and peace, they very clearly propagate a world view of India as a Hindu nation, Hinduism as a superior religion, and the need to make India (indeed the whole world) more Hindu. Given their underlying Hindu nationalism, it is not a surprise that the Sangh Parivar counts on them to use their charisma to bring moderate Hindus into the Hindutva camp.

Take the case of Swami Dayananda Saraswati. He seems to be equally at home in supposedly secular gatherings organized by chambers of commerce in Indian metropolises, as in the gatherings organized by the Hindu Swayamsevak Sangh in New Jersey. As reported by Christopher Fuller and John Harriss who attended his lectures to the Chennai elite, Swami Dayananda has openly mocked Christianity, declared the building of the Ram temple in Ayodhya as a non-negotiable demand of the Hindu majority, and supported the Tamil Nadu government's ban on conversions. On all these hot-button issues, his position is no different from that of the Sangh

Parivar. Yet, he has successfully cultivated the persona of a teacher of traditional wisdom and Vedic heritage.

Likewise, Sri Sri Ravi Shankar hides a Hindu nationalist passion behind the carefully cultivated image of playfulness, love, and joy. He has repeatedly displayed his Hindutva colours on matters of the Ram mandir and minorities. The British magazine *The Economist* described his politics quite accurately: 'Art of Living is open to people of all faiths. But, in fact, discussing the Ram temple, its guru starts to sound less like a spiritual leader and more like a politician, talking of the long history of "appeasement of the minority community", and of the unfairness of a system that subsidizes Muslims to go on the haj to Mecca.'

Given Sri Sri's underlying Hindutva, it is not surprising that Indian techies, who make up the biggest chunk of the followers, also show a distinct affinity towards Hindu nationalist parties. (This is not to say that their guru has directly caused these sympathies, but only that those with Hindutva biases can feel quite at home with Sri Sri and his organization.) In recent years, the open saffronization of IT workers has become large enough to constitute a trend in its own right. In an effort to mobilize IT and IT-enabled service providers, the RSS has been organizing IT-milans (meets) which are basically RSS shakhas exclusively meant for IT workers (only men are invited to join). According to media reports, these milans have started to become more common over the last three years. They started in Bangalore but have now spread to all the major cities with a substantial concentration of IT-related businesses. The milans are proving to be a great success for both sides: the Sangh Parivar gets its websites and databases updated, while the saffron techies get to meet like-minded people and get a sense of participating in something bigger than just punching keyboards all day.

Finally, consider the open Hindutva of Swami Ramdev.

Ramdev's admirers and followers get more than medical advice: they also get a lesson in Hindu traditionalism and Hindu pride. Interspersed with yogic postures and medical virtues of herbs and food items, Ramdev offers a steady harangue against Western culture, Western medicine, and Western corporations. He equates the promotion of the physical health and well-being of Indians with the promotion of *desh ka swabhiman* (national self-pride) through a revival of its 'ancient sciences'. He has made no secret of his association with the Sangh Parivar: a picture of him doing the RSS salute at a convention of the women's wing of the RSS is available in the RSS weekly, the *Organiser*. But Ramdev's open embrace of Hindu right wing ideas has not diminished the enthusiasm of the masses, which is a strong indication of how normal and ordinary the world view of Hindu supremacy and revival has become.

Supporters of Hindutva, incidentally, are fully aware of the usefulness of the new gurus for their cause. They realize, in the words of Swapan Dasgupta, an ex-Trotskyite historian who now supports Hindu nationalist causes, 'the real energy of contemporary Hinduism does not lie in Brahmanical institutions like the Shankaracharya of Kanchi'. What drives Hindus are either venerated temples or individual preachers and 'living saints'. They are to Hinduism what evangelical preachers are to Christianity and Dasgupta urges the leaders of the Sangh Parivar to invite them to lead the Hindutva cause:

There is a thriving tradition of what can be loosely called evangelical Hinduism. It comprises the likes of Asaram Bapu, Murari Bapu, Swami Ramdev, Amma, Satya Sai Baba, Sri Sri Ravi Shankar, and many others who feature on the various religious channels on TV. *They are the Pat Robertsons and the Billy Grahams of modern Hinduism.* They are able to inspire and motivate individual Hindus far more successfully than purohits and pontiffs.

The failure of organized Hindu nationalism lies in not being able to link the congregations of individual evangelists with bodies like the Hindu Acharya Sabha. (emphasis added)

It seems as if the Sangh Parivar has paid heed to this advice. There were reports that the VHP enlisted Sri Sri Ravi Shankar, Baba Ramdev, Murari Bapu, Asaram Bapu, and Pranav Pandya of the Gayatri Parivar to create an alliance that would marry political, religious, and environmental causes in the run-up to the 2009 elections. (Indeed, all of these gurus, except Sri Sri Ravi Shankar, were members of the VHP's Dharma Raksha Manch which campaigned for a Hindu vote bank and the BJP in the 2009 elections.) Rather than embark upon communally charged yatras over the Ram temple and other hotspots, they engaged in 'constructive agitations' around issues of cleaning the Ganga, saving Adam's Bridge and 'saving' temples from government interference. The idea is to use the goodwill these gurus have among the middle classes to reach out to moderate Hindus who may be fed up with the Ram temple but may be more open to concerns about the environment and temple affairs in general.

Sources of Enchantment

One conclusion that can be safely drawn from the survey of new religiosity is this: education and upward mobility has not led to any serious questioning of the reality of supernatural beings/powers, the possibility of miracles, or the efficacy of rituals and prayers. Indian middle classes are proving Max Weber wrong who thought that being modern—above all —meant believing that:

The world is disenchanted. That one need no longer have recourse to magical means in order to master or implore the spirits, as did the savage, for whom such mysterious powers existed. Technical means and calculations perform the service. This above all is what intellectualization means.

The Indian middle class is showing that one can very well make a good living out of mastering 'technical means and calculations', *and* continue to have 'recourse to magical means in order to master or implore the spirits'.

How to explain this phenomenon? What motivates educated, well-to-do urban sophisticates who continue to believe in miracles and supernatural beings?

Social theory has only two standard answers, neither of which fits the Indian data very well.

The first answer has to do with economic well-being. As has been shown with great sophistication and care by two Harvard sociologists, Pippa Norris and Roland Inglehart, the level of belief in modern, post-industrial societies bears a strong correlation with the level of 'existential insecurity'. On mapping religiosity against income data from societies in North America, Europe, and Japan, Norris and Inglehart found that the higher the income level, the lower the religiosity as measured by frequency of prayer: in aggregate terms, the poor turn out to be twice as religious as the rich. The data from the US, for example, shows that 67 per cent of the least well-off prayed, compared to 47 per cent of the highest income group. According to this view, religiosity falls off and people generally become more secular in modern industrial economies, except when they are caught in the lower rungs of the economy in those societies that do not provide for public welfare.

This explanation does not adequately explain the Indian data. Here we have the case of rising religiosity among the already wealthy and the upwardly mobile, whose level of material well-being is fairly decent even by Western standards. Clearly, the gains in existential security from improved material *dispense?*

well-being are not translating into a decline in religiosity in India.

The second explanation is that the growing religiosity is a defensive reaction to modernization and westernization. Pavan Varma, the author of the much cited *The Great Indian Middle Class,* for example, treats religion as a refuge for the alienated and lonely urbanites, uprooted from the old, warm little communities they left behind in villages. Varma simply assumes that the transition to modern life in the cities *must* be traumatic and drive the new middle classes to seek out the consolation of God in the company of fellow believers. Even the otherwise astute Achin Vanaik accepts the basic idea that those who are receptive to Hindu preachers are in need of a 'balm' for the 'social despair...due to loss of dignity and typically male self-respect' which comes with neo-liberalism.

But 'social despair' is not the first thing one thinks of when one looks at the Indian middle classes. There *is* anxiety and insecurity among the newly well-to-do as they face an increasingly competitive economy with declining job security. But there is *also* a sense of expanding horizons and multiplying opportunities. The upwardly mobile in urban India have, as Maya Warrier puts it quite accurately:

> ...have done well for themselves by seizing the educational and career opportunities that came their way. Their experience of the unprecedented pace and scale of change had resulted not so much in a sense of despair and alienation as in a sense of optimism about multiple opportunities in most spheres of life.

It is not despair or alienation, but rather ambivalence over their new-found wealth that seems to be a more plausible

104

explanation of the growing religiosity. Like in other religions, there are many contradictions between Hindu theology and the actual social practice. While Hindu textual and philosophical traditions tend to demote materialism in favour of renunciation, popular Hindu traditions worship wealth and material riches. Even when Indians are acquiring wealth at an unprecedented pace, they seem to be doing it with a bad conscience, as if they are breaking the cardinal virtue of their culture, namely, to renounce and to extricate themselves from the illusions created by the material world. Middle-class respondents in Baroda used the word 'good' to describe someone who they saw as 'simple', 'non-modern', and someone who 'lives frugally and seeks neither enjoyment nor status through consumption'. Even though they do not live by Gandhian philosophy, they still uphold Gandhian simplicity as a cultural ideal.

As we have seen above, modern gurus seem to ease this ambivalence by giving new wealth a divine stamp of approval. 'To be rich is divine', seems to be the message coming from modern gurus who minister to the upper crust. The Bhagvad Gita and the Yoga Sutras have been turned into self-help manuals for making money and achieving success.

While they bless worldly desires and pleasures, modern gurus also seem to help to take away the edge of guilt or bad conscience by teaching how to balance them with spiritual pursuits. Gurus like Mata Amritanandamayi teach that 'Western' consumerism creates bad karmic burden which can be negated, or at least 'balanced', by performing some of the rituals and pujas she prescribes. To put it somewhat flippantly, the cure for shopping is more shopping—this time for spiritual products and services of gurus and priests. Surely a win-win situation for all involved!

There is, however, another factor that is making public expressions of religiosity fashionable, namely, the rising levels of triumphalism and nationalism among the upwardly mobile. Indians top the list of all nations when it comes to a sense of cultural superiority: the 2007 Pew Global Attitudes Survey revealed that as many as 93 per cent of Indian respondents —highest in the world—agreed with the question 'our people are not perfect, but our culture is superior to others'. In comparison, the Chinese, Japanese, and American public opinion was far more self-critical and ambiguous over the superiority of their cultures. (More on the triumphalism of the middle classes in Chapter 4.)

Having grown up on a steady diet of religious, media, and other cultural discourses that constantly package *Hindu* signs and symbols as the essence of *Indian* culture, it has become almost second nature for educated Indians to conflate the two. Now that India is becoming an important player in the global market, many are beginning to ascribe the country's success to the superiority of 'Hindu values'. This sentiment is being aggressively promoted by gurus and tele-yogis whose work we have examined above. Indeed, the public sphere is replete with these messages of becoming more Hindu in order to become more successful in the global race for money and power.

Conclusion

This chapter has tried to provide representative samples of three different dimensions of middle-class Hindu religiosity, namely, invention of new rituals, gentrification of gods, and the booming guru culture.

It is clear that popular Hinduism is extremely innovative in how it is adapting to India's fast changing economy and society. Temples are getting renovated and together with worshippers, they are remaking old gods and rituals and inventing entirely new ones altogether. The local deities who were once considered guardians of the village, and who protected against scourges like smallpox and other illnesses, are now being beseeched for blessings for success and sanctity in an increasingly competitive, urban environment. Old and new god-men and gurus are doing thriving business in India's spiritual supermarket. They offer a theology of prosperity which combines fashionable new age spirituality with discourses on the Bhagvad Gita and Vedanta, all suitably reinterpreted as successful management tools.

It would be a mistake, however, to interpret the picture presented here as one more proof that Hindu Indians are 'naturally' or 'innately' more spiritual than other people. On the contrary, the explosion of popular Hindu religiosity is the result of years of the open and often hidden support Hinduism has received—and continues to receive—from the supposedly secular Indian government and India's corporate elite. The next chapter provides a closer look at this state–temple–corporate complex.

3

The State–Temple–Corporate Complex and the Banality of Hindu Nationalism

> Religion is not only good for business...it is the best business of all: start-up costs are low, there are never any problems with supply or inventory and one receives tangible goods for intangible ones.
>
> Lise McKean

> Over 90 per cent of Hindus are religious. We will convert that religiosity into a Hindu vote bank.'
>
> Praveen Togadia

Popular Hinduism is undergoing a great resurgence. As we described in the previous chapter, the rich and the poor alike are turning to gods and gurus; pujaris, astrologers, vastu shastris, spiritual advisers are all doing a thriving business.

What may seem like a paradox, the resurgence of popular Hinduism is happening not *against* the grain of Indian secularism, but *because* of it. The Indian brand of secularism has allowed the state to maintain an intimate and nurturing relationship with the majority religion. As the neo-liberal state has entered into a partnership with the private sector, a cosy triangular relationship has emerged between the state, the corporate sector, and the Hindu establishment.

The state–temple–corporate complex is creating new institutional spaces where Hinduism is renewing itself so as to remain relevant to the new social context created by the global political economy. But in the process of renewing itself, it is also taking on nationalistic overtones by turning rituals into politicized assertions of Hindu identity. This process of converting ritual spaces into politicized public spaces is so commonplace, so banal, and so much a part of our collective common sense that it passes unnoticed—and unchecked. This chapter will show how ordinary Hindu rituals end up merging the worship of god with the worship of the nation.

There are two broad areas where the state and the private sector are working together to promote Hinduism: education and tourism. Many of the newly minted English-speaking, computer-using pujaris, astrologers, vastu shastris, and other providers of religious services are products of new priest training schools and deemed universities that have benefited from the commercialization of higher education. Another sector where the state and the corporate sector are making a common cause with Hinduism is the rapidly growing and lucrative market for religious tourism. The seemingly innocent and perfectly secular agenda of promoting tourism has become a channel for pumping taxpayers' money into promoting temples, ashrams, and pilgrimage spots.

In spite of the glaringly obvious examples of state and corporate sponsorship of the majority religion, many Hindus have come to believe that the 'pseudo-secular' state panders to the Muslim and Christian minorities at their cost. 'Hinduism in danger' and 'protect our temples against government takeover' have become popular slogans of the Hindu right. This chapter challenges these myths by showing how the state–temple–corporate complex works to the advantage of Hinduism.

Government spending on religion and related infrastructure is a politically sensitive issue and exact facts and figures are hard to come by. This chapter will piece together the evidence that is available in the public domain to make visible the hidden nexus between the state and temples.

The State and Temples: Historical Background

The nexus between the state and the religious domain is a product of the peculiar nature of Indian secularism. Article 26 of the Constitution allows every religious denomination to 'establish and maintain institutions for religious and charitable purposes'. But this freedom extends only to the religious aspects of these institutions. The state reserves the right to intervene in the secular affairs of all religious institutions of all faiths, if it deems it necessary to bring them in line with the relevant set of laws that equivalent non-religious institutions have to obey. Examples of secular affairs of religious institutions include such issues as: Who owns the cash and other material offerings devotees make to the deity? How is temple wealth to be spent? Who will hand out contracts for temple renovations and/or construction of temple properties? Who will decide temple policies regarding the qualification of the priests? On these kinds of issues, temples, ashrams, and other religious institutions of public nature are not allowed to hide behind any special privileges: they have to open themselves to the same level of scrutiny and auditing that is required of secular institutions. In nearly all the states of the republic, there is some kind of government bureaucracy which oversees Hindu temples that exist in that state. The Supreme Court has accepted the argument that temples are public trusts accountable to the state. The court has affirmed the legitimacy of government oversight bodies over temples in numerous cases, most notably in the well-known Shirur Mutt case in 1954 in which the head of the Shirur monastery had challenged the authority of the state's intervention.

A brief historical elaboration may be useful here to understand why the Indian state got itself involved in this tricky business of overseeing temple affairs.

At the time when the Constitution was adopted, all religious communities were required to clean up the rampant corruption that existed in their places of worship, charities, and trusts. Sikh affairs were already covered by the Gurudwara Act of 1925, Muslim mosques and charities were brought under the Wakf Act of 1954, and Christian churches under the oversight of the National Council of Churches. Since Hindus lacked any single authority that was binding upon the thousands of sects and schools, the state was practically invited to step in by Hindu reformers themselves.

Hindu temples were so out of step with the times, and hereditary priests had become so entrenched in extortion and money-lending that Brahmins of the state of Madras (now Tamil Nadu) started an agitation for temple reforms in the early 20th century. According to Christopher Fuller, who has written extensively on this subject, a group of Brahmin lawyers led by S. Subramania Aiyar, a theosophist and an associate of Annie Besant, formed the Dharma Raksha Sabha in 1908. The Dharma Raksha Sabha brought lawsuits against corrupt temple priests and urged the British government for legislation to establish local bodies to oversee proper management of temple affairs. (The East India company, and later the British government, had managed temple endowments in the state from 1817 until 1888 when they had to retreat under pressure from the Christian critics at home.) The legislative council of Madras passed the first Hindu Religious Endowment Act in 1925, which took its final shape only in 1951 as the current Hindu Religious and Charitable Endowment (HRCE) Act. The HRCE Act put the management of temples' endowments and religious services under a management body made up of career bureaucrats (IAS officers) and trustees, some of whom come from among the temple priests while others are appointed by the government. As the historian Franklin Presler describes it, people in Tamil Nadu welcomed the creation of the HRCE Act:

Temples desperately needed state's protection...Without an active vigilant state, temples are corrupted, preyed on by unscrupulous trustees, priests, land tenants and politicians—all exploiting the temples for political gain. Only a centralized administration under the government can check this tendency.

The problems that plagued temples in Tamil Nadu were widespread throughout India. Not surprisingly, states all over the country have followed the model of Tamil Nadu's HRCE Act and established their own regulatory bodies to oversee the affairs of Hindu, Jain, and Buddhist temples. Consider some well-known examples:

- The fabled Jagannath temple in Puri in the state of Orissa, for example, was well known for theft and corruption, before it was brought under state control.
- The enormous wealth of Thirumala Tirupathi temple was completely controlled by 12 families of hereditary priests for centuries who were raking in as much as Rs 4.5 crore every year from the sale of laddoos sold as prasad, to say nothing of the cash donations. The Supreme Court in 1996 put its seal of approval on the abolition of the hereditary priesthood, opening the door to the formation of the Thirumala Thirupati Devasthanam which was entrusted with the task of managing the temple donations and professionalizing the priests.
- The enormous wealth of the Vaishno Devi temple, one of northern India's most popular pilgrimage sites located in the state of Jammu and Kashmir, was shared by the 1000 families of priests, with nothing was left for the temple's upkeep. The temple had fallen into disrepair and had come to stand for 'superficial, soul-less, action-less and deed-less India at its worst', in the words of Jagmohan, the then governor of the state of Jammu and Kashmir.

Governor Jagmohan pressed for the Mata Vaishno Devi Ordinance and the Mata Vaishno Devi Shrine Board was set up in August 1986. In 1988, the Supreme Court ratified the establishment of the Shrine Board.

- The success of the Vaishno Devi Shrine Board cleared the way for setting up a similar oversight body for another popular pilgrimage spot in Jammu and Kashmir, the Amarnath temple. Sri Amarnath Shrine Board was established in 2000 and took over the management of the pilgrimage to the shrine. In this case, the shrine board dislodged the descendants of Butta Malik, a Muslim shepherd who discovered the cave in 1850, who used to manage the shrine along with two Hindu organizations. The Muslim caretakers used to receive one-third of the offerings of the shrine.

Under the watchful eye of state-level religious endowment departments, temples are now required to use the wealth they acquire from the donations of the devotees to improve the quality of religious services they provide. The temples that do not have sufficient income from donations are supposed to be subsidized by the richer temples.

There are two main areas of concern when it comes to improving the quality of religious services. The first has to do with the education and training of priests. The second has to do with acquiring land for building facilities for the worshippers and charitable institutions for the lay public, including dharmashalas, public reading rooms, schools, dispensaries, hospitals, etc.

In both of these areas, the interests of the state, big businesses, and temples are becoming one and the same. This is turning temples into profit-making centres for the state economy and private businesses, and turning the state and businesses into accessories of the cultural–political agenda of the temples. The usual pattern of collaboration between the three partners seems to be this: the government provides land either as a gift or at a throwaway price for temples' investments in schools, universities, hospitals, and other charities, and/or directs its infrastructure projects to suit the needs of temple properties. At this stage, industrialists and business houses step in: they make donations to build and sustain these religious institutions headed by the holy man/guru they may happen to revere. The state in turn, makes the investment worthwhile by providing modern credentials by creating 'deemed universities', funding training and refresher courses, starting new academic programmes, recognizing new degrees etc. The net result is deeper penetration of distinctively Hindu institutions into the public sphere where they end up substituting for secular educational and health services which the state is obligated to provide for all its citizens.

There are three types of Hindu traditionalist institutions that are the main beneficiaries of this three-sided nexus:

- The first category is dedicated to propagating priestcraft (karmakanda) and 'Vedic sciences'. The variety of priest training schools (variously referred to as gurukuls, rishikuls, or Vedic or Agamic pathshalas) that are mushrooming around the country fall in this category.

- The second category straddles the secular–religion divide. Here one would have to look at the many deemed universities established by tax-exempt ashrams and temples which offer degrees in conventional science, engineering, and other secular subjects.

- The third category includes outright grants to temples. This category also includes cases of open diversion of public sector infrastructure projects to suit the needs of temples, religious festivals, and pilgrimages.

Prominent examples of each case will be provided in this chapter. But first we have to deal with a serious objection to our thesis.

The Secular State's Deference to Hindu Orthodoxy

We have argued that there is a nexus between the state and temples which is proving to be good for the temples. But many Hindu right organizations and activists have taken the exactly opposite position. They see the 'takeover' of temples by state-managed shrine boards as 'anti-Hindu'. The US-based Global Hindu Heritage Foundation, for example, seeks the abolition of all versions of the HRCE Act adopted by different states, which it calls a ploy to 'drive Hinduism out of India'. Organizations like the Bharat Jagran Forum accuse the Indian state of a 'conspiracy to de-Hinduize India'. The forum claims that government control over Hindu institutions has 'seriously interfered with spiritual and cultural activities, violated religious sentiments, suppressed Hindus' human rights of religious freedom, demolish[ed] ancient religious infrastructure by gross government mismanagement and sale of endowment lands, and stopped the essential activities of sewa and dharma prachar'. The idea that temples need to be 'saved' has taken an ominous turn as it is one of the demands of the Hindu Janjagruti Samiti, a Maharashtra-based group that has been implicated in the recent terrorist attacks against Muslims. These critics protest too much. They completely fail to acknowledge the great solicitousness and deference the state agencies routinely show for the orthodoxy of temple priests in matters relating to temple rituals and worship. They also fail to notice how the material interests of the government oversight bodies for revenue and status end up coinciding with the interests of temple priests in increasing the wealth and prestige of their institutions. The state bureaucracies have only encouraged—often with public funds coming from tourism and other cultural-educational activities of the state—pilgrimages and other expressions of devotional religiosity. A bit of history might be useful to dispel the idea that the government-appointed oversight agencies are 'anti-Hindu'. Deference to the authority of priests and their orthodox and often superstitious interpretation of Hindu scriptures was built into the state policy for temple management right from the beginning. The 1962 Report of the Hindu Religious Endowment Commission, which served as the basis of state-level oversight agencies for Hindu temples, provided a justification for unquestioning obedience of scriptural authority. Members of the National Commission on Religious Endowments toured 150 Hindu religious institutions in north India, and 82 in the south in about a year, interviewed a large number of priests, circulated 12,000 questionnaires, and offered a detailed analysis of the state of the temples in the country. The members of this commission report great disappointment over the 'ignorance and incompetence' of the priests, combined with their efficiency in 'extorting money'.

The commission issued recommendations for improvements which became the basis of nationwide reform of temples' secular affairs. These recommendations were modelled after the policies that already existed in the state of Tamil Nadu. Basically what the commission recommended was this: the temples should try to improve the education of priests by making them experts in carrying out rituals exactly as prescribed in the ancient texts. In other words, 'improvement' meant going back to the Vedas, Agamas, and other holy books and following their directions literally and faithfully. Here is the relevant excerpt from the commission's 1962 report, quoted here from the renowned scholar of religious law in India, Duncan Derrett:

> *Temples may be defined as occult laboratories* where certain physical acts of adoration coupled with certain systematized prayers, psalms, mantras, and musical invocations can yield certain

physical and psychological results as a matter of course. *And if these physical processes are properly conducted, the results will accrue* provided the persons who perform them are properly equipped. One of the essentials for the proper conduct of rituals is the proper ordaining of the priest. Also, the efficacy of prayers, poojas, archanas, abhisekas, festivals, etc., very much depends upon the expertness of the priestly agents employed in the physical process and ritualistic details. *It is therefore essential that the correct approach and proper conditions should be rigidly followed* to enable the temples to fulfill their purposes... *And if these physical processes [of worship] are properly conducted, the results will accrue'.* (emphasis added)

This is a statement only the most orthodox believers in the efficacy of temple rituals can make. The government commission of highly educated, well-known public servants assumed, without any equivocation, that delivering 'physical results' in 'occult laboratories' constitutes a legitimate and essential function of religion which the state must protect and encourage (by recommending that the priests should rigidly follow the ritual tradition). As Derrett wryly observed, the commissioners wanted better trained priests because they 'themselves may at any time visit the temple and wish to make offerings'. Clearly, policymakers approached the temples as devotees, and not as officials of a secular state with an interest in creating a secular public culture, equally removed from all religions as was the intent of the Constitution.

Over time, state-level temple management agencies/ departments/ministries seem to have moved closer to the worl-dview and the sensibilities of the priesthood. As Joanne Waghorne observed after an exhaustive study of religious revival in Tamil Nadu, 'the executive officers [appointed by the HRCE Board] appeared to work in tandem with the trustees in a mutual project to enhance and direct the growing interest in temple culture in the city...the officer's home values were closer to those of the temple trustees and devotees. No officer or devotee whom I met devalued ritual, or tried to spiritualize worship.' The same sentiment is expressed today by the spokesmen of state oversight agencies who assure their critics that they are respectful of all 'traditional rights of pujaris' and are only trying to improve the quality of services. One can say with some confidence that the state-appointed overseers share the religious world view of the temple trustees, priests, and worshippers.

Over and above the shared belief, there is a shared material interest between the state oversight agencies and temples: both want to increase the temples' revenues and prestige. Thus it is quite common to see temple management departments actively trying to turn some remote temple into a pilgrimage spot by inventing a 'pracheen itihas' (ancient history) for it, and actively involving the state-funded tourism departments to create roads and hotels to make pilgrimage easier. Some of the newly-invented temple rituals described in the previous chapter—the gold car in temples in Tamil Nadu, the re-enactment of the Shiva and Parvati wedding—are pure money the spinners put in place with full knowledge of the government overseers. These rituals fade in comparison with the massive fraud that the Devaswom board of the Sabarimala temple in Kerala, in full complicity with the Communist government of the state, has been perpetuating for many years. Every year, millions of pilgrims turn out to witness the 'divine light' (called Makravilakku) that is actually lit by the officials of the temple, the Devaswom board, and the Kerala State Electricity Board in connivance with forest officials and the police. In 2008, the temple made Rs 72.52 crore in the pilgrimage season, a good chunk of it on the day of 'divine' lights. Involvement of the state authorities in inventing new traditions and encouraging people to participate in them is nothing new. Writing in 1982, Franklin Presler described how Tamil Nadu's HRCE tried to 'turn several temples in the state into pilgrim centres by publicizing them and making it easier to travel to them'. (Presler was however, critical of the politicization of the HRCE.) Likewise, in his study of the Chandi temple in Cuttack, Orissa, James Preston found out that the temple priests, local merchants, and the state endowment commission worked together to 'maximize the temple's margin of profit', so that more land could be purchased to set up the temple's expanding charities. The revenue of the Chandi temple went up from 100,000 in 1968 to Rs 350,000 in 1972 after it was brought under the control of the Endowment Commission of the state of Orissa.

If more evidence is needed, consider how major pilgrimage spots are thriving today under the state-appointed management boards:

- The oversight of the famous Tirupati temple in Andhra Pradesh by a joint state–temple management committee has by no means hurt the temple's fortunes. On the contrary, reports suggest that Tirupati has overtaken the Vatican as the wealthiest and the most popular religious institution in the world. The temple has grown substantially in its reach into the society: it runs 12 colleges, with 30,000 students, churns out 600 priests in its Veda schools every year, and runs a string of charitable hospitals.
- As in the case of Tirupati, the state-appointed shrine board has done wonders for the Vaishno Devi shrine: the number of pilgrims has gone up from 1.3 million in 1986 to 6 million in 2004, and nearly 7 million in 2007. The numbers are expected to cross 8 million in 2009.
- Under the solicitous care of the Sri Amarnath Shrine Board, Amarnath has emerged from a little-known temple drawing barely 12,000 pilgrims in 1989 to a major pilgrimage spot attracting 400,000 pilgrims in 2007.

- The Shiv Khori temple in Jammu which was little known till about fifty years ago has now become one of the most popular temples in Jammu, second only to Vaishno Devi. In just two years since it was brought under the control of the Shri Shiv Khori Shrine Board modelled after the Vaishno Devi and Amarnath shrine boards, the number of pilgrims to Shiv Khori crossed the 500,000 mark in 2008. Incidentally, all the growth is not self-sustained from the temple's coffers: the Ministry of Tourism of the state of Jammu and Kashmir has approved a project plan for Shiv Khori at a cost of Rs 5 crore.

Such government intervention has been so successful that many temples are clamouring for more of it. There are calls to replicate the success of pilgrimages to the Vaishno Devi and Amarnath temples by creating new government boards for additional temples and indeed, for all the temples of Kahsmiri Pandits. Indeed, even L.K. Advani is on record defending the need for government intervention in temple affairs. He told *Hinduism Today* that 'there can come a stage when degradation of institutions makes it obligatory for the government to step in. The actual experience of Vaishno Devi is that government intervention has certainly helped the pilgrims.'

The critics' objections out of the way, it is time to examine the details of how the state–temple–corporate complex works in the three categories mentioned above: namely, priest training and 'Vedic science' schools, 'secular' institutions affiliated with Hindu temples and ashrams, and direct subsidies to temples.

Gurukuls and Vedic Pathshalas

Given that 'ignorance and incompetence' of temple priests was one of the motivating forces for temple reforms, it is not surprising that priest training schools have been at the leading edge of modernization and renewal of Hinduism.

Today there is literally an explosion of all kinds of gurukuls, 'rishikuls', and Vedic pathshalas which take in young boys of all castes (even though some still prefer Brahmins). After about 12 years of memorizing Sanskrit mantras for doing pujas, yagnas, and mastering the physical performance of rituals, they are certified to enter the booming market for priests.

Overall, these schools have remained true to the conservative philosophy that informed the 1962 national commission on temple reforms, that is, to improve the education of priests by making them experts in carrying out the rituals exactly as prescribed in the ancient texts. But at the same time, the graduates of these schools have at least the trappings of modern education, especially English language skills, and the use of computers. Some modern gurukuls have started offering regular school subjects in the sciences and mathematics as well, but it is a safe bet that science is being taught more to affirm the traditional Vedic sciences than inculcate habits of critical thinking among the priests-in-training. When the University Grants Commission, the highest educational policy making body of the land, can propose 'focused research in occult sciences', right alongside biotechnology and genomics, one cannot expect gurukuls not to treat occult as a legitimate science. These schools are producing, to use Chris Fuller's words, 'professionally trained guardians of tradition', an oxymoron, if ever there was one. Their aim is to produce a new crop of priests who can speak in the preferred language (English) and idiom ('science') of the new middle classes.

The Government of India has put in place all the regulatory mechanisms that ensure financial support for, and official recognition of, suitably 'modern' priests. The process started in February 2001 when the University Grants Commission decided to introduce college-level courses in Jyotir Vigyan (astrology) and Purohitya (karmakanda or priest craft). The UGC, with the support of the BJP-led government, and the blessings of the Supreme Court, succeeded in institutionalizing astrology courses in higher education. But for Purohitya degrees, the institutional infrastructure already existed in the form of the Rashtriya Sanskrit Sansthan and Maharishi Sandipani Rashtriya Veda Vidya Pratishthan.

The BJP-led NDA government gave the status of full-fledged 'deemed university' to three institutions which specialize in offering advanced degrees in Sanskrit, yoga, and 'Vedic sciences'. These institutions don't directly train priests, but serve as affiliating institutions for gurukuls and Vedic pathshalas which train pujaris and practitioners of Vedic sciences like yoga and astrology, but are not authorized to offer degrees.

The most well known and important of the three is the Rashtriya Sanskrit Sansthan. This institute was established in 1970 as an autonomous organization for the development, preservation, and promotion of Sanskrit. In May 2002, the Sansthan, along with eight of its campuses—in Allahabad, Garli (Himachal Pradesh), Jaipur, Jammu, Lucknow, Puri, Sringeri, and Trichur—were deemed as full-fledged universities, with complete freedom to set their own curricula and the authority to confer degrees. In addition, two Kendriya Vidyapeeths associated with the Sansthan, one in Delhi and the other in Tirupati, have been converted into deemed universities.

The Rashtriya Sanskrit Sansthan and institutions affiliated with it are entrusted with the task of propagation of Sanskrit learning—undoubtedly a worthy task. But a part of their curricula involves training in Purohitya as well. These institutions offer courses and degrees equivalent to degrees in secular subjects: the title Shastri is equivalent to having a Bachelor's degree, Acharya a Master's degree, while Vidya Varidhi means a doctorate. Apart from receiving instructions in Sanskrit grammar and the six traditional darshanas, students receive hands-on training in carrying out the rituals prescribed by the shastras. According to the Rashtriya Sanskrit Sansthan's website, institutions affiliated with it receive 'financial assistance (from the government's Human Resource Development department) for organizing short-term vocational training to students of Sanskrit in jyotish, karmakanda, paleography, cataloguing, Sanskrit shorthand, typewriting, etc.' Training in astrology, karmakanda, and other traditional sciences have always been impatted as a part of a college-level degree in Sanskrit. Giving the status of universities to Sanskrit teaching institutions did not start new courses geared exclusively at priest training.

Two other newly 'deemed universities' are attracting priests-in-training from gurukuls and Vedic pathshalas: Swami Vivekananda Yoga Anusandhana Samsthana (SVYAS) in Bangalore, which was given the status of a university in 2001; and Bihar Yoga Bharati in Fort Munger in Bihar, deemed in 2000. Both of these universities offer advanced degrees, all the way to Ph.D.s in 'yogic sciences'. Gurukuls and pathshalas which take in young school-age children to become pujaris and priests channel their students to these universities, or any of the other Sanskrit Sansthan institutions, to round off their purohitya training with a course in yoga and allied sciences. A degree from these universities enhances the professional profile of the pujari.

But government money and resources are also used more directly in training priests, who may or may not go for an advanced degree in yoga or Sanskrit. Purohitya is funded by the Maharishi Sandipani Rashtriya Veda Vidya Pratishthan based in Ujjain, Madhya Pradesh. Established in 1987 as an autonomous organization of the Ministry of Human Resource Development, the Sandipani Pratishthan funds gurukuls all across the country and serves as their accrediting body.

Media reports suggest that funding and accreditation from the Pratishthan has become a selling point for new priest training schools that are cropping up all across the country. A good example is Navi Mandal Veda Vidya Mandir in Ujjain which takes in about 80 boys, between 8 and 18 years of age, and trains them in Yajurveda, the Veda that specializes in ritual arts. The school receives grants from the government through the Sandipani Pratishthan and the degree it awards is considered equivalent to a standard high school degree so that a graduate of purohit school can enter a college if he so chooses. A similar Vedic school in Palakkad in Kerala gets funds and accreditation through the Sandipani Pratishthan. The exact number of priest training schools that receive government money through the Pratishthan is not known.

In addition, a number of state governments have started funding Vedic gurukuls directly out of their own funds without going through central government agencies like Sandipani. Under the reign of the BJP chief minister Vasundhara Raje Scindia, the state government of Rajasthan set aside Rs 260 million (Rs 26 crore) for temple renovations and training 600 Hindu priests. It organized training camps for priests in order to 'enable them to conduct temple rituals in accordance with the Shastras', and providing them with the right equipment to conduct these rituals. The state of Andhra Pradesh has recently announced creation of 8 new Vedic schools which will provide free training of temple priests drawn from all castes. The state has promised to release Rs 60 crore to the religious endowment department for the welfare of temple priests in the state. The BJP government of Gujarat routinely allows funds marked for infrastructure development to be used for training priests and paying their salaries. (More on Gujarat's initiatives below.)

In what can be described as a progressive development, training for priesthood is now being offered as a part of social welfare, especially for Dalits. But linking priestly education with social welfare has further legitimized the idea of the state spending public money on teaching mantras and yagnas. A case in point is Tamil Nadu. After the Supreme Court decided in 2002 that Dalits had a right to officiate over pujas in temples, M. Karunanidhi's government in 2006 decided to open 6 priest training institutes with a mandate to admit Dalits and people from the backward castes. The state opened two Vaishnava and four Shaivite schools. Some 207 students were trained in all methods of temple worship and rituals and given a certificate in Agama shastras. All told, there are at least 22 priest training schools, most of which are run by temples and charitable endowments but at least part of the money comes from the state's coffers. According to the official report for 2006–07, the state gives out Rs 7,500,000 every year to the state's Hindu Religious and Charitable Endowments department. The official report for 2008–09 shows that the government increased the grant it gives for temple renovations from Rs 45 lakh per year to Rs 3 crore per year. It is not unreasonable to expect that at least a part of these grants finds it way into schools for priests.

The commercial/industrial elite are key partners in at least some of these priest training enterprises. As an example, consider the magnificent sandstone temple called Shri Hari Mandir that opened in 2006 in the city of Porbandar, Gujarat. Attached to the temple is a priest school (a 'rishikul', a school for rishis or sages) called Sandipani Vidyaniketan. As for the land grant, the website of Sandipani Vidyaniketan (http://www.sandipani.org/trusts/index.asp) contains the following information: 'The Shree Bharatiya Sanskruti Samvardhak Trust (the parent trust of Sandipani) then set out to acquire the existing piece of land. A request was made to the government of Gujarat who very generously granted 85 acres of land close to the Porbandar airport.' The temple and the school are founded by Ramesh Bhai Oza, a well-known kathakar, a singer-preacher of the Bhagvat Purana, Ramayana, and Bhagvat Gita. His other claim to fame is that he is the personal guru of the Ambani family, India's richest and best-known business dynasty.

This is how the triangular relationship between the guru, the government, and the industrialist works, at least in this case. The temple and the priest school stand upon the 85 acres of land gifted to Oza by Gujarat's chief minister, Narendra Modi. The late Dhirubhai Ambani, the founding patriarch of the Ambani business empire, provided the financial resources for building the temple-'rishikul' complex.

Other examples of such triangular relationships are not hard to come by. Swami Ramdev, the popular tele-yogi, who has created a massive Rs 4000 million empire selling yoga and Ayurvedic medicines, is building two universities on land gifted to him by the state governments of Madhya Pradesh and Uttarakhand. The state of Jharkhand has gifted him another 100 acres of land recently. Despite the fact that the medical claims he makes for the medicines he sells have not been scientifically tested in appropriate double-blind studies, his Patanjali Yog Peeth has been granted the status of a university with Ramdev being appointed as its 'vice-chancellor for life'. The business elite, in India and abroad, including big names like Lakshmi Mittal, the Hinduja brothers, and Anil Agarwal of the Vedanta group, have been generous patrons and promoters of Ramdev's yoga peeth. Ramdev's yoga–Ayurveda empire is a paradigm case of the seamless merging of state, business, and religious-cultural elites and the openly communalist, xenophobic Hindu right. (Ramdev is a frequent and honoured guest of the RSS and was part of the core group of VHP's Dharma Raksha Manch that tried, without much success, to grow the size of the Hindu vote bank in the 2009 elections.)

Modernization of priesthood has been a fond dream of the VHP, one of the leading members of the Hindutva family. Setting up short-term priest training camps is a common practice of both the VHP and the RSS. Ominously, heads of mainstream religious ashrams and mutts show up to bless priesthood camps run by the Sangh Parivar, showing the close ideological congruence between the two. Reports in *The Organiser*, the weekly newspaper of the RSS, reveal that the Kanchi Shankaracharya, Sri Shankara Vijayendra Saraswati, himself came to bless the trainees at a village priest training camp organized by the VHP. The popular Bangaru Adigalar Shakti 'Amma' who we encountered earlier in our discussion of gentrification of gods, was also well represented at the VHP priest training camps in Tamil Nadu.

Special attention must be paid to the teaching style and content of these schools for priestcraft and Vedic sciences. After all, these institutions are responsible for producing the crop of household priests, astrologers, yoga teachers, vastu shastris, and peddlers of all kinds of dubious Ayurvedic drugs.

Overall, priest training schools offer an orthodox and conservative curriculum which emphasizes two virtues above all—rote learning and unquestioning obedience. The best description of how these schools function comes from Christopher Fuller's 2003 monograph *The Renewal of Priesthood*, which provides a detailed look at the modernization of priestly education in the state of Tamil Nadu. What follows here is based upon Fuller's work, supplemented with reports from the US-based magazine *Hinduism Today*, and news reports in the Indian media.

Vedic schools admit only boys and young men, preferably but not always Brahmins. Young boys, 12–14 year-olds, go through the traditional gurukul training which requires that they accept their guru's word as God's command.

('There is only duty of the disciple: Obey your guru! Obey your guru! Obey your guru!' This was the advice given by Satguru Sivaya Subramuniyaswami, the American-Hindu founder of *Hinduism Today*, to the monks of the Sarangpur sadhu school in Gujarat.) The emphasis is on correct memorization and the correct reproduction of the sound of Sanskrit verses, because the sound is supposed to carry 'divine vibrations' which have been ricocheting around the cosmos since the beginning of time. The future priests learn the correct words and the correct hand gestures that go with the words. Some of them learn the meanings of these gestures, but many don't. The entire programme is one long exercise in rote learning, with no room for critical reflection on the validity of the metaphysical presuppositions behind the hand gestures and the mantras. Training in astrology is considered an essential part of training for priesthood. Agamic education, Fuller concludes:

> has helped to strengthen the priests' traditionalism, so that compared with twenty years ago, they more forcefully express their ideological commitment to the authority and legitimacy of the tradition, as embodied in Agamic texts and also vested in the Temple's [Meenakshi temple in Madurai] ancient customs and their own hereditary rights.

Fuller's description of the state of priest education in Tamil Nadu is fully corroborated by independent accounts of other gurukuls. According to G.K. Ramamurthy, the 'head principal' of Sri Venkateshwara Veda Pathshala in Dharmagiri near Tirumala, which is considered one of the finest priest training centres in India, the priests-in-training are 'not taught philosophy, although they do learn all about worship and its practice and cultivation of personal devotion...The students

are also taught astrology, Sanskrit, and the Dharmashastra.'
The only concession to 'modernity' is teaching how to
speak in English: 'A few years back, English was introduced
as a part of the curriculum. We are becoming increasingly
aware of the importance of English as a second language.
Specifically we are teaching students how to read, write,
and speak in English (as well as in Sanskrit).' This pathshala
(school) operates on the principle of hereditary priesthood
and innate priestly samskaras (subconscious impressions)
which are encouraged through rituals performed on babies
still in their mothers' wombs: 'A priest at Balaji's temple must
be born the son of...a priest who is himself fully trained
in the Vaikhansa Agama. He must also be taught certain
priestly samskaras while still in the mother's womb. This
is accomplished through a ritual called the "Vishnu Bali".'
This school proudly produces 35 students each year, all of
whom find solid middle-class employment in temples in
India or in the mushrooming Hindu temples among the
diaspora in the West.

Another priest training school in Pillaiyarpatti in Tamil
Nadu is run by K. Pitchai Gurukkal, and with 250 students,
it is considered the largest in the country. Both Fuller
and other commentators describe hands-on training in
rituals, combined with training in astrology, Sanskrit
grammar, and devotional singing. The special feature
of this school is the emphasis on practical training from
early on. The students, even the youngest among them,
earn their tuition by assisting the teachers in conducting
yagnas and prayers in temples and private homes. Priest-
students are trained in re-enacting the fire rituals exactly,
literally, and in the same detail as they are prescribed in
the Vedas. The popular Ganpati homa (yagna for Ganesha)
performed by the priests-in-training involves 21 people,
16 to recite the correct number of mantras and five for

adding oblations to the fire. Rather than simplifying the ceremonies, the emphasis is on 'flawless execution' of elaborate details.

Deemed Universities and other 'Modern' Institutions

This section looks at how distinctly Hindu teachings, rituals, and so-called 'Vedic sciences', coded as universal spiritual and moral values, are riding piggy-back on private sector investments into higher education.

Hindu charitable trusts have a long history of providing education, either in gurukuls or in state-aided schools and colleges. What seems to be new is that they are now entering the lucrative market for higher education among the urban elite. Charitable endowments of temples or foundations established by gurus are opening state-of-the-art educational facilities that purport to blend Western science and technology with Hindu wisdom. They offer degrees in sought-after subjects like management, media studies, information technology and engineering, all of them infused with moral and spiritual values explicitly derived from Hindu sacred texts and traditions. Even those who welcome these 'swamiji schools' admit that these schools are nurseries of soft Hindutva:

> Even though trustees and managers as well as liberal citizens who enroll their offspring in the new age swamiji schools tend to stress that these institutions promote Indian cultural and spiritual values, it is self evident that these schools promote Hindutva and are essentially Hindu revivalist institutions. But it is also patent that their promoter saints and seers have been influenced by Nehruvian legacy of secularism, and at best promote soft, liberal Hindutva which is becoming universally popular.

There is no definite accounting of how many such swamji colleges and universities exist in the country. There is a general consensus that their growth has been dramatic. For example, the Sri Adichunchanagiri Mahasamsthana math or trust has moved from rural education into urban and technical education in the states of Karnataka, Tamil Nadu, and Maharashtra. Today it operates 375 educational institutions in several states with 40,000 students on their rolls. Its institutions range from Veda and Agama colleges for training priests and training Ayurvedic doctors to colleges of modern medicine, nursing, pharmacy, engineering, and management. The crown jewel of this math is the thoroughly contemporary BGS International Residential School in Bangalore with branches in Delhi and Mangalore. The school is not for ordinary folks: its annual tuition runs over Rs 100,000. The Chinmaya Mission runs another successful chain of schools. Founded by the same Swami Chinmayananda who was one of the founding members of the Vishwa Hindu Parishad, the Mission runs 75 schools, including the International Baccalaureate programme offered at the five-star Chinmaya International Residential School in Coimbatore.

What interests us here are those distinctively Hindu educational institutions which enjoy the largesse of the state and the corporate world. Some prominent examples are given below.

The Art of Living Foundation of Siri Siri Ravi Shankar, the favourite guru of the 'techies', is a huge beneficiary of government largesse. His multi-million dollar ashram sits atop a hill 40 km from Bangalore on lease from the Karnataka government for 99 years. According to Edward Luce, the author of *In Spite of the Gods*, 'the funding for this extravagant construction had come from the software companies in nearby Bangalore and the revenues the foundation earns from its hugely popular courses in breathing technique and meditation'. Here again, we encounter the familiar triangular relationship—the guru, government, and corporate deep-pockets.

But the Bangalore operation of the AOL is not the end of the story. In 2006, the Orissa government gave the AOL Foundation 200 acres of land on the outskirts of the capital Bhubaneswar at an undisclosed concessional rate to set up a Sri Sri University of Art of Living. The university plans to blend traditional subjects like Ayurveda, yoga, and Vedic studies into its regular curricula of modern science and engineering. The land on which the university will be built comes from three existing villages. The fate of those who will have to be parted from their land is not known.

The AOL deal is puny compared to the 8000 acres of prime land that the government of Orissa has promised to make available to Vedanta University, along with promises of providing the most up-to-date infrastructure, including an airport and a four-lane highway. This university is bankrolled by Anil Agarwal, an Indian-born billionaire, who owns Vedanta Resources, a metals and mining group headquartered in the UK with mining operations in aluminium, copper, zinc, and lead, principally in India and a number of other countries. Vedanta University plans to become a modern institution of higher learning supposedly at par with Stanford, Oxford, and Harvard. But going by the past record of the Anil Agarwal Foundation, it is not clear how secular his Indian venture will really be. This foundation is deeply involved in creating the Krishna-Avanti school, the first government-funded Hindu school in the UK, which is seen by many as having a strong traditionalist flavour imparted by the Hare Krishnas (or the International Society for Krishna Consciousness) who have a leading role in deciding who qualifies as a 'practising Hindu'. Anil

Agarwal is an adviser to the I-Foundation, an ISKCON charity based in the UK which describes itself as:

> a charity that aims to establish sustainable projects that promote and advance Vedic culture and philosophy in the modern world. The culture and the philosophy of the Vedas, which originate in ancient India, bring with them a depth and richness to life, as well as a wholesome approach to living in harmony with nature.

To take another prominent example, Maharishi Mahesh Yogi has been able to headquarter his 'university' (a complete misnomer in this case) in his native state of Madhya Pradesh, with full support from the state government. In 1995, the government of Digvijay Singh, the Congress party chief minister of Madhya Pradesh, unanimously voted to grant the status of a state university to Maharishi Mahesh Yogi Vedic Vishwavidyalaya (MMYVV). According to its own promotional materials, the MMYVV 'has been established as a statutory university like any other UGC recognized university. It is an affiliating university with jurisdiction spread over entire Madhya Pradesh. Hon'ble Maharishi Mahesh Yogi Ji is the first Chancellor of the University.' In 2002, a sister institute, Maharishi University of Management and Technology, was established by a decree from the state government in Chhattisgarh.

It is safe to assume that having been established as 'statutory universities like any other UGC recognized university', Maharishi's institutions are eligible for all the benefits, funds, and grants that all other public universities receive from the UGC. And yet, the nature of education offered by them scarcely qualifies for the label of 'higher education' that universities are mandated to provide. The MMYVV offers education based upon the Vedic science of natural law as taught by Mahesh Yogi. Anyone with a high school diploma, with sufficient money to pay the fees, can receive graduate and postgraduate degrees, including a doctorate, in the following subjects: 'Maharishi Ved Vigyan, Jyotish (astrology), Yog, Sthaptya Ved Vastu Vidya (Vastu shastra), and Vedic Swasthya Vidhan.' According to the MMYVV's own data, 'thousands of students have been awarded degrees' and many of the alumni of this school are establishing their own businesses and centres for teaching astrology and vastu. Career advisers in the magazine *Education World* would agree: they rate the Maharishi University among the top eight institutions that offer diplomas, degrees, and doctorate-level courses in astrology.

While institutions like the AOL and MMYVV at least make an attempt to appear non-communal and even 'secular', or 'scientific', a university run by the RSS can have no such fig leaf. And yet, that has not prevented the state of Rajasthan from making 2300 acres of land and infrastructure available to the proposed Keshav Vidyapeeth Vishwavidyalaya. This RSS-affiliated university promises to propagate cultural nationalism and offer college-level courses in 'Vedic sciences'. It got the green light from the Rajasthan government in March 2006 and it is only a matter of time before we begin to encounter new college graduates with their minds imprinted with the Sangh ideology.

Religious Tourism, Temple Construction, and 'Hindukaran'

In this category, state funds and resources are used to fund the construction of new temples, pay salaries for temple priests, promote pilgrimages and religious tourism, and even promote open Hindukaran, or Hindu proselytization.

Take the example of Akshardham temple, a grand sandstone structure occupying 100 acres of prime land on the banks of the Yamuna in Delhi, which was inaugurated with much fanfare in 2005. To build a temple in Delhi was apparently a long-standing desire of the late Yogiji Maharaj, the preceptor of BAPS Swaminarayan Samstha who wrote in 1969:

> Delhi is the throne. The flag [of Swaminarayan] should fly high in Delhi. Now Yamuna is waiting. She has become restless. With certain surety, land on the banks of Yamuna ji will be acquired. The Lord will fulfill this in His divine way.

The 'Lord's divine way' led through Jagmohan, the same Jagmohan who had earlier involved himself in Vaishno Devi temple management, and who served as the Union Cabinet Minister for Urban Development from 1999 to 2001 under the NDA-government led by the BJP. Yogiji Maharaj advised his followers to cultivate Jagmohan: 'Garland the Saheb, the land will be granted.'

The land was, indeed, granted. The Delhi administration under Jagmohan altered the master plan of Delhi, rezoned parts of the Yamuna riverbed to allow commercial development, demolished the Yamuna Pushta slum dislocating thousands of poor people, and allotted 30 acres of land to the temple at a reportedly 'throwaway price'. (Secular buildings like the Commonwealth and an IT park were also allowed to be built.) That was not all: the temple managed to acquire another 50 acres of land—and get all environmental clearances—in an ecologically sensitive area managed by the neighbouring state of Uttar Pradesh. Serious concerns regarding recharge of groundwater were set aside by the state government and the courts to allow the temple to be constructed. The state clearly bent backward, broke its own laws, and sold public land at below the market price to a Hindu sect.

In addition to facilitating temple building, public funds are being used in some states for directly paying the salaries of Hindu priests.

In the state of Rajasthan, 390 of the state's less famous and poorer temples fall under the 'direct control of the government, all expenses paid from the state budget', to cite the state's Devasthan department report. The report further states that the Devasthan department 'spends Rs 63.65 per day, per government temple (total 390) on puja, bhog-rag, utsav, deity dress, electricity, and water bills'.

In the state of Gujarat, to take another example, Hindu priests have been on the government payroll since 2001. The BJP-led government of the state announced in 2001 that it will pay a monthly salary of Rs 1 200 to all the priests working in the 354 temples that are under the care of the state's temple management, or Devasthan, department.

In the state of Madhya Pradesh, the government has decided to make pujaris employees of the state. According to media reports, 'Madhya Pradesh will soon be the first state to have government appointed priests (pujaris) to conduct worship and supervise the affairs of thousands of Hindu temples.' Apparently, this scheme was initiated on the behest of priests who wanted to be 'brought under the government's umbrella to secure their future and ensure the upkeep of temples, the majority of which are crumbling with neglect'.

In the state of Tamil Nadu, the HRCE department runs the Oru kala puja (one prayer a day) scheme for temples that cannot afford it. Anyone wishing to have pujas done in the temple of his or her choice can send in a cheque for Rs 2500, to which the HRCE department promises to add a 'matching grant' of Rs 20,500. (It is not clear if the matching grants come from the government or from the temple funds.)

All these initiatives are pale as compared to the level of state involvement in religious tourism. With grants from the central government, states like Jammu and Kashmir, Himachal Pradesh, Uttaranchal, and Punjab are rushing to create new 'pilgrimage circuits'. To take just one representative example, the state of Himachal Pradesh has received a grant of Rs 7.8 crore from the central government to promote pilgrimages to the well-known mountain temples that exist in the state. The state aims to replicate the success of Vaishno Devi in Jammu and Kashmir. These kinds of pilgrimage circuits are typically very attractive to the private sector as well. Notable examples include the Ford Motor Company's involvement in building the Hare Krishna temple in Mayapur in West Bengal and the TVS Group's involvement in temple renovations in Tamil Nadu.

Public funding of religious tourism is generally justified on economic grounds. Often, purely pragmatic considerations of providing basic facilities to millions of pilgrims are cited to make a case for government spending. Public funds, however, are used not just to take care of the existing demand, but also for actively encouraging people to participate in religious festivals and pilgrimages. Traditional festivals are being reinvented and popularized with full involvement of the state with an express purpose of encouraging pilgrimage and religious tourism.

The state of Jammu and Kashmir, for example, gives out hefty matching grants to the Vaishno Devi temple to organize and popularize Navratra festivals held during the peak of the pilgrimage season. Thus, at the 2004 pilgrimage to Vaishno Devi, the state governor S.K. Sinha officiated over a yagna, offered puja, and led the pilgrims for the first sighting of the goddess before announcing a matching grant of Rs 850,000 from the state government to the temple board. With the funds from the state, the Navratra festival is being promoted as a tourist attraction in its own right, separate from the pilgrimage to Vaishno Devi: the state agencies put up a cultural show complete with classical dances, folk dances, poetry recitals, and even wrestling matches, and 'Maha car loan melas'.

But this case is far from unique. The state of Gujarat officially sponsors Navratri and Makar Sankranti festivities as a part of its 'Vibrant Gujarat' programme. According to media reports, major corporations including Reliance, Birla, and Essar make big donations to the state government for these festivals. The notorious case of the Communist government of Kerala participating in lighting the so-called divine light at the Sabarimala temple has already been mentioned.

The state of Jammu and Kashmir has been especially aggressive in promoting temple tourism in this politically and ecologically sensitive state. As mentioned earlier, the state government is trying to replicate the success of Vaishno Devi and Amarnath temples by pouring in money into the Shiv Khori temple complex. Going completely against the recommendations of environmental groups worried about the carrying capacity of this ecologically sensitive region, the state and central governments went out of the way to promote the pilgrimage to the Amarnath temple. In 2006–07, the central government offered to spend Rs 7 crore on infrastructure development for the Amarnath pilgrimage route. In addition, the pilgrimage was extended from one to two months with new facilities like helicopter flights to the shrine added. In the summer of 2008, the shrine board tried to divert 40 hectares of forest land to build temporary shelters for pilgrims, leading to political unrest all over the state.

The final example comes from the state of Gujarat where state funds were made available for what can only be called Hindu proselytization or Hindukaran. Groups affiliated with the BJP and the RSS organized a massive gathering at a newly invented 'pilgrimage' (the so-called

'Shabri Kumbh') in the adivasi area of the Dangs. The temple of Shabri (and Ram) was built on land acquired by dubious means and the bathing ghat for the pseudo-Kumbh was built with check dams and other infrastructure provided by the Gujarat government. As the Citizens' Inquiry Committee that visited the area found out, 'even the pretense of distance between the state apparatus and the Sangh [was] abandoned'.

The near-complete merging of the state machinery with forces of 'Hindukaran' has been going on for some time. The infamous Ekatmata yagna (sacrifice for unanimity) organized by the VHP in 1983, for example, was marked by enthusiastic participation and encouragement by state functionaries, including district magistrates and high-ranking police officials who presided over the yatra and religious ceremonies.

To sum up: the actual practice of secularism in India seems to be replicating the pre-modern, pre-Mughal Hindu model of the state–temple relationship. Elected ministers and bureaucrats see themselves in the mould of Hindu kings of yesteryears who considered it their duty to protect dharma. The temple priests and gurus, in turn, think nothing of treating elected officials as VIPs, if not literally as gods. The seamless partnership of faith and politics continues under the thin veneer of secularism.

The Banality of Hindu Nationalism

On the face of it, contemporary popular Hinduism appears to be the very epitome of a dynamic and inventive religious tradition which is changing to keep pace with the changing time. Clearly, all the new gods, god-men/women, new temples, and rituals add up to an impressive inventory of creative innovations that are allowing men and women to take their gods with them as they step into the heady, though unsettling, world dominated by global corporate capitalism.

But there is an underside: the same innovations in religious ritual and dogmas that are enabling the so-called Great Indian Middle Class to adjust to global capitalism, are also deepening a sense of Hindu chauvinism, and widening the chasm between Hindus and non-Hindu minorities. The banal, everyday Hindu religiosity is simultaneously breeding a banal, everyday kind of Hindu nationalism. This kind of nationalism is not openly proclaimed in fatwas, nor does it appear on the election manifestos of political parties. Its power lies in structuring the common sense of ordinary people.

*[handwritten margin note: more dangerous **]*

The idea of banal nationalism is from Michael Billig's 1995 book with the same title. Billig argues convincingly that nationalism is not merely an ideology of peripheral movements of separatists, ultra-nationalist fascists, and the extreme right. There is *also* the nationalism of the already well-established nations whose states have confidence in their own continuity—nation-states like the US, which is Billig's paradigmatic example. In these countries where the existence or continuity of the nation-state is not in doubt, symbols celebrating the nation nevertheless provide a continual background for making sense of everyday political discourse. As Billig puts it:

In many little ways, the citizenry are daily reminded of their national place in the world of nations. However, this reminding is so familiar, so continual, that it is not consciously registered as reminding. *The metonymic image of banal nationalism is not a flag which is being waved with fervent passion; it is the flag hanging unnoticed on the public building.* (emphasis added)

Gods are to India what the red-white-and-blue flag its to America. In India, public worship of Hindu gods and the

140

public performance of distinctively Hindu rituals serve the role of 'flagging' the national identity of the citizenry as Indians. Whereas the 'religions of the book', that is, Islam and Christianity, bind the faithful by demanding obedience to the letter and the spirit of their revealed dogmas, Hinduism deploys familiar rituals, festivals, myths, and observances—the kind of things children learn on their mothers' knees—to knit a many-stranded rope that binds the faithful to the faith with so many little ties, at so many different points that one loses sight of the ideological indoctrination that is going on. Ordinary worshippers and the three partners described above—the state, the temples, and the corporate or business interests—perform a choreographed dance, as it were, in which each element merges into another smoothly and effortlessly. The net result is a new kind of political and nationalistic Hinduism which is invented out of old customs and traditions that people are fond of, and familiar with. Because it builds upon the deeply felt religiosity, it sucks in even those who are not particularly anti-Muslim or anti-Christian. Religious festivals, temple rituals, and religious discourses become so many ways of 'flagging' India as a Hindu nation, and India's cultural superiority as due to its Hindu spirituality.

The best way to describe the banality of Hindu nationalism and the role of religion in it is to show how it works.

The example comes from the recent inauguration of Shri Hari Mandir, a new temple that opened in Porbandar in Gujarat on February 4, 2006. As described in a previous section, this grand sandstone temple and priest training school called Sandipani Vidyaniketan attached to it is a joint venture of the Gujarat government, the business house of the Ambanis, and the charismatic kathakar, Ramesh Bhai Oza. The inauguration ceremony of this temple–gurukul complex provides a good example of how Hindu

141

gods end up serving as props for Hindu nationalism and Hindu supremacy.

According to the description provided by the organizers themselves, the temple was inaugurated by Bhairon Singh Shekhawat, the then vice president of the country, with the chief minister Narendra Modi, in attendance. Also in attendance were the widow of Dhirubhai Ambani and the rest of the Ambani clan whose generous financial donations had built the temple. Some 50,000 well-heeled devotees of Oza from India and abroad crowded into the temple precincts to watch the event.

The elected representatives of 'secular' India, in their official capacity, prayed before the temple idols—something so routine that it hardly evokes a response from anyone any more. The prayer was followed by the national anthem sung before the gods, followed by a recital of the Vedas by the student-priests, followed by Gujarati folk dances. This was followed by speeches that liberally mixed up the gods with the nation, with quite a bit of rhetoric about the greatness of Hindu 'science' thrown in for good measure. Modi, under whose regime Gujarat witnessed the worst-ever communal riots, spoke glowingly of the 'tolerance' and 'secularism' of Hinduism. He went on to recommend that yagnas and religious recitals be held all over the country before undertaking any new construction because Hinduism is 'inherently ecological'. Next came Mrs Kokila Ambani, who, using her late husband as an example, urged mixing spirituality with work ethic and industry. The vice president, in his turn, spoke of how modern and scientific Hindu traditions were, comparing the gods' weapons with modern missiles and their vehicles to modern-day helicopters.

The theme of the superiority of ancient Hindu science was taken up a week later when the president of India, Abdul Kalam, came down to the temple–ashram complex to inaugurate its 'science museum' which highlights ancient Hindu discoveries in astronomy/astrology, medicine (Ayurveda), architecture (vastu), and so on. Without ever questioning what validity the earth-at-the-centre astronomy/astrology of Aryabhatta has in the modern world, the nuclear physicist president went on to claim not only the greatness of antiquity but also the continued relevance of the ancients for 'enriching' modern astronomy. The ancients—regardless of the fact that their cosmology has been falsified by modern science—were smoothly turned into the guiding lights of modern science.

This is a representative sample of how India's state–temple–corporate complex works: the gods become the backdrop, and the traditional puja becomes the medium, for asserting the Hinduness of India and the greatness of both. Worship of the gods becomes indistinguishable from the worship of Hindu culture and the Indian nation. Devotees come to sing hymns to gods, but end up singing hymns to mother India—and cannot tell the difference. The cult of the nation, furthermore, is simultaneously turned into a cult of 'reason' and 'science', but without the critical and empirical spirit of science.

Once the beloved and popular gods become identified with the land and its culture, Hindu nationalism becomes a banal, everyday affair. No one has to pass fatwas and there is no need to launch a militant battle against the West. Hindu nationalists have no use for such crude tools. They would rather turn the worship of gods into the worship of the nation and they would rather beat the West by appropriating the West's strengths in empirical sciences and other advances for their own gods. The tragedy is that the religiosity of ordinary believers provides the building blocks for this banal, but far from benign, Hindu nationalism.

This is the more polite, urban, and urbane face of everyday Hindu nationalism.

Conclusion

Economic globalization and neo-liberal reforms have created the material and ideological conditions in which a popular and ritualistic Hindu religiosity is growing. The three-sided partnership between the state, the temples, and the corporate interests is working in harmony to promote Hinduism in the public sphere. Popular religiosity, in turn, is being directed into a mass ideology of Hindu supremacy and Hindu nationalism.

This trend is a symptom of a deeper, more fundamental malaise, namely, the failure of secularism. For all its professions of secularism, the Indian state has developed neither a stance of equal indifference, nor of equal respect, for all the many religions of India. It has instead treated Hinduism, the religion of the majority, as the civic religion of the Indian nation itself. The result is a deep and widespread Hinduization of the public sphere, which is only growing under the conditions of globalization.

4

India@superpower.com: How We See Ourselves

We, the Indians, as Guru of all nations. Yes, I believe in that...

A.B. Vajpayee

Yad ihasti tad anyatra, yan nehasti na tat kavcit
Whatever is here might be elsewhere, but what is not here could hardly ever be found.

Mahabharata, 1.56.33

Mirror, Mirror on the Wall...

Of all the people in the world, guess who are the most bewitched by their image in the looking glass?

We are.

Indians rank number one in the world in thinking that we *are* number one in the world. Or rather, that our culture is.

This ranking comes from the 2007 Global Attitudes Survey carried out by the well-known American think tank, Pew Research Center. The survey asked people in forty-seven countries if they agreed or disagreed with this question: 'Our people are not perfect, but our culture is superior to others.'

Indians topped the list. A whopping 93 per cent agreed that our culture was superior to others, with 64 per cent agreeing without any reservations. The survey involved 2043 respondents, all of them from urban areas which means a higher proportion of literates, English speakers, and relatively well-to-do. Within the limitations that apply to all public opinion surveys, the figures reported by Pew give us a rough idea of how relatively privileged Indians see themselves vis-à-vis the world.

All people have a soft spot for their own culture and it is therefore not surprising that we Indians should think well of ourselves. But to see how off-the-charts our vanity is, let us compare ourselves with other 'ancient civilizations' in our neighbourhood. Compared to our 93 per cent, only 69 per cent of Japanese and 71 per cent of Chinese believed that their culture was the best in the world. Indeed, close to a quarter of the Japanese and the Chinese—as compared to our meagre 5 per cent—*denied* that their ways were the best. The US, a country universally condemned for its cultural imperialism, comes across as practically suffering from a severe inferiority complex: only 55 per cent of Americans believed in the superiority of their culture, 24 per cent expressed self-doubt, and 16 per cent completely denied that their culture was superior. (The corresponding numbers from India are 93, 5 and 1 per cent.)

This unquestioning belief inthe superiority of 'our culture' is why so many otherwise sensible people seem to buy into the glib talk of India as an emerging superpower. If one were to believe the political, business, and religious leaders, India is barely a couple of decades away from becoming the Number One in everything from IT, science (or 'knowledge' more broadly), technology, higher education, medicine, economy, culture, and of course spirituality. By 2050 or so, India will finally achieve the status of jagat guru in the realms of both the spiritual and the material.

In this chapter, I will look at how the cheerleaders for neo-liberalism and globalization—who come in secularist and Hindu nationalist flavours—are laying India's success in the global economy on the feet of our ancient Vedic Hindu sanskriti: everything from India's success in information

146

technology to its democracy is being ascribed to the great and wondrous Hindu Mind.

Not only is this Hindu triumphalism factually unwarranted, it is also dangerous because it often comes with its evil twin called communalism. Obviously, those who buy into Hindu triumphalism don't necessarily buy into communalism: there are many upright, liberal, and perfectly secular Indians who are proud of their Hindu heritage but who don't have a communal bone in their bodies. But by accepting Hindu triumphalism so readily and uncritically, they unwittingly end up endorsing the Islamophobic and anti-Christian rabble-rousers who are only too eager to grab the achievement of Indians—of *all* Indians, of *all* faiths and creeds—for the glory of Sanatan Dharma. Hindu triumphalism is the shared ground between the secular neo-liberals and their Hindu nationalist counterparts.

'Gen Next' and the Clash of Civilizations

Social scientists classify the worldwide responses to globalization into two broad categories: one based on fear and mimicry of the West, the second based upon national pride and defiance of the West.

The first generation of modernizers in non-Western societies, who were fighting for independence from Western colonial powers, fall into the first category. But the second generation that came of age in free, postcolonial societies, tends to adopt the stance of self-pride and defiance of the West. This rising self-awareness and pride of the second generation modernizers is partly responsible for the clash of civilizations that the American sociologist Samuel Huntington described in his well-known and controversial book *The Clash of Civilizations*.

What is this famous 'clash' all about? In his much-debated book, Huntington has argued that globalization does not erode cultural identities and create a McDonaldized world. Rather, it encourages 'civilizational consciousness' and makes people more intensely aware of and proud of their distinctive cultures. Against those like Francis Fukuyama who predicted that after the end of the Soviet Union, history itself will come to an end and the whole world will adopt American-style capitalist democracy, Huntington predicted that globalization will *split up* the world into eight major civilizational blocks: Western Christianity (both Protestant and Catholic, including Latin America), Orthodox or Eastern Christianity (Russia), Islamic world, Chinese (or Confucian), Japanese, Buddhist, African, and Hindu civilizations. Future friends and foes on the world stage will be determined no so much by ideologies but by civilizational affinities or clashes. Huntington predicted that the Chinese will make military alliance with Islamic countries and challenge the cultural and economic power of the 'the West' (the US, Europe, and Britain). India, along with Japan and Russia, will become 'swing civilizations' that will ally themselves with the Western–Jewish axis against the Confucian–Islamic axis.

Why do civilizations clash? Huntington gives two main reasons: human nature and the 'rise of the Rest' against the West.

Civilizations will clash, Huntington says, because 'people define themselves by what makes them different from others in a particular context… people define their identity by what they are not', Thus as non-Western cultures become familiar with Western ways, they begin to accord greater —not lesser—relevance to their own civilizational identities. That is just human nature and there is no reason to expect anything else.

But another reason 'the Rest' will clash with 'the West' is that it is modernizing without westernizing. In the past, the elite of non-Western societies used to believe that in order to modernize, their societies will have to adopt Western cultural values and Western tastes. But that is no longer true. As non-Western societies acquire the technological hardware of modernity, they begin to reconcile this modernity with their own traditions and cultural values. What it means in practical terms is that rather than trying to imitate the West as the first generation of modernizers used to do, the second generation seeks the secret of their success in their own culture:

> ...they attribute their dramatic economic development not to their import of Western culture, but rather to their adherence to their own culture. They are succeeding because they are different from the West...The revolt against the West is being legitimated by asserting the superiority of non-Western values.

This is exactly what is going on among the emerging urban middle classes—the kind whose views are captured in the Pew survey. This generation of Indians sees no reason to feel awed by the West, or to hold it as a model to emulate. On the contrary, they have very good reasons to be proud of what India has managed to achieve in the sixty plus years since it won its independence. Proud of their own achievements, they think that the West has something to learn from them.

While Huntington's thesis has been very influential—especially after 9/11 which was explained as a clash between Islam and the West—it has obvious problems. For one, it assumes the world's 6 billion plus people can be neatly divided into seven groups defined by cultural values which have supposedly endured through thousands of years. Moreover, this way of understanding the world turns cultures, or civilizations, into destiny: like genes, you are either born in the right civilization, or you are destined to remain a laggard.

The Great Hindu Mind and the IT Miracle

As with the rest of 'the Rest', India, too, is undergoing second-generation indigenization and refusing to Westernize as it modernizes. As it acquires the usual hallmarks of modernity —wealth, machines, nuclear bombs, McDonald's, shopping malls, beauty pageants, and such—it is simultaneously putting a distinctively Indian imprint on them. More often than not, this imprint is distinctively and self-consciously Hindu.

This process of domesticating and Hinduizing modernity did not start with the current phase of globalization. Treating new and foreign ideas *as if* they are simply a restatement of ancient Hindu wisdom has been India's unique way of dealing with change. The neo-Hinduism of people like Swami Vivekananda, Sarvepalli Radhakrishnan, and Mahatma Gandhi is based on this very Indian process of mixing and matching. Indians take whatever they find admirable or simply fashionable in the West but afterwards, they somehow or the other connect it to the 'eternal' Hindu tradition, and claim it to be a product of their own native genius since the beginning of time! The new is made old and the alien is made native—and whatever challenge the new may have posed to the ancient order is blunted, and all contradictions denied. It is as if modern Indians are unconsciously fulfilling the *Mahabharata*'s boast quoted in the beginning of this chapter that there is nothing outside of the tradition that it represents.

This method of making-new-old never ends. New and perfectly secular (i.e., non-religious, this-worldly) developments and challenges thrown up by the process of modernization end up getting framed in 'Vedic', or elite Hindu ways of thinking which are held to be sanatan, or eternally true. The wild leaps of logic this process involves will become clearer from the following examples:

- India is a parliamentary democracy. From this fact, many leap to the conclusion that Indians are democratic by nature. The fact that there were reasons of political expediency at the time of Independence that made us embrace democracy is simply set aside. The visible phenomenon is supposed to be already contained in the invisible cause which is the svabhava, or essential nature of things and people: like a seed cannot help become a tree of its own kind, Indians cannot help becoming democratic because it is their *svabhava*, their innate nature to do so.

  Once a social phenomenon gets defined in terms of innate natures, or cultural essences, the question 'naturally' arises: where do Indians get this sweet democratic essence? The answer invariably is: from Hinduism which supposedly teaches democratic values. Any mention of *chaturvarna*, the very anti-thesis of democracy, is considered to be in bad taste and proof that you are trying to tarnish the motherland's image.

- There are many religions in India. From this fact, it is concluded that Indians are tolerant by nature. They are tolerant because Hinduism teaches that all religions are equally true. Any mention of the fact that traditional Hinduism actually treats the Vedas as the Absolute Truth and all other forms of worship based upon lower levels of truth as providing illusionary benefits, is brushed off as nonsense.

- Gandhi led us to freedom using non-violent means. From this fact, it is concluded that Indians are non-violent by nature. Why are we so non-violent? It is all thanks to the Hindu teaching of ahimsa. Anyone who mentions that the *Bhagvat Gita* in fact condones himsa even against your own brothers and family members, is declared to be incapable of plumbing the depths of the Divine Song.

- India has the third largest scientific workforce in the world. From this fact, it is concluded that Indians are innately good at science. Why are we so innately scientific? Well, modern science is only rediscovering what our Vedic forefathers already knew. If you were to show serious contradictions between modern science and the spiritual monism of the Vedas, you will be declared to be a nastik communist to the boot!

And so it goes.

Not everyone indulges in such wild leaps of logic, of course. On the contrary, India has produced some of the finest social scientists and historians who do not fall in this trap of explaining social phenomena in terms of innate cultural-religious essences. But in the wider culture, there are any number of gurus and political pundits who have honed this reasoning to perfection. In this they have been aided by Western Indophiles and Orientalists who look to India for creative alternatives to some of the problems of their own societies. It is by a constant and cumulative use of this style of reasoning that the new is turned into ancient Hindu wisdom, and secular developments of science, democracy, and even secularism itself, are gobbled up by high Hinduism. Invariably, it is not the glory of the Indian civilization which has many streams flowing into it, but the glory of our Vedic-'Aryan' forefathers that is invoked to explain the 'innate' virtues of Indians. The achievements of India for which *all* Indians —Muslims, Christians, Sikhs, Buddhists, animist adivasis, nonbelievers—have toiled and sacrificed are simply declared to be Hindu achievements. Like the good book said, there is simply nothing outside the Hindu universe!

Perhaps a parallel with the US can bring out the full extent of how exclusionary this way of thinking is. What if all of America's achievements were to be ascribed to its Christian pilgrim fathers, and to its Protestant Christian culture? It is a safe bet that a vast majority of non-Christian Americans —including the very vocal Indian immigrants—will be up in arms if such an idea was to become as mainstream in that country as the idea of India-as-Hindu is in this country? (Another safe bet: many of the same NRIs who will scream racism if such a scenario were to come to pass in the US will have no problem funding Hindutva causes in India.)

This conflation between India and Hinduism can be seen at work in the heart of India's most prized achievement: its IT industry. The basic plot will be familiar by now:

- Indians are good at writing software: why, we are practically running the back offices of the whole world! Why are we so great at this stuff? It is our Hindu heritage which has endowed us with an intuitive grasp of interconnections between isolated bits of information.

This is not a hypothetical scenario meant to bolster the thesis presented here. A great many computer professionals, important scientists, and well-respected intellectuals have bought into this idea that Hinduism predisposes Indians to become great software engineers. Computing is all about writing code, some argue, and our rituals carry coded knowledge about the cosmos; others claim that we are the people who invented '0' and computer code is all about manipulating '0' and '1'; or alternatively, Sanskrit is the language of computers etc. Here is a sampling of some of the more serious arguments of this kind.

Gurcharan Das, the celebrated author of *India Unbound*, has this to say:

We proved by our history that we are inveterate tinkerers, people who can make things work in different ways at different times. That is perfect for software and other knowledge applications...

153

in fact, the immense complexity of Hinduism makes us tinkerers, hairsplitters, debaters, people who communicate, network and talk and get to know what works and what doesn't. That is perfect IT-world behaviour and that's why we are the best at it.

One can't help wondering if we are the best in 'IT-world behaviour', why didn't we invent the Internet in the first place? If our religion makes us such great tinkerers, why is it that the vast majority of our people still use woodstoves and ploughs which our celebrated Vedic forefathers would feel at home with, if they could be reincarnated into 'India's century'.

Here is Pavan Varma, the otherwise astute observer of Indian society, waxing eloquent about the Hindu Mind's inner computer nerd:

> The essential point is that the Hindu seems to have a congenital inclination to differentiate the database around him. He cannot resist the impulse to segment, to break down, all empirical phenomenon into constituent units, to arrange them into compartments what may appear to be seamless wholes...such an exercise presupposes the ability to continually structure a link between a sum and its parts...The Hindu is, therefore, not fazed by the sheer accretion of data or the elusiveness of a paradigm; like a beaver collecting pieces of wood, he proceeds to deconstruct both...

Really? One is naturally inclined to ask why did this beaver-like Hindu mind have to wait for western scientists to make all the breakthroughs that we today take for granted?

Finally, here is Daniel Lak, BBC South Asia correspondent for many years, and author most recently of *India Express*, ruminating over the connection between a Brahmin upbringing and computer prowess:

...the arcane, impenetrable nature of Hindu lore and practice somehow predisposes its former priestly class to flourishing in information technology. Like Hindu ritual, IT involves coded language and a veritable priesthood of initiates to resolves problems and to reconcile the mysterious and the mundane...

But even if all the Brahmins in the country were to become software engineers, what does that have to do with 'Hindu lore', impenetrable or not? It is Brahmins' superior access to modern science and engineering education—made possible by the cultural capital they have accumulated through exclusive control of all learning for centuries—that can more than adequately explain their disproportionate presence in this profession.

These ideas seem to be percolating down into the Indian street. It is commonplace to hear ordinary folk extolling the innate virtues of Indians in mathematics, science, and 'computers'. Interestingly enough, the fulsome praise we heap upon ourselves often comes paired with derogatory statements we heap upon Westerners, especially Americans, as materialist gluttons who are too busy having fun to put in the kind of hard work Indians do in developing their skills. Many of them seem to really think that if it were not for the brainy Indians, the wheels of industry and commerce in the United States will come to a grinding halt!

This hype about the Hindu mind is preventing a more realistic assessment of the state of Indian science and technology including the much-admired IT sector. While the general impression is that India is making great strides towards becoming a 'knowledge economy', facts on the ground tell a more sobering story.

Indian science and technology is not faring very well when compared to our Asian neighbours or even when compared to its own earlier record. Consider the fact that none of India's top institutes of science or technology has ever made into the top 100 of the prestigious Shanghai ranking of the top 500 universities of the world. Only three Indian institutions have ever made it into the list at all, but at a very low rank: the Indian Institute of Science in Bangalore scored in the 251–300 range, and IIT-Delhi and IIT-Kharagpur figured in the lowest bracket (451–500). In contrast, five of Japan's universities figured in the top 100 universities and two Chinese universities ranked higher than India's. The irony is that the quantity and quality of scientific research has been steadily declining even as the number of universities and deemed universities has been growing, and even as the budgets for research and development have been getting bigger. The number of research papers from India in peer-reviewed journals fell from 14,987 to 12,227 between 1980 and 2000, while China's grew from merely 924 to 22,061. When measured for quality (or impact) of Indian research, the data is equally dismal: only 0.33 per cent of research papers published from India make it in the top 1 per cent of the most cited papers in the world, while the corresponding figure from China is about twice as high. Even the much-hyped IT sector has created stupendous amount of wealth not because of superior innovations, but because it is cheap. It is true that the IT industry has come a long was from its techo-coolie days, but still the engine driving it remains relatively routine information tinkering at a relatively low cost.

All told, invoking the Hindu Mind does not take us very far in understanding the modern world that we are creating through the blood, tears, and sweat of all Indians.

Majoritarian Common Sense

Laying the achievements of modern India at the feet of Hinduism may boost the ego of Hindu Indians, but it does

no other useful work. As we saw above, <u>invoking the Great</u>
<u>Hindu Mind creates delusions of grandeur which prevent an</u>
<u>honest, self-critical appraisal of the real state of affairs.</u>

But <u>there is an even bigger danger: that of *unwittingly*</u>
<u>agreeing to play on Hindutva's turf.</u> The conflation of Hinduism
with Indian culture has become so much a part of the prevailing
common sense that it is easy to forget that this is actually what
the Hindu right has been agitating for since its birth.

This does *not* mean that all those who have a soft spot
for the virtues of Hindu culture are communal and harbour
anti-Muslim or anti-Christian feelings. No, that does not
follow. <u>Religious belief or even the rather common feeling</u>
<u>of pride in one's own tribe, by itself does not make anyone</u>
<u>hate: if that were the case, India would have ceased to exist</u>
<u>long time back.</u>

Imagining and explaining Indian achievements in Hindu
terms, or using Indian and Hindu interchangeably, does
<u>not make you communal.</u> *But it does contribute to a Hindu*
majoritarian mindset.

A <u>majoritarian is someone who believes that the 'numerically</u>
<u>larger community has the democratic right of asserting its</u>
<u>wishes on the rest of the society'.</u> Thus, a majoritarian would
insist that <u>the culture of the majority community is the culture</u>
<u>of the whole nation, and the minorities ought to adopt it as</u>
<u>their own.</u> Not surprisingly, a majoritarian would oppose any
special provision by the state to protect minority cultures as
unfair appeasement.

It looks like the majoritarian strain is growing in Indian
politics. Ironically, the widespread acceptance of democracy
as the rule by majority gets confused with the idea that
the community with larger numerical strength has the
democratic right to assert its will on everyone else. India's
most reliable and respected <u>pollsters from the Center of Study</u>
<u>of Developing Societies carried out a survey of voters in the</u>

2004 elections on the issue of majoritarianism. They asked a cross-section of voters this question: 'In a democracy, the opinion of the majority community should prevail.' They found that 35 per cent of respondents agreed with this idea, 35 per cent disagreed, and the remaining 30 per cent had no opinion (one hopes because they don't think in terms of majority minority). Muslims, for obvious reasons, were much less majoritarian: 60 per cent of the Muslim respondents disagreed when asked if the opinions of the majority should prevail in a democracy.

What is surprising is that more education seems to make people more majoritarian. More college graduates (44 per cent) were majoritarian as compared to those with high school education (40 per cent). But it was religiosity that was found to make the biggest difference: twice as many more highly religious Hindus (42 per cent) agreed that the will of the Hindu majority ought to prevail, as compared to less religious Hindus (26 per cent). (Incidentally, this correlation between religion and majoritarianism is not particularly Hindu, but was found to hold true for all religions in all South Asian countries. A recent survey of the state of democracy in all the countries of South Asia showed that 'those who participate in religious organizations are twice more likely to be majoritarian as compared to those who are not engaged in religious organizations.')

The voting trends from 2004 suggested that those with more majoritarian attitudes were slightly more inclined to vote for the BJP and its allies (39 per cent) as compared to Congress (34 per cent). The data from earlier elections in 1996, 1998, and 1999 also indicated that the urban middle class voters were beginning to desert the Congress and vote for the BJP.

The 2009 elections have defied this trend. In a metropolis like Delhi, all seven seats, regardless of whether the constituency

158

was a slum or a well-to-do community, have all gone to the Congress Party. Voters don't go to ballot boxes only as Hindus but also as people with a diversity of clashing interests. Electoral fortunes of political parties do not give a true assessment of the long-term cultural shifts in the world view and values of voters.

In any case, Hindu majoritarianism does not necessarily break down along the Congress–BJP lines. The Congress and its allies have a fair share of voters and leaders who treat Hinduism as the *de facto* way of life for the entire nation. As we saw above, the phenomenon of absorbing everything into Hinduism has a long and complex history that cuts across the secular–communal/BJP–Congress divide.

The danger of this cultural majoritarianism is not that the majority community will necessarily become a Hindu vote bank and vote for communalists, or become actively hostile and violent towards the minorities. The real danger lies in indifference and insensitivity towards the members of minority communities; in seeing state measures for protecting minority rights as 'appeasement'; and in seeing the minorities as an alien 'them' with inferior culture. Sociologist Dipankar Gupta makes this point as well:

> For the ordinary Indian who comes from the majority community of Hindus, what happens to Muslims periodically is of no great interest... an overwhelming majority will not go out to kill Muslims but would look kindly upon those who do so under state support.

This is exactly right: Those with a majoritarian attitude find it easier to accept that India is a Hindu country, with a Hindu culture and that minorities need to fall in line or face the consequences. It is this tolerance of intolerance that is the real danger of Hindu majoritarianism.

Theology of Hatred: Hindutva against 'Semitic Monotheism'

Thankfully, at least so far, the Hindu majoritarian mindset described above has been more of a diffused and widely shared cultural sensibility, rather than a full-blown political project. It has been prevented from sliding into chauvinism by the pluralism and diversity within Hinduism itself. Moreover, the familiar rhetoric of *sarva dharma samabhav* has served to moderate open expressions of Hindu supremacy: even the most hardened communalists feel compelled to say some good things now and then about other religions, if only to show how tolerant and liberal Hinduism is. Even though, as this book has shown, the state functionaries often treat Hinduism as if it were the *de facto* state religion, the constitutional principle of the state being equi-distant from all religions still acts as a moderating influence.

To convert the diffused cultural majoritarianism of Hindus into a unified political majoritarianism which openly reduces non-Hindus to the status of second-class citizens has been the fond dream of the Hindu right. Towards that end, there are voices within the Hindutva camp that are openly fermenting hatred of Islam and Christianity.

A relatively new, deeply Islamophobic and anti-Christian faction is emerging within the Hindutva camp that is so extreme right that it accuses the RSS of being soft on Muslims and Christians. It is made up of a group of writers and journalists associated with the publishing house called Voice of India (VOI). The VOI circle of writers is producing what can best be described as a theology of hatred, for they are offering theological arguments that are deeply insulting to all Abrahamic or monotheistic religions.

The earlier generation of Hindu nationalists who were influenced by Vinayak Damodar Savarkar and Guru Golwalker, justified their hatred of Muslims and Christians on the foreign origins of their religions: Muslims and Christians were not full members of Bharatvarsha because their holy lands lay elsewhere. The new generation of Hindu extremists is not satisfied with *merely* decrying Indian Muslims and Christians as aliens. They go on to condemn the monotheistic God that Muslims and Christians worship as 'defective and inadequate' because, to quote Ram Swarup, a major theoretican of the Hindu right, '[their God] is "one", male, exclusive and intolerant [who inspires] *tamsika* and *rajasika* worship but lacks *sattvika* worship,' and because, to quote Sita Ram Goel, the founder of VOI, '[their God] is a construct of the outer mind drawing strength as it draws upon dark drives of unregerate consiousness'. According to the VOI school of thought, Hindus can only acquire self-confidence vis-à-vis the West and Islam when they begin to openly criticize monotheistic religions from the perspective of Hindu or yogic spirituality in order to 'save' Muslims from the 'disease of Islam... and help them realize how false and diabolical is the creed of Muhammad, how it is holding them prisoner and how it deserves not their loyalty but their contempt'. The same idea is expressed by Koenraad Elst, a Belgian champion of Hindu nationalism and other anti-Islamic movements, when he told an interviewer recently that 'Every Muslim is a Sita, an abductee who must be liberated from Ravana's prison... We should help Muslims in freeing themselves from Islam.'

Secondly, the earlier generation of RSS communalists grew up on the discredited Nazi-era language of 'race spirit' and 'racial pride' their gurus (especially Guru Golwalker) had borrowed from the fascists in Germany and Italy. The newer generation uses the liberal vocabulary of tolerance and reason: it sees monotheistic religions as being 'innately' intolerant and irrational because of their conception of divine as One True God. Only Hinduism, with its many gods and respect for many levels of truth, can be truly tolerant and respectful of difference. Only Hinduism that does not remove God from nature (the way monotheism's do), can combine science with spirituality. To take a fairly representative example, this is how Sita Ram Goel describes the god of monotheistic religions:

> Supreme Being of monotheism (whether Jehova or Allah) comes out as a despot who is also an arbitrary partisan, a jealous gangster...The One God is simply another name for Satan and that is why devotees of One God invoke him while committing all kinds of atrocities.

This conception of God who is despotic and jealous is contrasted favourably with Vedantic ideals of equality of all truths and 'friendship of all gods with each other and with their worshippers. This reading of monotheistic religions completely denies the sources of tolerance, love, and equality that these religions have in them. But what is remarkable is that it foments intolerance against Islam and Christianity in the name of the superior tolerance of Hinduism. This kind of thinking is described as 'designer fascism' which uses the language of tolerance and enlightenment, but considers these values to be the exclusive and innate virtue of only one kind of people—the Hindus in this case.

Who are these Hindu triumphalists? They prefer to call themselves *bhaudik kshatriya*, or intellectual warriors. This term was coined by David Frawley, a.k.a. Vamadev Shastri, an American convert to Hinduism, to describe those dedicated intellectuals who can serve as global brand managers of Hinduism and present a positive picture of the faith. These self-proclaimed warriors on behalf of Hinduism share two noticeable features:

One, nearly all the prominent Hindu triumphalists are associated with the New Delhi-based publishing house called Voice of India (VOI). VOI was founded by two anti-Communists turned Hindu nationalists—Sita Ram Goel (1921–2003) and his friend and intellectual soulmate, Ram Swarup (1920–1992). Influential journalists writing for the mainstream media, including Girilal Jain (1924–1993), Arun Shourie, S. Gurumurthy, and François Gautier have been associated with VOI either directly as published authors (Jain, Shourie, and Gautier) or indirectly as admired fellow travelers (Gurumurthy). The VOI group has managed to attract a number of Western writers. Koenraad Elst, a writer with links with Vlaams Belang, the fanatically anti-immigrant and Islampohobic far right party of his native Belgium, is the acknowledged intellectual heir of Sita Ram Goel and Ram Swarup. François Gautier, a follower of Sri Aurobindo, and more recently of Siri Siri Ravi Shankar, served for many years as the India correspondent for the French newspaper *La Figaro*, which has been described as the mouthpiece of the French New Right. Vedic astrologer and Ayurvedic doctor, David Frawley, is among the best-known authors of VOI. VOI has also attracted a number of US-based Indian engineers, computer scientists, and other professionals who see themselves as Hinduism's global brand managers.

VOI brings out inexpensive, relatively well-produced books that carry the views of writers and journalists who specialize in putting a Hindu supremacist spin on Hindu philosophy and history. The official website lists a grand total of 107 books, mostly in English but also in Hindi. It offers complete texts of 26 of its more popular books, especially the works of Sita Ram Goel, Ram Swarup, Koenraad Elst, and David Frawley online as well. It has also started publishing Indian editions of works by Daniel Pipes, the well-known anti-Islamic American neoconservative. VOI has practically become a brand name for publishing books on two themes very dear to the Hindu right, namely, India as the original homeland of the 'Aryans', and Vedas as containing modern cosmological ideas in coded language. All the arguments and evidence they produce in support of this revisionist history have been discredited by well-known historians of ancient India.

The second feature that unites the VOI-affiliated triumphalists has already been mentioned above: they stand on the right of the RSS. Their main complaint against the RSS is that it has not openly renounced the Gandhian ideal of sarva dharma samabhav and that it continues to try to prove that it is more authentically secular as compared to the 'pseudo-seculars'. The VOI stalwarts, especially Sita Ram Goel, Ram Swarup, and Abhas Chatterjee, are vehemently opposed to even the suggestion of showing equal respect for Islam and Christianity because they consider them to be adharmic and 'asuric' (demonic) 'creeds', fit only for those with tàmsik vritti (dark nature). The following is a representative sample of their utter contempt for the idea of equal respect for all faiths:

> Islam and Christianity follow a path of adharma of *tamasika vrittis* (traits of darkness) or *asuric vrittis* (demonic traits) which can only lead a person away from the God of Sanatan Dharma…Putting dharma and adharma on the same pedestal by labeling them both as 'panths' and holding such 'panths' in equal respect amounts to the principle of *dharma-adharam samabhava*, i.e., equality of respect for virtue and vice, righteous and unrighteous, good and evil. It can only make a mockery of 5000 years of Indian spiritual thought. It cannot but sink the society to the lowest depths of viciousness and moral bankruptcy.

They are opposed to even paying lip service to equal-respect rhetoric because it undercuts their opposition to religious conversions: if they admit all religions are equally true and worthy of respect, on what grounds can they oppose any Hindu opting for other religions? The VOI authors' vehemence on this matter also reflects the anxieties of many American NRIs who are getting nervous that their own children will use the logic of sarva dharma samabhav to adopt other religions and drop out of the Hindu fold.

The VOI circle's vehement condemnation of monotheistic religions is matched only by their absolute and total admiration of Hindu spirituality, tolerance, and rationality. Their aspiration to make Hinduism the jagat guru represents the most extreme Hindu-centric response to Samuel Huntington's thesis of clash of civilizations discussed above.

The intellectual warriors of VOI share Huntington's basic idea that each civilization has an enduring, unchanging core which is formed primarily by religion. In their mind, just as 'the West' is defined by Christianity, the civilizational core of India (or 'Greater India' which extends over all of South Asia and much of South East Asia) is defined by Hinduism. As L.K. Advani put it recently, Hinduism is the 'cultural life current' that animates India and that 'words like Hindu and Bhartiyata, Hindu Rashtra and Bharatiya Rajya are synonymous.'

But while Huntington sees the major clash of civilizations as taking place between the 'Christian West' and Islam (aided by the Chinese), Hindu triumphalists one-up Huntington and pit Hinduism against both Islam *and* Christianity. The real source of intolerance and other evils in the world, they insist, is not Islam alone but rather monotheism of the 'Semitic' type (i.e., of West Asian origin) which includes Christianity and Judaism as well. Their claim is that because Semitic monotheistic religions believe in only One True God for the whole world, they are *innately* intolerant of diversity and pluralism. (Judaism is exempted from this critique of

165

monotheism because even though Jews believe in One God, their God is exclusively the God of Jews alone.)

In this reading, the clash between monotheism and polytheism is the most fundamental clash in the whole of human history. The two are locked in an eternal conflict because their very essences are opposed to each other: the essential instinct of Semitic monotheism is supposed to be 'exclusive and annihilative' while the essential instinct of Hinduism is 'assimilative and inclusive'. This clash was hidden from view while the world was busy fighting the Cold War.

Now that the Cold War against Communism is over and the Hot War against 'Islamofascism' is on, the civilizational conflict between the two conceptions of God takes on a new urgency. Hindu triumphalists believe that in the post-9/11 world, 'Hindu India' has valuable lessons to teach to the West about how to defeat Islam, because as S. Gurumurthy put it, 'the Hindu society is perhaps the only society in the world that faced and then survived the Islamic theocratic civilization'. The underlying idea is that the world will have to learn Hindu values if it is to defeat 'Islamic theocratic civilization'.

VOI-style triumphalism has also drawn a lot of fresh energy from the rising profile of India in the world economy and politics. There is a general feeling aboard that this is 'India's century'. VOI wants to make the so-called Indian century a Hindu century.

Rising Islamophobia

VOI can publish whatever it wants—India is a free country, after all. But just how effective have their diatribes against the great monotheistic religions been?

The fact that Indian voters have delivered the Hindu communalists a resounding defeat in two general elections in a row (2004, and again in 2009) is a cause for hope that the communal virus has been contained. But electoral trends don't always reflect the changes in mentalities and attitudes. People may not vote for the BJP for many reasons having to do with calculations about political stability, continuity in governance, economic policies, and similar secular issues. But that does not mean that they don't see eye to eye with the BJP and Hindutva allies on matters related to religion and religious minorities.

Long-term trends in the social conditions of Muslims have been adequately and very carefully described by the Sachar Committee report. But one doesn't need a committee report to realize that something has changed: the kinds of things 'people like us' say in polite company these days would have been unthinkable some years back. Just in the last six months of my stay in India this year, I've come to realize how respectable open expressions of Islamophobia have become.

In a big and well-stocked bookstore in the upscale Connaught Place, New Delhi, I found books on Islam stacked in the section marked 'War/Military/Islam', while books on Hinduism and Buddhism grace the shelves marked 'Religion/Philosophy/Spirituality'. When I complained to the owner of the bookstore, he could not understand what my problem was. Islam doesn't have much of spirituality, he said, so he couldn't possibly place books on Islam in the religion/spirituality section. And isn't it a fact that the Koran teaches violence, he asked me point-blank. So what was I complaining about? There were a couple of other customers who agreed with me that it was disrespectful to Islam. But it seems to have made no difference to his business: by all appearances, the bookstore seems to be thriving. (The VOI hardliners would be thrilled.)

On a visit to Chandigarh earlier this year, I happened to witness an honour kidnapping of a young woman by her relatives (which I reported in *The Hindu* later). It turned out that the woman who is a Sikh wanted to marry a Muslim man, and her father had her kidnapped outside the court-house. What shocked me was how everyone—from other witnesses to the police officers—agreed that the father did the right thing, because how could anyone respectable allow their daughter to marry a Muslim? It was eerie sitting in the police office listening to the old man assuring the cops (who didn't need much assurance on this count anyway) that he wasn't narrow-minded, and that he would have allowed his daughter to marry a *churra-chamar*, but letting her marry a Muslim was another matter. That is when the truth of the Sachar Committee's finding that Muslims were faring worse then Dalits hit me: Muslims had become the new untouchables in India.

And then there was a conversation with an old school friend. He lives in a posh high-rise apartment block in Mumbai. I happened to mention that a Dalit–Muslim couple I knew were practically homeless because no one would rent them an apartment in the great metropolis of Mumbai. Suddenly an aspect of my friend's personality came to the surface that I did not know existed. With great passion and vehemence he defended why Muslims should not be allowed to rent or buy in 'Hindu areas': they are dirty, violent, meat-eating people and have no business living with good people like himself. I later discovered that my friend was quite sympathetic to Hindutva causes, and spent his spare time trawling the VOI and other anti-Islamic websites.

 Three vignettes don't prove a trend. Neither do they prove that VOI-style triumphalism is a direct cause of what is going on. All one can say is that such ideas are in the air—more than they used to. And this ought to give us a pause. History shows us that terrible things happen when otherwise good people feel no empathy for a vulnerable minority and when they see that minority as a source of backwardness dragging them down from their rightful place in the world.

Pride without Prejudice

Pride in the achievements of your own tribe is a legitimate emotion. But when pride is fuelled by—and contributes to —prejudice against others, it becomes jingoism.

As this chapter has argued, the self-congratulatory conflation of all of India's achievements into Hinduism is contributing to the emergence of a jingoistic Hindu majoritarian mindset.

There are two big dangers of this mindset. The first is an exaggerated sense of our achievements as a people. This may be a good ego booster in the short run, but it can lead us into a self-defeating complacency.

The second danger is potentially deadlier, and that is the growing tolerance of intolerance towards non-Hindu minorities. Those who are convinced that all that is worthwhile and commendable in India is a product of the Great Hindu Mind will not have much respect and fellow feelings for non-Hindu minorities, especially if there is a history of bad blood between them. They will not get too upset or angry when their elected leaders allow occasional pogroms, so long as they can promise to make India a Great Nation, a jagat guru. They will consider it perfectly normal and right that Hindu women be abducted if necessary to prevent them from marrying Muslim men. They will consider it just right that Muslims don't move into their neighbourhoods, and so on.

The only way to challenge the majoritarian mindset is to reclaim all of India's achievements for *all* its people. India is what it is not because of Hindu genius, but because Indians of all faiths, and of no faith, have struggled and toiled and sacrificed.

India is a secular democracy not because Hinduism makes us democratic by nature. But we are a democracy because we made a social contract in our Constitution to set aside all pre-existing notions of high and low, the great Hindu system of sanctified hierarchy included. We are tolerant, not because we are Hindus but because all of India's religious faiths found ways to live with each other without compromising on the tenets of their faith. And today, if we are succeeding in IT (to the extent that we really are), it is not because of our Hindu lore, but because so many children of all faiths were deprived of primary education so that India could build the IITs and other institutions of higher education.

Rather than allow the Great Hindu Mind to absorb the secular achievements of India, it is time to reclaim them for the blood and sweat of all Indians. Only then can we be proud without being prejudiced.

5

Rethinking secularization
(with India in mind)

'God is dead,' Nietzsche
'Nietzsche is dead,' God

God on a Winning Streak

So far we have concentrated, single-mindedly, on understanding the growth of popular Hinduism in India in the era of globalization. But India is not alone: a rising tide of religiosity seems to be sweeping the whole world. Consider the following:

- Traditional Christian beliefs in a personal God, heaven, hell, and the resurrection of the soul are growing even in some of the most secularized countries in Europe. Evangelical churches preaching a more passionate and participatory Christianity are showing a strong growth in such bastions of secularism as Sweden, Holland, Germany, and Britain. American-style tele-evangelicalism and mega-churches are cropping up within the Church of England in Britain and Germany. Continent-wide programmes in Christian education are attracting new members. Even Roman Catholicism, which has been declining most sharply all across Europe, is showing a growth in charismatic movements like the Emmanuel Community which started in France and now operates in 50 countries. Catholic shrines, especially those devoted to Virgin Mary, are attracting huge numbers of pilgrims to the extent that Europe has been described as 'living in the golden age of pilgrimage'.
- Belief in reincarnation, the new age, and the occult remains

high in most of Europe, including France, the home of the Enlightenment.

- Russia is witnessing a growing clericalization of the public sphere. The Russian Orthodox Church, richer and more powerful than at any time in almost a century, has become the spiritual arm of the Russian state. The power of the Church has grown to the point that it has succeeded in introducing Russian Orthodox teachings, complete with Bible reading and liturgy, in public schools. Despite the government's attempts since 1997 to curb all competitors to the Russian Orthodox, religious movements like Jehovah's Witnesses, Hare Krishna, and Scientology, along with evangelical and Catholic churches are growing.

- The once atheistic China has emerged as 'one of the most religious countries in the world where all kinds of religions, old and new, conventional or eccentric, are thriving'. Rationalism and a favourable attitude to science give way to a growth of belief in God, spirits/ghosts, ancestors, and fate.

- New transnational religious networks are emerging as globalization disembeds religions from their historic homelands and scatters them around the world. African and East Asian (especially Korean) churches are booming in Europe and North America. Hindu temples and ashrams are becoming increasingly transnational.

- Online religions are growing. Today, anyone with a computer and a credit card can do a virtual darshan, complete with virtual arti and flower offerings, to any of the multitude of gods and goddesses in the Hindu pantheon. (As an experiment, Google 'online puja'.)

- Religious belief remains widespread among scientists. A recent study of Indian scientists (1100 participants, all Ph.D.s in basic sciences, engineering, and medicine) by the

US-based Institute for Study of Secularism in Society and Culture found that 26 per cent of them firmly believed in the existence of a personal God, while another 30 per cent believed in an impersonal spiritual power. Close to 40 per cent of Indian scientists believed that God performs miracles, while 24 per cent believed that men and women with special divine powers can perform miracles. A significant number believe in karma (29 per cent), life after death (26 per cent) and reincarnation (20 per cent). Many scientists who would be counted in the category of 'eminent scientists' of the country participate in public prayers and follow miracle-mongering gurus.

- Similar trends are reported from the Western societies as well. In the US, for example, 40 per cent of scientists, but only 7 per cent of 'eminent scientists' surveyed proclaimed belief in a personal God. Recent data from the UK shows that about 20 per cent of scientists and about 4 per cent 'eminent scientists' believe in God.

- Use of science to affirm the literal truth of holy books is rampant. Campaigns to teach creationism as 'scientific' in American schools are well known. 'Vedic creationism' is a new trend in the US where the Hare Krishna movement has taken a lead and Deepak Chopra has defended intelligent design from a Hindu perspective. Scientific creationism is spreading in the Islamic world, which has a long tradition of looking for modern science in the verses of the Koran. The belief that astrology, yagnas, and yogic siddhis are somehow scientific continues to be widespread in India.

- The great resurgence of popular Hinduism with nationalistic overtones has already been described in great details in Chapters 2 and 3 of this book.

God is clearly on a winning streak these days.

173

Bye-bye Secularism?

This resurgence of religion raises one hugely embarrassing question: how could we all be so wrong?

It has been one of the fundamental assumptions of modern social theory that as the world becomes more modern, people will no longer need to believe in supernatural beings, religions will lose their importance, and people will become more secular. All the giants of social philosophy—Karl Marx, Max Weber, Emile Durkheim, Sigmund Freud, and Friedrich Nietzsche—agreed that religion's days were numbered and the future belonged to secularism. India's own great secularists, Jawaharlal Nehru and Bhim Rao Ambedkar, struggled mightily to redefine a new Constitution for India based entirely on a secular morality pertaining to *this life*, with no reference to religious conceptions like karma and dharma. They exhorted us to cultivate a scientific temper and critical thinking so that we could become more secular. Becoming secular was good, we were told, because it meant the very opposite of narrow-minded communalism and superstitious obscurantism. Secularism was something to cherish and strive for.

What were these secularists celebrating? What *is* secularism, anyway?

Secularism is basically an *attitude of minimalism* which, with regard to, one: belief in God; two: social significance of religion; and three: both of them together.

With regard to belief in God, secularists are sceptics. They believe that as modern women and men learn to trust the judgement of their own senses and reason, they will find the idea of a being with supernatural powers rather implausible. God will not completely die, but will lose many of the awesome powers ascribed to Him or Her. Such a God will come closer to what Richard Dawkins calls an 'Einsteinian God' who is more like a poetic metaphor for the wonderment and awe. A secular society is one where, in the words of Peter Berger, 'increasing number of people look upon the world and their own lives without the benefit of religious interpretations'. By this standard, a society can be called properly secular when more and more people learn to live good and fulfilled lives without the consolation of belief in supernatural powers which they accept on faith.

With regard to the scope of religion, secularists are separatists. They believe that modern societies undergo a process of separation (or differentiation, as sociologists call it) by which sectors of society and culture are removed from the domination of religious institutions and symbols. Secularization means that religion ceases to be the 'sacred canopy' (to use Peter Berger's famous description) under whose shade the rest of the society flourishes. Rather than provide overarching meaning for all of life, religion recedes to the private sphere, leaving politics, economics, sciences, arts, and other social endeavours to begin to operate by their own internal logic. Religion is to be protected and even cherished, but strictly within its own sphere of metaphysical speculations, weddings and funerals, and poetic pleasure and consolation. Secularism is a stance of setting limits on what religion can and cannot be allowed to do.

India's Constitution is a good example of setting limits on religion: while it respects people's right to believe in their chosen gods, it abolishes, at the stroke of the pen, the authority of the Dharmashastras to lay down rights and duties of the different varnas. The equal rights of Indian citizens regardless of their caste, creed, and gender is a result of secular authority setting limits on what religion can and cannot be allowed to do.

With regard to both of the above, secularists see a link. In the secularist world view, the decline of personal piety is linked to decline in the social significance of religion. In other words, when people begin to understand the world rationally, without invoking divine beings or powers, they no longer see the need to beseech them for fulfilling their wishes, or look to religious authorities to derive their sense of right and wrong, duties, and responsibilities. Religion begins to decline in social significance when more and more people create meaningful lives without God(s).

That, however, does not mean that believers can't be secularists: they may not be sceptics, but they can be separatists. The traditional liberal position has been that as long as believers can keep their faith safely tucked away in their private lives, they are secular. While this position makes theoretical sense, it is full of contradictions, for it creates a split between the believers' deepest beliefs and his/her actions: she is basically being asked not to act upon what she holds to be the highest truth. A liberal society like the United States with very high walls separating the state from the Church did succeed for a while in living with this kind of a split consciousness. But even there, it has begun to show serious stresses and strains and religion has been increasingly bleeding into the affairs of the state.

Indian secularism offers its own peculiar twist to the idea of secularism: it does not erect a wall of separation between religion and the state. What makes the Indian state secular, instead, is its commitment to religious neutrality, that is, not having an official religion of the state and treating all religions with equal respect.

This, in broad strokes, is what secularism is all about.

Clearly, we don't live in a religiously minimalist world: the world is getting more, not less, religious. People all around the world are turning to religion not only in their private lives, but they are bringing their religious interests into the public sphere as well. The evidence from India shows how religious identities are getting politicized and how religious rituals are becoming as much a part of political mobilizations as they are of weddings and funerals. Moreover, as the evidence of a thriving Indian supermarket of gods and god-men shows, modern men and women still find supernatural and miraculous powers to be entirely credible. All over the world, religious maximalism seems to be the order of the day.

In this chapter, we will try to understand the changing and growing religiosity in India by looking at it through the wider lens of social-scientific theories of secularization. This engagement with social theory may seem a bit daunting and even irrelevant to the rest of this book. But it will enable us to develop a deeper understanding of what makes a society more or less secular at any point of time. It will also help to enrich the domestic debates over secularism with fresh insights from the global debates where a new paradigm of market-based, supply-side theory of religious revival is emerging.

For many years now, the Indian debate over secularism has been firmly stuck between the Gandhian pole of *sarva dharma samabhav* (equal respect for all religions) and the Nehruvian pole of *dharma nirpekshta* (equal indifference to all religions). New theories regarding the role of competitive free markets in the realm of religion/spirituality are, however, important to understand the kind of blockbuster growth in the demand and supply of religious services that India is experiencing. This chapter will try to introduce the reader to these new ways of thinking about the resurgence of gods in the era of globalization. Since these theories about the return of religion in the modern world have emerged as a result of intellectual debates with the earlier theories that predicted the death of religion, we will necessarily have to look at the various theories in succession. In what follows the older theories of secularization (or decline of religion) and the newer thinking about *de*-secularization (or resurgence of religion) are examined in terms of their relevance to the Indian experience.

The Classical Theory: The Inevitability of Secularism

The classical theory of secularization flows out of the Enlightenment project which believed that as men and women begin to understand the underlying order of nature without invoking God, they will learn to outgrow their faith in God. Rational control of nature will make supplications to divine powers superfluous, and religion will begin to wither away. It was this understanding of secularism that informed the outlook of the modernist architects of India's Constitution.

The birth and death of this classical theory of secularization can be telescoped into the exceptionally productive career of Peter Berger, a renowned sociologist of religion at Boston University. He wrote his path-breaking book, *The Sacred Canopy,* in 1967 in which he showed why the decline of religion was inevitable in modern industrial societies. Almost thirty years later, in 1999, he edited a book titled *The De-secularization of the World* in which he recanted his belief in secularization and accepted that the world was actually becoming *more* religious as it was becoming more modern.

In *The Sacred Canopy,* Berger described secularization as a global process built into the functioning of modern industry: *any society that industrializes will end up secularizing as well.* Religion, Berger said, 'stops at the factory gate' and modern industry is 'something like a "liberated territory" with respect to religion' and spreads secularization outward through the rest of the society.

What makes the industrial sector a 'liberated zone'? The short answer is: rationalization of the work process, that is, making it calculable and predictable, removing all scope of divine intervention or magical action. Modern industrial society requires the presence of a large cadre of scientific and technological personnel whose training and ongoing social organization presupposes a high degree of rationalization, not only on the level of infrastructure, but also on that of consciousness. The upshot of Berger's argument is that over time, the state itself dissociates itself from religious constraints in order to protect and promote the rationalized core of the economy. Whether this process is accompanied by organized anti-clericalism (as in France) or not (as in America, Britain, India), varies with the national context. But the *core* of secularization, namely, the emancipation of the state from the sway of religious rationales for economic activity, law, and politics is a universal characteristic of all modernizing states.

In Berger's account, once a secular state is in place, secularization of the society, culture, and lifeworld follows almost automatically. What happens is this: the state takes over more and more of the civilian sectors and services that used to be previously controlled by religious institutions. Simultaneously, many of life's misfortunes which used to be seen as a result of divine intervention—diseases, destitution, and natural catastrophes—are brought under rational control.

This slow but steady differentiation of the domains of the state, economy, education, health, scientific research, and technological development from the overarching 'sacred canopy' of religion constitutes the very essence of secularization. As institutions break free from the sway of religion, so does the consciousness of the people:

As there is a secularization of society and culture, there is a secularization of consciousness. Put simply, this means that the

179

modern West has produced an increasing number of individuals who look upon the world and their own lives without the benefit of religious interpretations. (emphasis added)

Once religions are forced to cede control over enculturation to the state, the sacred canopy they once provided is shattered and religions can no longer take the allegiance of the population for granted. Privatized religions become a choice and not an obligation. Under these circumstances, Berger argues, religious institutions become marketing agencies, and religious traditions become consumer commodities.

Berger sees this pluralistic market in religion as making people *less* religious. The idea is that when people are faced with so many clashing accounts of God, they can no longer accept their own religious tradition as the only valid tradition. Berger believes that religious relativism breeds doubt.

The Indian Constitution is based upon this classical view of secularization. India's democratic revolution was premised on the assumption that religion must decline in its influence on the public sphere, and that the state must step in to remedy the religious sources of caste and gender inequities. The Constitution's promise of equal citizenship regardless of caste, creed, class, or gender meant a clean sweep of Hindu laws, taboos, and customs that had regulated socio-economic relationships for centuries. The Indian Constitution, moreover, is completely nastik: its principles of 'Justice, Liberty, Equality and Fraternity' invoke no divine power, no holy book(s) and no sacred tradition. But ironically, democratizing access to high Hinduism, *without simultaneously democratizing access to secular education*, has led to the creation of a *less* secular civil society. Thus while the social dynamic that led India to embrace secular nationalism conforms to Berger's theory, it has not produced 'secularization of consciousness' that Berger predicted.

Science, Socialism, and Secularization

The Sacred Canopy is justifiably considered a classic and it influenced a whole generation of thinkers. But the classical theories of secularism tend to leave out two important factors: the role of scientific advances in changing the popular intellectual climate; and the historical affinity between secularism and working class movements. Given the importance our secularist founding fathers placed on the cultivation of a scientific temper in creating a culture of secularism in India, it is important to dwell on the reception of science by the working people in Western societies where struggles for secularism started much before they did in India.

The curious thing about the mainstream secularization theory is that it left very little room for culture and ideas to influence the technical and institutional infrastructure. Berger is very clear on this issue. He grants that the biblical tradition played a historical role in starting the process of secularization in the West. But once the process gets going, religion has no direct role to play. Rather, religion becomes purely dependent on political economy and loses the ability to act back on, or influence, the institutional structure of a society. Writing in the heydays of the Cold War, Berger was equally dismissive of 'scientific atheists' in the Soviet Bloc and Christian evangelicals in the US in stemming the tide of secularization. Neither rational critique nor apologetics could save religion, whose ultimate fate was oblivion, if not death.

The other curious feature is the lack of importance attached to the growth of modern science and scientific outlook in the larger society. Science makes a difference only as technology which, leads to rationalization of work, which in turn, spills over into other spheres of the society. The *cultural* influence of science—the rational questioning of the truth of the claims religious dogmas make about the world—hardly plays any role in the mainstream account of secularization. Indeed, in Berger's account, it is not truth but *plausibility*, or believability, that is the key: any idea, true or false, can be made to appear plausible by the process of socialization which includes constant repetition through rituals and ceremonies. Secularization, on this account, is not the result of people judging the evidence for and against their gods and adjusting their beliefs in proportion to the evidence. Rather, societies secularize because of the breakdown of religion's monopoly on the socialization processes that made gods look plausible. This view is widely shared by other supporters of secularization, most notably Steve Bruce who is one of the most outspoken and prolific defenders of secularization.

It is useful to read Berger together with Owen Chadwick's 1975 classic, *The Secularization of the European Mind in the Nineteenth Century*. Chadwick reminds us that what was distinctive about the process of secularization in **nineteenth** century Europe was that the working people took the revolution in ideas brought about by modern science seriously: scientific critique of religion was not confined to the salons of the intellectual elite but rather spread into the working class culture: 'The free thinkers of the 1840s were different from the free-thinkers of the 1740s. They were lower in the social scale and *they associated the religious cause with the social cause.*' Even the word 'secularism', Chadwick reminds us, was coined by George Holyoake in 1851 to prevent the British socialists from being tarred by the negative connotations of atheism. European secularist movements of this era were inspired by the writings of Karl Marx and Charles Darwin and espoused the materialist philosophy of well-known German scientists, especially Karl Vogt, Ludwig Buchner, and Ernst Haeckel who were fighting a battle against vitalism (i.e., the idea that living organisms need some kind of vital energy—what we in India call 'prana' over and above the play of biochemical molecules). These movements had the enthusiastic support of the lower-middle-class artisans, weavers, shopkeepers, and booksellers and the labouring classes who were either indifferent to the official churches or identified religion with opposition to the aspirations of the worker.

Similar developments took place across the Atlantic in the US as well. During the heyday of progressivism (1875–1914), American freethinkers joined forces with the working classes for issues that appealed to broad cross-sections of people including freedom of speech, separation of church and state, eight-hour workday, and free secular public schools which appealed to a broad constituency among the working classes. The American evidence confirms the idea that secular movements succeed only in so far as they are able to offer practical, this-worldly, and rational solutions to everyday problems that affect the lives of ordinary people.

Chadwick describes how Marx himself came to embrace this practice-oriented conception of secularism. In his younger days, Marx engaged with the intellectual content of religion: he saw it as an error which could be corrected by reasoned argument. But in his more mature writings, Marx began to see that no amount of sceptical demystification could promote real secularization under the conditions of capitalism. If we want to change men's ideas, Chadwick writes summarizing Marx's views in *German Ideology*, 'we shall not do it in preaching atheism, or in undermining their beliefs by philosophizing. To make religion vanish, we need not science but social revolution.' But even though rational critique by itself was not sufficient, Marx and Marxists always considered it a necessary element of working class struggles.

The lasting impact of these revolutionary movements was not political revolutions per se, but rather a slow and steady *intellectual transformation of the popular culture* in the West. These movements brought before the working people and the middle classes the idea that there was an alternative explanation to the world, different from what they had inherited. They succeeded in sowing seeds of doubt regarding the picture of the universe that the Bible assumed.

These debates regarding rationalism and social struggles for justice are as relevant to India as they are for the West. The political left in India has long been preoccupied by the question of what comes first—demystifying religion or social revolution? This was the main bone of contention between the Dalit and Shudra thinkers-activists and the Marxists. For Dalit intellectuals like B.R. Ambedkar, any radical change in social relations *first* required the demolition of the Hindu legitimation for innate human inequality. Ambedkar asked: how can a new base (democratic socialism) be put in place before the existing superstructure (Hindu justifications of caste) is knocked down? Indian Marxists, on the other hand, while being philosophically committed to materialism and atheism, have generally followed Marx's lead: they have given priority to anti-capitalist and anti-imperialist revolution. It is not that they are opposed to the project of sceptical demystification of religious beliefs: Marxist thinkers like M.N. Roy, Debiprasad Chattopadhyaya, and D.D. Kosambi have taken the lead in drawing attention to the long-denigrated rationalist and materialist elements in Hinduism. While sympathetic to rationalism, Indian Marxists tend to subordinate a critique of religion to political calculations which can sometimes ally them with populist anti-modernist movements. As a result, a distinct politics of rationalism, frontally aimed at religion's many mystifications, has not been a prominent feature of the Indian left. Even the Dalit movement today is putting the Ambedkarite project of ideology-critique on the back burner in order to make opportunistic alliances with upper castes that have never renounced their support of the fundamentals of varna dharma, nor revised the metaphysics that justifies hierarchy. But, as this chapter will argue, struggles for truth and justice are deeply intertwined, and one is incomplete without the other.

Is secularization a Western Idea?

Another question that has puzzled those who think about such things is whether secularization is a universal phenomenon. Do all societies undergo a separation of different spheres of society from the sacred canopy of religion as they industrialize?

Jose Casanova, a sociologist at the New School for Social Research in New York, provided a useful way to look at this question in his widely acclaimed 1994 book *Public Religion in the Modern World*. His insights are relevant to the debates that have been going on in India over what kind of secularism is appropriate for India.

Casanova defended the fundamental core of secularization, namely, the increasing autonomy (or differentiation) of the state, the economy, and scientific research and development from religious injunctions: what distinguishes *modern* state bureaucracies and markets is the fact that they function *as if* God did not exist. This process of the growing autonomy of different aspects of social life from religious sanctions and taboos is what makes any society modern.

While this process of differentiation is universal, Casanova argues, that does not mean that religions in all societies will experience the same extent of privatization and decline. His thesis is that all modernizing societies go through a similar *process* of differentiation, but whether or not differentiation will bring about similar *consequences* of decline in popular religiosity and/or a decline in the cultural authority of temples, churches, or mosques depends upon the cultural and political preconditions which differ in different societies. He correctly points out that the original secularization theory was flawed in 'confusing the historical processes of secularization proper with the alleged and anticipated consequences of these processes'.

Why does the same process of modernization/institutional differentiation lead to different consequences in different societies? Why is it that in some societies, especially in Western Europe, religions began to lose their social influence with modernization? And why does religion continue to flourish in other societies like the US and India even after formal separation from the state?

Casanova tries to explain such differences by looking at four cultural 'carriers' of secularization: the Protestant Reformation, the rise of modern nation-states, the rise of modern capitalism, and the rise of modern science. Since each of these carriers developed different dynamics in different places and at different times, the patterns and outcomes of the historical process of secularization should be different in different societies.

Casanova outlines how Protestantism helped set in motion other carriers of secularization in the West, namely, capitalism and modern science. But over time, the connection with Protestantism was broken and science and capitalism became independent forces in the birth of secular nation-states. *All* modernizing societies, Christian or not, with or without cultural analogues of Protestantism, participate in global capitalist markets managed by their nation-states and all want to promote scientific education and technical training. Today, no modernizing nation-state can afford to shut itself off either from capitalism or from science, both of which

186

tend to insulate the secular aspects of state and economy from religious injunctions.

The kind of nuance Casanova provides is relevant for the Indian situation. Some Indian critics of secularism have condemned the very idea of confining the sacred in the private sphere as a Christian idea which is unsuited for the holistic Indic religions which claim 'all of a follower's life, so that religion is constitutive of society'. Those who make a case for Hindu exceptionalism forget that throughout the Middle Ages, Christianity was no less 'totalizing' than Hinduism. Before the forces of modernization and secularization broke the sacred canopy, *all* religions were totalizing in the sense that they regulated all aspects of life. It is true that Hindu metaphysical doctrines complicate matters because they do not allow a differentiation of matter and spirit, or between creatures and the creator, as clearly as monotheisms do. But following Casanova, it is clear that the nature of religious doctrine is only *one* among the four major carriers of secularization. For the last three centuries, India has been drawn into the other three global forces of secularization, namely, global spread of science, global capitalism, and the global emergence of modern nation-states. These global carriers of secularization are no longer tied to Protestant Christianity, even though their emergence in history was encouraged by Protestantism. This being the case, the claims of Hindu exceptionalism do not apply. Secularism understood as separation between religion and the public sphere is as valid for India as for any other society.

Secularization, Rest in Peace

By the close of the 20th century, theories of secularization lost steam. Predictions of the decline of religion became impossible to sustain in the face of the resurgence of religion in public and private spheres all over the world. The phenomenon that needed explanation was not decline of religion, but rather the stubborn persistence of full-blooded religions complete with supernatural beings that listen to prayers and perform miracles.

The death of secularization theory was first announced by none other than Peter Berger himself, the great theorist of secularization. Writing in 1999 in a book of essays titled *The Desecularization of the World,* Berger admitted that he was proven wrong:

> the key idea [was] that modernization necessarily leads to a decline of religion, both in society and in the minds of individuals. It is precisely this idea that has turned out to be wrong.

The world today, Berger correctly points out, is not a secular world rather, it is 'as furiously religious as it ever was'. Berger went on to say what was becoming pretty obvious to many sociologists: *not only is our world religious, it is religious in the old-fashioned supernaturalistic way.* In fact, those religions that have tried to rationalize their beliefs by underplaying the miracles and other supernatural elements have lost members, while 'religious movements dripping with reactionary supernaturalism have widely succeeded'.

Berger's point about the growth of religions 'dripping with reactionary supernaturalism' is the crux of the problem. Even the staunchest secularists can accept that religions do not simply give up and wither away in modern industrial societies. Take for example the work of Steve Bruce, the best-known defender of secularization theory today. Bruce is perfectly willing to grant that religions innovate, adapt, and find newer, more secular, or this-worldly things to do, for example, legitimize the nation, bless new business enterprises, legitimize the acquisition of riches, mobilize in defence of 'traditional family values', etc. But he believes that religions end up paying a price for their new profiles by *diluting,* or ignoring, the supernatural aspects of their teachings which are no longer plausible to the moderns. Religions survive the secular world by becoming more secular themselves, by giving up or minimizing beliefs in the supernatural, the miraculous, and the other-worldly. They become gentle prosperity religions, analogues of 'karma capitalism' described in earlier chapters, whose role is 'not to question the modern world's riches but to bring them within the reach of everyone', as Alan Wolfe, a well-known sociologist of religion put it recently. But this is exactly what Berger is denying.

This then is the crucial claim of the new theory of de-secularization: *the supernatural has not lost its plausibility in the modern world.* Religions continue to find new work to do in secular societies, *without* giving up, or even diluting, the essential religious impulse which seeks help and solace from beings with extraordinary powers who are supposed to exist beyond the confines of time and space. The current upsurge in religious fundamentalism, in Berger's view, is not some secularized, politicized 'corruption' of true religions, but actual 'restoration' of a full-blooded, strongly felt belief in the supernatural revelation of the faith. Islam is not alone in this fundamentalist impulse, of course. Berger finds the evangelical upsurge across the world, including wide swathes of East Asia, Latin America, and sub-Saharan Africa to be equally a sign of serious religious quest by masses of ordinary people.

The 'rush hour of the gods' in India that we examined in Chapter 2 is a pretty good example of Berger's argument. The earlier attempts of neo-Hindu reformers to moderate or rationalize the supernatural by emphasizing the impersonal world-soul, or Brahman, over personal, wish-fulfilling gods, have failed to gain popular support: it is the *saguna* gods, the human-like manifestations of the divine that the masses of Hindus line up to pray to. The supernatural has not lost its plausibility in modern India.

This naturally raises the question: why now? Berger's explanation is based upon economics. Modernity undermines life's certainties, more so under the current phase of globalization. The new global class of super-rich—the 'Davos set', as Berger calls them—have the economic and cultural resources to deal with and even profit from these uncertainties. The non-elites, on the other hand, resent the secular elite for looking down on their religiosity and that is the reason, Berger says, they are drawn to religious movements with a strongly anti-secularist or even a fundamentalist bent.

While it makes intuitive sense, this explanation fails to persuade. It is not clear if religiosity so closely coincides with class. In India, it is clearly the rising middle classes who are becoming more religious. It is not clear, moreover, that the 'Davos set' is such a bastion of secularism as Berger makes them out to be, for then it would be hard to explain the growing popularity of karma capitalism taught by saffron-clad swamis quoting from the Vedanta and Bhagvat Gita to CEOs of business conglomerates all around the world. The evidence from India should also disabuse us of the idea that class resentment is a significant motivator of mass religiosity. Far from resenting them, it looks like the masses aspire towards the consumption habits of the elites and the new rich. Both the elites and the masses are turning to gurus and pujaris who are more than willing to find religious justifications for getting rich.

Neo-liberal Theory of Religion's Persistence

Perhaps as a sign of the dominance of neo-liberalism in the US, *laissez-faire* thinking has spilled over into debates over secularization as well. A new paradigm is emerging which argues that those societies which allow a competitive free market of religious service providers will be least secularized; and conversely, societies which distort the free market of religions by creating monopolies will appear to be most secularized. In other words, the same forces that drive the success of market capitalism—competition and choice–drive the surge of religion.

The chief architect of this supply-side theory is Rodney Stark, who teaches sociology at the Baylor University in Texas. Starting with a provocative essay titled 'Secularizatisn, R.I.P.—Rest In Peace' that appeared in 1999 and has been reprinted many times since then, Stark and his colleagues (including Roger Finke, Williams Brainbridge, Stephen Warner, and Andrew Greeley) have succeeded in bringing about a paradigm shift in the sociology of religion. The new ideas offer insights which are relevant for understanding the religious supermarket that is thriving in India.

The supply-side theory of religion assumes that religion is an innate human trait which is never going to go away or even decline. Because human beings will always want to make bargains with gods for protection against unforeseeable dangers, the *demand* for religion is a human constant and stays pretty much unchanged across time and place. The *supply* of religious services, however, varies in different societies. In those societies where there are religious monopolies due to sponsorship by the state, the supply will be of poor quality. In such societies, religious demand will remain unmet, people will stop going to churches or temples, and societies will look *as if* they have become more secular. But in those societies where there is free competition between different religious 'firms', there will be ample supply of religious services and the level of religiosity will be higher. In other words, the societies we think as secular are only suffering from a lack of supply of religious services.

The implications of this market view of religion are quite striking and unsettling.

To begin with, this turns the traditional understanding of secularism on its head. As we saw above, the classical theories of secularization argued that the demand for religion will decline as societies modernize because increased emphasis on scientific explanations will lead people away from supernaturalism. But the new paradigm starts with the assumption that the urge to establish 'exchange relations' with supernatural powers is a perfectly rational human need built into the human condition. The idea is simple and quite familiar: Stark and his colleagues argue that human life is so uncertain, fragile, and full of tragedies that human beings will *always* and *everywhere* seek compensation and consolation from supernatural powers which exist above and beyond this world. No amount of rational and empirical knowledge can dislodge the idea and the need for God. Religion is eternal.

If we assume that all people are naturally religious, then it follows that there are no secular societies and the very idea of secularism—understood as the decline of religiosity—is doomed.

On the face of it, this thesis seems to contradict overwhelming evidence of widespread indifference towards religion and decline of religiosity in Europe. While huge, mall-like mega-churches that can accommodate tens of thousands of worshippers at a time are the rage in the US, most churches and cathedrals in countries like Sweden, Holland, France, Germany, Great Britain, and even Canada are going empty. Western Europe certainly *looks* far more secularized than the US. Defenders of secularization theory have long held up the high degree of secularization achieved by Europeans as representing the universal end point for all modernizing societies, with the religious US as an exception.

But supply-side theorists argue that the decline in church attendance only means that Europeans don't like their state-run churches, not that they have become less religious in their hearts and minds. Stark offers telling data from Iceland: only 2 per cent of Icelanders attend church weekly, making it the world's least religious country. And yet 82 per cent of those asked said they prayed, 81 per cent believed in life-after-death, 88 per cent said that the human soul is eternal, and 40 per cent believed in reincarnation. Measured by subjective religiosity, Europeans are no less religious than the highly religious Americans or for that matter, Indians. Europeans 'believe without belonging' is the conclusion expressed succinctly by Grace Davie, a British sociologist.

But the question arises: Why don't Europeans care to belong if they continue to believe? The problem is with the quality of the supply, supply-siders argue. If Europeans are not going to church, it is because until very recently, traditional churches in much of Europe have been *state churches*, as for example the Lutheran Church of Sweden, or the Anglican Church of England, where the king or the queen is also the head of the church. Like any other state-protected monopoly, state churches have become complacent and lazy. Because they take their survival for granted, they simply do not care to make a serious effort to sustain the interest of their congregations. Their status as official churches, moreover, dampens competition from other Christian denominations and other religions, creating a shortage of attractive alternatives. As a result, the religious needs of ordinary people are going unmet.

Although the supply-side theory has many critics, it has acquired the status of a new paradigm in the sociology of religion. For all the unresolved issues, this theory does a good job of explaining why the official policy of secularism has actually been very good for religion in India. The key word is competition: The Indian brand of secularism has not been the kind that dampens competition within and between the many religions that exist in the country. By not officially adopting Hinduism as the state religion and imposing it upon everyone else, and by protecting (within limits) the freedom of all religions, the Indian state prepared the conditions for a great flowering of all kinds of old and new religious movements/institutions. The net effect is that India today has perhaps the largest supermarket of religions anywhere in the world.

Indeed, even when the Indian state directly intervened in the affairs of Hinduism, it managed to remove the traditional rigidities of caste and gender from it, thereby enabling it to compete better against other religions. To begin with, the Constitution in effect deregulated Hinduism: it threw open the temples that were closed to Shudras and untouchables, increasing the demand enormously. Secondly, even when the state intervened to control the secular affairs (cash donations, properties, and religious endowments) of Hindu temples, the net effect has been to make the temples less corrupt and more responsive to the needs of the worshippers and pilgrims. As we have seen in earlier chapters, the joint state–temple management committees have vastly improved the fortunes of many of India's important pilgrimage spots. Thirdly, while reformist in intent, the Indian brand of soft secularism is not hostile to religious expression even in state-funded public forums. Hinduism being the religion of the majority often ends up as the *de facto* religion of the state. Fourthly, whatever formal constraints there were on the government regarding open sponsorship of religion have weakened under the current neo-liberal economic regime. The public–private partnerships that have replaced public sector agencies in education, tourism, and infrastructure development have developed an active partnership with temples and religious endowments. This state–temple–corporate complex whose workings we have tried to lay bare in this book is providing a huge boost to the supply of all varieties of Hinduism, from temple worship to new age spirituality.

Apart from the state, there are other features of India's religious landscape that are religion friendly. The long co-existence of Islam and Christianity with India's native religions has created conditions of competition and syncretism. The central ideas of neo-Hinduism, for example, are deeply influenced by Protestant Christianity, while Christians and Muslims have adopted some Hindu practices of caste, style of worship, and yoga. On top of it all, Hinduism itself has enormous internal pluralism when it comes to beliefs, rituals, and styles of worship. In traditional Hinduism, this pluralism was frozen within caste boundaries, which were unfrozen by the secular Constitution. All of these factors have contributed to making India a veritable supermarket which can cater to all religious tastes and inclinations.

Towards a Modest Theory of Secularization

The theory of secularism is at an impasse. Can we still assume that modern men and women can live without the consolation of God(s), as the classical social theory told us? Or is the demand for God really an unchanging constant that no amount of modernity can dislodge or even moderate? Should we declare secularization theory dead and murmur 'rest in peace' as we bury it in the graveyard of failed theories, as Stark and his colleagues recommend?

Obituaries for secularization are premature. The core of secularization theory—namely, the need or demand for belief in supernatural beings will decline with modernity—can be saved if we do not see it as an iron law, but as a *tendency*. Religiosity is not *guaranteed* to decline, or to rise: religiosity, like other cultural trends, is most likely to wax and wane in intensity.

One such nuanced defence of secularization is offered by Pippa Norris and Ronald Inglehart in their 2004 book, *Sacred and Secular*. Among many of their findings, two observations stand out: one, even though belief in God, heaven, and hell are still significant even in the supposedly 'post-Christian' Europe, they *have* been falling over time; and two, whether you continue to believe or not bears a strong correlation with the 'existential insecurity' you experience, which has to do with the kind of society you live in and the economic class you happen to fall into. Both of these points warrant a closer look.

Norris and Inglehart do not dispute the claims of Stark (and co.) that large proportions of Europeans continue to express belief in God and life-after-death, even after they have stopped being practising Christians. But they argue that if we look at these beliefs not at any given time, but in a wider time span of about 50 years—from 1947 to 2001—we will find that the number of people holding these beliefs *has* declined.

Their long-term analysis is based upon data for 19 countries (covering most of Europe also including Great Britain, US, Canada, Brazil, Japan, and India) obtained from Gallup polls (for the period 1947–75) and World Values Survey (for the period 1981–2001). Their analysis shows that in 1947, eight out of ten people in the countries sampled believed in God, with the highest level of belief in Australia, Canada, the US, and Brazil. Their regression models show a decline in faith in God in all but two nations (the US and Brazil), with the sharpest decline in Scandinavian countries, the Netherlands, and Great Britain. (Data for India is inconclusive because pre-1990 data does not exist.

Available data show that 93 per cent of Indians reportedly believed in God in 1995.) Similar patterns are also reported for belief in life-after-death, where again an erosion of subjective religiosity takes place in 13 out of 19 countries (Indian data are not available). Even today, the number of believers exceeds 50 per cent in all European countries. But the trend shows a decline.

This finding is important as it shows that the fall in church participation is not entirely due to supply-side factors (lazy state churches and all that). Rather, there has been an actual decline in the belief itself. The demand for religion is not as constant and steady as the supply-siders make it out to be.

This brings us to the second important finding, namely, the influence of socio-economic factors on levels of religiosity. Norris and Inglehart argue that since one of the most important functions of all religions is to provide reassurance of help from a higher power, it follows that some socio-economic contexts increase the need for this reassurance, and others minimize it. They predict that:

> All things being equal, *the experience of growing up in less secure societies will heighten the importance of religious values,* while conversely, *experience of more secure conditions will lessen it…*The process of human development has significant consequences for religiosity. (emphasis in the original)

Norris and Inglehart test this hypothesis using data from a cross-section of industrially advanced countries. They summarize their conclusions as follows:

> *The level of economic inequality proves strongly and significantly related to religious behaviour.* The United States is exceptionally high in religiosity in large part, we believe, because it is also the most unequal post-industrial society under comparison…

Americans face greater anxieties than citizens of other advanced industrialized countries about whether they will be covered by medical insurance, whether they will be fired arbitrarily, or whether they will be forced to choose between losing their job and devoting themselves to their new born child.

The correlation between income inequality and religiosity also shows up among the rich and the poor in aggregate numbers *within* each post-industrial society. Norris and Inglehart found that higher the income level, lower the religiosity as measured by frequency of prayer. In aggregate terms, the poor turn out to be twice as religious as the rich. When they narrowed the analysis to the US alone, a similar pattern emerged: two-thirds (66 per cent) of the least well-off prayed, compared to 47 per cent of the highest income group.

There is another component of life in post-industrial societies that breeds despair and encourages religiosity. In an extensive survey involving in-depth interviews with thousands of working people from a wide variety of workplaces in America, Michael Lerner, the editor of progressive Jewish magazine *Tikkun* and the author of the recent *Spirit Matters*, reported that workers found their work, even if well paying, meaningless because:

> They wanted more than 'making it in the rat-race.' Spiritual meaning, not money or power, was the thing they were missing and they made no bones about how painful it felt to be wasting their lives for no purpose except 'the almighty paycheck'.

American workers looking for meaning turn to the churches and not to their unions, because 'there was no meaning to be found there, except during negotiations, when they could fight for more money'. Workers are hungry for community which unions have failed to provide, except in purely economic matters like wages (and there, too, unions are failing). Lerner fears that this lack of meaning is part of the reason why the message of the religious right resonates with the average worker in America.

Existential insecurity and meaninglessness are no doubt important motivators for turning to religion. But religiosity is too complex to be explained by any one factor. The poor may be more religious than the rich, but the rich do not give up on God just because they have creative jobs with health insurances. As this book has shown, the middle classes are becoming more religious as their income levels are going up and existential insecurities coming down. Even in Norris and Inglehart's careful analysis, close to half of those in the highest income group in America continue to pray. It is also clear that the newly emerging middle classes in fast growing economies like India, China, Brazil, or Russia are displaying more religiosity, not less.

In other words, *if poverty makes people pray, so does prosperity.* The so-called 'prosperity religions' which put the sacred teachings to use in order to obtain and sanctify wealth have a long history. No religion has shown any great compunction when it comes to making their holy books available for legitimating naked self-interest and enjoyment of the materialistic life. India leads them all in this department: It is after all the homeland of Deepak Chopra, Mahesh Yogi, and Bhagvan Rajneesh! A new crop of Vedanta and Gita-toting management gurus is emerging who are bringing spirituality to the moneyed classes the world over. Their clientele comes from the rich who want to get richer, while balancing their prosperity with spiritualism which can be packaged, sold, and bought like any other consumer product.

The point of bringing class and economics into the discussion of religiosity is not to reduce religion to a sideshow of economic imperatives. The point is to challenge all attempts to eternalize religion, to turn it into a primordial impulse which supposedly stays constant and unchanging in a changing world. Granted that because of its long evolutionary history, and its many-millennia-long intertwinement with all aspects of social and intellectual life, belief in the supernatural is extraordinarily well adapted to the human psyche. But however well adapted it may be, the religious impulse is by no means isolated from the rest of the social, political, and intellectual world.

Lessons for India

Our exercise of viewing Indian experience through the prism of secularization theory has proven to be quite fruitful.

It is remarkable how the experience of secularism in India can be mapped on the rise and fall of the mainstream of secularization theory. Expectations of creating a secular society have waxed and waned in India, pretty much as they have in the rest of the world. And as with the rest of the world, it is the new paradigm of de-secularization that explains India better than the older paradigm of secularization.

The classical theory of secularization was the founding assumption on which India's model of secularism rested. The modernists among the founding fathers, most notably Jawaharlal Nehru and B.R. Ambedkar and their many progressive allies among communists, socialists, radical humanists, and neo-Buddhists, were secularists in the strong, or the classical, sense of the word. That is to say, they welcomed the idea that modernity will erode the sacred canopy of religion and drive out the gods from the natural and the social world. Accordingly, they sought to minimize the jurisdiction of religion on as many personal and political aspects of life as they possibly could. (Unfortunately, due to the political circumstances right after Partition, they did not fight for reform of Muslim and Christian personal law with the same passion that they had for reforming Hinduism. This has created a perception of 'pandering' to the minorities. They favoured a sceptical approach to the metaphysical basis of religion and clearly encouraged the cultivation of critical thought in the public sphere. To their great credit, they tried to balance a critical outlook towards religions with freedom of belief and practice of all the many religions of India.

But despite the strong influence of principled rationalists and secularists in the founding of the Republic and the writing of the Constitution, rationalism failed to link up with other social movements. 'Scientific temper' remained more of a slogan and never really became an operating principle of institutions of the government and civil society.

In the aftermath of the Emergency, starting around 1980 or so, many Indian intellectuals began to lose confidence in the Nehruvian model of modernization, including its commitment to secularism. The very idea of separation of spheres from the sacred canopy of religion was considered inappropriate for Indic religions. Along with secularism, science and rationalism also came under critical scrutiny, often verging on outright hostility. This phase of traditionalism in India coincided with the flourishing of postmodernism in social theory which questioned the entire trajectory of the Scientific Revolution and the Enlightenment.

However, developments on the ground jolted the critics of secularism out of their romantic reveries. In India, as in many other parts of the world, religious nationalists and conservatives began to gain political power. The rise of the BJP showed that the religious idiom resonated well with the electorate.

These concerns were reflected in the radical rethinking of secularization that started happening in academic circles in the West around the turn of the millennium. The pendulum has now swung to the other side: it is not the decline, but the persistence of religion that sociologists are now trying to explain. The new idea is that the *demand* for religion is never going to go away or decline, while the *supply* of religion will vary in different societies at different times. The new supply-side theory claims, as we have seen, that deregulation and free markets are not only good for improving the choice of cars and toothbrushes and such, but also for improving the choice of religions and gods.

The material provided in this book bears out this market theory of why religions are growing in a globalizing world. This book has shown that in India, neo-liberal economic policies have worked to the advantage of the God market. Economic reforms and rising wealth of the middle classes have increased both the demand for, and the supply of, religious services. The new market economy did not *create* the religious market—India always had plenty of choices when it came to gods, faiths, and modes of worship. But the new economy has opened up more spaces in the public sphere for religion to penetrate. In theory, of course, it should work in favour of *all* of India's religions. But in practice, it is the majority religion that is poised to make best use of the new opportunities as all the other leading institutions of society are aligned in its favour. Moreover, the increasingly triumphalist tone of mainstream Hinduism and the physical violence against Christian and Muslim minorities has created an atmosphere of fear and insecurity among these communities which is hardly conducive to the kind of vigorous growth that Hinduism is experiencing.

Where do we go from here?

If the booming and often bewildering God market that this book has described was just about people seeking spiritual solace in a manner of their choice, this market would be as welcome as, say, the growing market for books, or music.

But the God market is special, because religion is special: it confers the quality of sacredness and holiness on ordinary, mundane, and profane ideas and actions.

The danger in India today, as this book has tried to describe, is that the sacredness reserved for gods is getting transferred to secular entities like the nation. A Hindu majoritarian mindset is emerging which ascribes all of India's achievements, past or present, to the Great Hindu Mind. Moreover, with the penetration of Hindu rituals, symbols, and vocabulary in the public sphere, the secular space where people can interact simply as citizens, unmarked by their religious identities, is declining. Everything—from where you live, the schools and other public services that you have access to, the kind of jobs you can get, what political parties you vote for, etc.—is getting more and more dependent upon religious identities.

There is no bigger challenge for India today than to create meaningful secular spaces and a secular public culture. We have to create more spaces where Hindus and Muslims and everyone else can live as co-workers, neighbours, and friends. We have to create secular and inclusive explanations for India's achievements and flaws. We have to provide greater existential security to the poor and struggling masses so that they are not left at the mercy of gods and god-men alone.

This book has only described the workings of the God market in India. The bigger challenge is to bring it within the limits of public reason and collective good.

Notes

INTRODUCTION

p. 1   'As Robert Kaplan...', 'Trouble in the other Middle East', *The New York Times*, December 8, 2008.

p. 1   M.V. Kamath...', 'What's wrong with our Islamic community,' *The Organiser*, January 25, 2009.

p. 6   'There are some who say...', T.N. Madan, 'Secularism in its place', *Journal of Asian Studies*, 46 (November 1987).

CHAPTER 1

p. 12   Promotional slogan of Confederation of Indian Industry at the World Economic Forum, Davos, 2006. www.indiaeverywhere.com

p. 12   Mani Shankar Aiyar, 'I was always Leftist. Economic reforms made me completely Marxist', *Indian Express*, April 24, 2007.

p. 12   Aijaz Ahmad, *Communalism and Globalization: Offensives of the Far Right* (Three Essays Collective, 2003).

p. 13   'G.P. Sawant is an elderly man...', Anand Giridharadas, 'The ink fades on a profession as India modernizes', *The New York Times*, December 26, 2007.

p. 14   this man, Bilgay [sic]...', Gurcharan Das, *India Unbound* (Alfred A. Knopf, 2000).

p. 14   'Globalization can thus be defined as...', Anthony Giddens, *Consequences of Modernity* (Stanford University Press, 1990), p. 64.

p. 15   'Globality means that from now on...', Ulrich Beck, *What is Globalization?* (Sage, 2000), p. 11.

p. 15   'This small-ing of the world...', David Harvey, *Condition of Postmodernity* (Blackwell, 1990).

p. 16   'super-territorial space...', Jan Aart Scholte, *Globalization: A Critical Introduction* (Palgrave Macmillan, 2005), p. 62.

p. 17   'According to Jan Aart Scholte...', see above, p. 160.

p. 21   'Radical conservatives like Grover Norquist...', Robert Dreyfus, 'Robert Norquist: Field marshall of Bush Plan,' *The Nation*, April 26, 2001.

p. 21   'What the neo-liberals want . . .', Aijaz Ahmad, *Communalism and Globalization: Offensives of the Far Right* (Three Essays Collective, 2002), p. 105.

p. 22   'Chandrababu Naidu's regime . . .', D. Narasimha Reddy, 'Alliance of opportunism and people's distress', *Biblio*, November–December 2008. See also P. Sainath, 'Chandrababu: Image and reality', *The Hindu*, July 5, 2004.

p. 22   'The falling public investment...', P. Sainath, 'One farmer's suicide every 30 minutes', *The Hindu*, November. 15, 2007; V. Sridhar, 'Distress and kidney sale', *Frontline*, June 19, 2004.

p. 23   'Recent evidence gathered by John Harriss...', John Harriss, 'Middle class Activism and the Politics of Informal Working Class: A Perspective on Class Relations and Civil Society in Indian Cities', in Ronald Herring and Rina Agarwal (eds), *Whatever Happened to Class?: Reflections from South Asia* (Dannish Books, 2008).

p. 27   'According to Upadhyaya . . . ', Complete text of Deendayal Upadhyaya's lectures on integral humanism can be found on the website of the BJP, www.bjp.org

p. 28   'Nehru, the *bête noire* of Swatantra...', Howard Erdman, 'India's Swatantra Party', *Pacific Affairs*,

36, 4 (1963): 394–410, p. 394.

p. 28   'Since such well-known people…' Andy
          Mukherjee, 'Markets need to hear from conserva-
          tionists,' *Livemint*,June 29, 2007. Ravi Velloor,
          'Indian ITmogul 'eyeing role in politics,' *Business
          Times*, April 2, 2007.

p. 29   'Some scholars describe Swatantra Party…', Lise
          McKean, *Divine Enterprise: Gurus and the Hindu
          Nationalist Movement* (Chicago, 1996).

p. 30   'According to Howard Erdman…', Howard
          Erdman, 'India's Swatantra Party', *Pacific Affairs*,
          36, 4 (1963): 394–410, p. 409.

p. 30   'Swatantra liberals did not speak out…' Howard
          Erdman, 'India's Swatantra Party', *Pacific Affairs*, 36
          4: 394–410, p. 403.

p. 31   'Rid India of socialism and bigotry…', Indian
          Liberal Party, www.liberalpartyofindia.org

p. 33   'Dismissed by Indira Gandhi….', Deepak Lal, 'The
          Economic Impact of Hindu Revivalism', in Martin
          Marty and Scott Appleby (eds), *Fundamentalism
          and the State* (Chicago, 1993).

p. 34   'Golden summer of 1991…', Gurcharan Das, *India
          Unbound* (Knopf, 2000), pp. 213, 242.

p. 37   'According to the Columbia University econo-
          mist…', Arvind Panagariya, *India: The Emerging
          Giant* (New York, 2008), p. 95.

p. 38   'The recent economic data is grim…', *Frontline*,
          March 13, 2009.

p. 41   'According to a recent *New York Times* report…',
          Heather Timmons, 'Security guards become the
          front lines in India', *The New York Times*, March 3,
          2009.

p. 41   'In the words of Amit Bhaduri…', Amit Bhaduri,
          'Predatory growth', *Economic and Political Weekly*, April
          19, 2008.

p. 42   'India is rising in the Forbes…', P. Sainath,

'Shangri-La and sub-Saharan Africa', *The Hindu*, November 28, 2006.

p. 42 'Then there are the millionaires…', 'Indian millionaires over 1 lakh', *The Financial Express*, June 18, 2007.

p. 43 'Recent reports have revealed…', 'The black trillion', *Tehelka*, March 7, 2009.

p. 43 'According to the figures…', P. Sainath, 'HDI Oscars: Slumdogs versus millionaires', *The Hindu*, March 18, 2009; and 'Shangri-La and sub-Saharan Africa', *The Hindu*, November 28, 2006.

p. 43 'According to the 2007 *Human Development Report* …', Human Development Report (United Nations Development Programme, 2007), available at http://hdr.undp.org/en/statistics/.

p. 43 'One of the most respected studies…', Angus Deaton and Jean Dreze, 'Poverty and inequality in India: A re-examination', *Economic and Political Weekly*, September 7, 2008, p. 3729.

p. 43 'Although above the official poverty line…', National Commission for Enterprises in the Unorganized Sector (NCEUS), *Report on Conditions of Work and Promotions of Livelihoods in the Unorganized Sector* (Government of India, 2007), available at www.nceus.nic.in.

p. 44 'A process that has been dubbed…', Amit Bhaduri, 'Economic growth: A meaningless obsession?', *Seminar*, Number 569, month 2007, p. ??

p. 44 'Nano, the much-hyped, low-cost car…', Somini Sengupta, 'Razing farms for factory creates battleground in India', *The New York Times*, December 29, 2006; Shoma Chaudhary, 'Bengal shows the way', *Tehelka*, March 3, 2007.

p. 45 'Government's own data…', NCEUS, *Report on Conditions of Work and Promotions of Livelihoods in the Unorganized Sector* (Government of India, 2007), available at www.nceus.nic.in.

p. 45 'Their labour is extracted...', Barbara Harriss-White, 'India's Informal Economy: Facing the 21st Century', in Kaushik Basu (ed.)*India's Emerging Economy: Performance and Prospects in the 1990s and Beyond* (MITPress, 2004).

p. 46 'Even the government admits...', NCEUS, *Report on Conditions of Work and Promotion of Livelihoods in the Unorganized Sector* (Government of India, 2007), p. 8.

p. 46 'Manifesto for Dalit capitalism...', the Bhopal Declaration is available at www.ambedkar.org.

p. 46 'Proponents of Dalit capitalism ...', S. Anand, 'An epitaph for the bull-hull economy', *Outlook-Business*, June 8, 2008.

p. 46 'The fact remains...', Barbara Harriss-White and Nandini Gooptu, 'Mapping India's World of Unorganized Labour', *Socialist Register*, 2001, p. 99.

p. 47 'The recent Sachar Committee report...', *Social, Economic and Educational Status of the Muslim Community of India: A Report* (Government of India, 2006), available at http://www.minorityaffaris.gov.in.

p. 47 'Even as the revenues grew...', Prabhat Patnaik, 'Conservatism to the fore', *Frontline*, March 15–28, 2008; Jayati Ghosh, 'Stagnant sectors', *Frontline*, March 15–28, 2008.

p. 48 'The despair driven...', Dilip Thakore, 'Shame and scandal in primary education', *Education World*, December 2008; Amy Waldman, 'India's poor bet precious sums on private schools', *The New York Times*, November 15, 2003.

p. 48 'Critics point out...', Anil Sadgopal, 'Misconceiving fundamentals, dismantling rights', *Tehelka*, June 14, 2008.

p. 49 'In 2000, India had only ...', Pawan Agarwal,

Higher Education in India: The Need for Change,
Working Paper 180 (Indian Council for Research
on International Economic Relations, 2006).

p. 49 'The total number of private colleges…', Vijender
Sharma, 'Commercialization of higher education in
India', *Social Scientist*, 33 (2005): 65–74. p. 67.

p. 49 'In 2003, 86.4 per cent…', Devesh Kapur and
Pratap Bhanu Mehta, *Indian Higher Education
Reform: Erom Half-baked Socialism to Half-baked
Capitalism*, Working Paper 108 (Center for
International Development, Harvard University,
2004).

p. 50 'There is a push to allow…', Konark Sharma, 'FDI in
higher education: Aspirations and reality',
Mainstream, June 9, 2007; Shailaja Neelakantan, 'India
is shutting the door on Britain's top institutions', *The
Independent*, July 17, 2008.

p. 51 'There is absolutely no doubt…', Devesh Kapur
and Pratap Bhanu Mehta, *Indian Higher Education
Reform: From Half-baked Socialism to Half-baked
Capitalism*, Working Paper 108 (Center for
International Development, Harvard University,
2004).

p. 51 'The government invited…', Mukesh Ambani,
Kumar Mangalam Birla, *A Policy Framework for
Reforms in Education*, Prime Minister's Council on
Trade and Industry, available at www.nic.in.

p. 52 'Commercialization of education is backed by legal
rulings…', Devesh Kapur and Pratap Bhanu
Mehta, *Indian Higher Education Reform: From Half-
baked Socialism to Half-baked Capitalism*, Working
Paper 108 (Center for International Development,
Harvard University, 2004).

p. 54 'According to Rob Jenkins…', Rob Jenkins, 'Labour
policy and the second generation of economic
reform in India', *India Review*, 3, 2 (2004): p.21.

p. 54   'A representative example...', Ranabir Choudhury, 'Evolution of the swadeshi idea,' *Hindu Business Line*, April 5, 2004.

p. 54   'Even the Swadeshi Jagran Manch...', S. Gurumurthy, 'Making India an economic super-power', *The Tribune*, August 15, 1998.

p. 56   'The so-called "theocons"...', Damon Linker, *The Theocons: Secular America Under Seige* (Doubleday, 2006).

p. 57   'India becoming a global superpower...', Subramanian Swamy, 'In search for a Hindu agenda', *The Organiser*, November 20, 2005.

p. 58   'Jaithirth (Jerry) Rao, the founder-CEOof Mphasis ...', Jaithirth (Jerry) Rao, 'Revive the Swatantra Party', *Indian Express*, July 25, 2005; see also Rao, 'Tired of Socialists', *Livemint*, June 8, 2007.

p. 58   Narayana Murthy, the founder-CEOof Infosys...', 'Indian IT-mogul eyeing role in politics', *The Strait Times* (Singapore), April 2, 2007.

p. 58   'A new party that will put economics...', Gurcharan Das, 'The only alternative', *The Times of India*, December 28, 2002.

CHAPTER 2

p. 61   Peter Berger, *Desecularization of the World* (Eerdmans, 1999).

p. 61   Pavan Varma, *Being Indian* (Penguin India, 2004).

p. 63   'The expression "rush hour of the gods"...', Neil MacFarland, *The Rush Hour of the Gods: A Study of New Religious Movements in Japan* (Harper Colophon Books, 1967).

p. 66   'They are instead what...', Achin Vanaik, 'The new Indian right', *New Left Review*, May–June pp. 43–67.

p. 66   'According to the Indian National Council of

Applied Economic Research (NCAER)...', The
Great Indian Middle Class (GIMC) at business-
standard.com/ncr/ncr.php; see also 'Middle class
income group to grow by 13%, NCAER study', *the
Financial Express*, September 1, 2006.

p. 66　'But if middle class-ness is measured...', 'Indian
middle class happy with economic progress',
IBNLive at http://ibnlive.com.

p. 67　'Going by the recent...', Pew Global Attitudes
Project, 2007, 'World publics welcome global trade,
but not immigration',
http://pewglobal.org/reports/pdf/258.pdf.

p. 68　'Economists have shown...', Nirvikar Singh, 'The
idea of India and the role of the middle class',
available at the eScholarship Repository,
University of California, at
http://repositories.cdlib.org/ucscecon/597.

p. 68　'As Chakravarti Ram-Prasad observed...', Ram-
Prasad Chakravarti, 'India's middle class failure',
Prospect Magazine 138 (2007).

p. 69　'Analysis of election data....', Suhas Palshikar,
'Politics of Indian Middle-Classes', in Imtiaz
Ahmad and H. Reifeld (eds), *Middle-class Values in
India and West Europe* (Social Science Press, 2007).

p. 70　'According to the 2007 State of the Nation
Survey...', 'State of the nation: What makes
Indians keep the faith', January 24, 2007, IBN-
CNN–Hindustan Times, IBNLive, available at
http://ibnlive.com.

p. 70　'Based upon the National Election Survey of
2004...', Suhas Palshikar, 'Majoritarian middle
ground?', *Economic and Political Weekly*, December
18, 2004.

p. 71　'The number of registered religious buildings...',
Lise McKean, *Divine Enterprise: Gurus and the
Hindu Nationalist Movement* (University of Chicago

Press, 1996), p. 32.

p. 71   'In his much acclaimed…', Pavan Varma, *Being Indian* (Penguin India, 2004), p. 96.

p. 71   'According to a recent study…', 'Indians keep the faith: Religious tourism booms in India', Indian Brand Equity Foundation at www.ibef.org; see also, 'Thank God! Religious tourism grows at 25 per annum', *The Economic Times*, October 1, 2006.

p. 72   'As a scientist…', David Gosling, *Science and Religion in India* (Christian Literature Society, 1976), p. 80.

p. 72   'This is the phenomenon of compartmentalization…', Milton Singer, *When a Great Tradition Modernizes: An Anthropological Approach to Indian Civilization* (University of Chicago Press, 1972).

p. 72   'Indians are supposed to be…', Alan Roland, *In Search of Self in India and Japan: Toward a Cross-cultural Psychology* (Princeton University Press, 1988), p. 252.

p. 73   'In Singer's words…', Milton Singer, *When a Great Tradition Modernizes: An Anthropological Approach to Indian Civilization* (University of Chicago Press, 1972) pp. 336, 342.

p. 75   'What is unique about all invented traditions…', Eric Hobsbawm and Terence Ranger, *The Invention of Tradition* (Cambridge, 1983), p. 1.

p. 75   'Christopher Fuller's 2003 monograph…', Christopher Fuller, *The Renewal of Priesthood: Modernity and Traditionalism in a South Indian Temple* (Princeton University Press, 2003).

p. 76   'The state government's latest figures…', Tamil Development Culture and Religious Endowments Department, Hindu Religious and Charitable Endowments Department, Policy Note, 2006–2007, Demand No. 47, www.tn.gov.in/policynotes/pdf/hr_and_ce.pdf.

p. 78　'Joanne Punzo Waghorne describes...', Joanne P. Waghorne, *Diaspora of the Gods: Modern Hindu Temple in an Urban Middle Class World* (Oxford University Press, 2004), p. 25.

p. 79　'According to media reports...', 'Akshaya Trithiya: When the leitmotif is gold', *Business Line*, April 19, 2007; see also Meera Nanda, 'Is India a Science Superpower?', *Frontline*, September 13, 2005.

p. 79　'There are newspaper accounts...', Klaus Klostermaier, *A Survey of Hinduism* (State University of New York Press, 1994), pp. 155–158.

p. 79　'In 1970, there were even reports...', see above, pp. 158, 526.

p. 80　'Worldwide popularity of Gayatri Pariwar...', see website of All World Gayatri Pariwar, http://www.awgp.org.

p. 81　'As Dr Pranav Pandya, the spiritual head...', Archana Dongre, 'Hardwar institute tracks power of Gayatri yagna', *Hinduism Today*, September 1992.

p. 81　'In their unique and original interpretation...', 'Rajiv Malik, 'Wow! One million join Vedic rites', *Hinduism Today*, June 1994.

p. 82　'Gayatri Parivar's clients include...', 'Training programme for personnel' at http://missionvision.awgp.org.

p. 83　'The other notable redesign of Vedic ritual...', Timothy Lubin, 'Science, patriotism and Mother Veda: Ritual activism in Maharashtra', *International Journal of Hindu Studies*, 5, 3 (2001): 81–105.

p. 84　'A very brief summary...', ibid.

p. 84　'A culture of "political darshan"...', A.R. Vasavi, 'Political "darshan" as development in Karnataka', *Economic and Political Weekly*, July 28, 2007.

p. 84　'Even more blatant...', Neeraj Mishra, 'In God I trust', *India Today*, May 12, 2003.

p. 84　'Bhairon Singh Shekhawat is reported...', 'You can

mail order "prasadam"', *Hindu Business Line*, November 9, 2002.

p. 84 'Agitation to "liberate" the Guru Dattatreya Baba Bundan Dargah...', Parvathi Menon, 'Saffron mobilization', *Frontline*, December 20, 2004.

p. 85 'The VHP plans to organize a hundred yagnas...', Sanjana, 'Freedom of hate speech', *Tehelka*, April 11, 2009.

p. 85 'In Orissa where thousands of Christians...', Rohini Mohan, 'Killing the Phoenix', *Tehelka*, April 18, 2009.

p. 85 'In one of the most shameful examples...', Ashok Mitra, 'A sense of humiliation: Why the bhoomi puja in Singur is such a let-down', *The Telegraph*, February 2, 2007.

P 86 'A process that has been dubbed...', Joanne Waghorne, *Diaspora of the Gods: Modern Hindu Temple in an Urban Middle Class World* (Oxford University Press, 2004).

p. 87 'A recent study of roadside temples...', U. Kalpagam, 'Secularism, Religiosity and Popular Culture: Chennai's Roadside Temples', *Economic and Political Weekly*, November 4, 2006, pp. 4595-4.

p. 87 'A very similar process of gentrification...', Joanne Waghorne, *Diaspora of the Gods: Modern Hindu Temple in an Urban Middle Class World* (Oxford University Press, 2004).

p. 88 'To quote Joanne Waghorne...', ibid, pp. 132, 149.

p. 88 'The fast growing cult of Adi Para Shakti...', Vasudha Narayanan, 'Diglossic Hinduism: Liberation and lentils', *Journal of the American Academy of Religion*, 68, 4 (2000): 761–779.

p. 89 'Another phenomenon of note...', Anna Portnoy, 'A Goddess in the Making', *The Whole Earth Catalogue*, 2000, www.wholeearthmag.com/ArticleBin/395.html.

p. 89   'The TVSGroup is a major benefactor...', 'Nine
        temples on pilgrim circuits', *The Hindu*, March 4,
        2002.

p. 90   'The growing popularity of Hanuman ....', Philip
        Lutgendorf, 'My Hanuman is bigger than yours',
        History of Religions, 33, 3 (1994): 211–245.

p. 91   'As Chris Fuller puts it...', Christopher Fuller, *The
        Camphor Flame* (Princeton University Press, 1992),
        p. 72.

p. 91   'Deities like Hanuman...', Philip Lutgendorf,
        Hanuman's Tale: The Messages of a Divine Monkey
        (Oxford University Press, 2007), p. 373.

p. 93   'Mata Amritanandamayi, or Amma...', See the fol-
        lowing essays by Maya Warrier: 'Modernity and its
        imbalances: Constructing modern selfhood in the
        Mata Amritanandmayi Mission', *Religion*, 36
        (2006): 179–195; 'Guru choice and spiritual seeking
        in contemporary India,' *International Journal of
        Hindu Studies*, 7 (2005): 31–54; and 'Process of secu-
        larization in contemporary India: Guru faith in the
        Mata Amritanandmayi Misison', *Modern Asian
        Studies*, 37 (2003): 213–53.

p. 94   'She urges her followers...', ibid.

p. 95   'Through his magic, Sai Baba...', Hugh Urban,
        'Avatar for our age: Satya Sai Baba and the contra-
        dictions of late capitalism', *Religion*, 33 (2003):
        73–93.

p. 95   'He runs a gurukul...', see the website of Arha
        Vidya Gurukulam at www.http://arshavidya.org.

p. 96   'Swami Dayananda has a substantial following...',
        Christopher Fuller and John Harriss, 'Globalizing
        Hinduism: A "Traditional" Guru and modern
        Businessmen in Chennai', in Jackie Assayag and
        Christopher Fuller (eds) *Globalizing India:
        Perspectives from Below* (Anthem Press, 2005), pp.
        211–236.

p. 96 'A trend that has been dubbed 'karma capitalism...', Pete Engardio and Jena McGregor, 'Karma capitalism', *BusinessWeek*, October 30, 2006.

p. 97 'Corporations like Oracle...', 'A guru teaches techies how to breathe', *BusinessWeek*, September 22, 2003.

p. 98 'Reportedly 60–70 per cent of its members...', Suma Verghese, 'Sri Sri Ravi Shankar: Life-coach to the next generation', *Life Positive*, February 2006.

p. 98 'Another reason that followers...', 'A guru teaches techies how to breathe', *BusinessWeek*, September 22, 2003.

p. 99 'When examined objectively...', Meera Nanda, 'Ayurveda under the scanner', *Frontline*, April 8, 2006.

p. 99 'He seems to be equally at home...', See Hindu Swayamsevak Sangh, 'Tri-state Hindus come together for Hindu Sangam in New Jersey', www.hssus.org.

p. 99 'As reported by Christopher Fuller and John Harriss...', Christopher Fuller and John Harriss, 'Globalizing Hinduism: A "Traditional" Guru and Modern Businessmen in Chennai', in Jackie Assayag and Christopher Fuller (eds), *Globalizing India: Perspectives from Below* (Anthem Press, 2005), pp. 211–236.

p. 100 'The British magazine, *The Economist*...', 'The swamis', *The Economist*, December 20, 2003.

p. 100 'According to media reports...', 'Saffron techies', *Tehelka,* November 1, 2008.

p. 101 'He has made no secret...', 'Report: National Convention of Rashtra Sevika Samiti', *The Organiser*, December 11–18, 2005; 'Sangh Samachar: 15th National Convention of Rashtra Sevika Samiti in Nagpur: No empowerment without power—Swami Ramdev', *The Organiser*, November 27, 2005.

p. 101 'Supporters of Hindutva…', Swapan Dasgupta,
Evangelical Hindutva', *Seminar*, 545, 2005.

p. 102 'There were reports…', Priyanka Narain, 'God,
godmen and BJP and co. for political, religious and
environmental causes', *Livemint*, August 8, 2008.
See also '250 religious leaders flag off Save Ganga
campaign', *The Economic Times*, August 18, 2008.

p. 102 'Indian middle classes are proving Max Weber
wrong…', Max Weber, 'Science as Vocation', *From
Max Weber: Essays in Sociology*, H.H. Gerth and C.
Wright Mills (eds) (Oxford University Press, 1958
[1922]).

p. 103 'As has been shown …', Pippa Norris and Ronald
Inglehart, *Sacred and Secular: Religion and Politics
Worldwide* (Cambridge University Press, 2004).

p. 104 'The second explanation…', Pavan Varma, *The
Great Indian Middle Class* (Penguin India, 1998).

p. 104 'Even the otherwise astute…', Achin Vanaik, 'The
New Indian Right', *New Left Review*, May–June
2001: 43–67.

p. 104 'The upwardly mobile in urban India…', Maya
Warrier, 'Modernity and its imbalances:
Constructing modern selfhood in the Mata
Amritanandmayi Mission', *Religion*, 36 (2006):
179–195, p. 184.

p. 105 'Middle-class respondents in Baroda…', Margrit
van Wessel, 'Talking about consumption: How
Indian middle class dissociates from middle-class
life', *Cultural Dynamic*, 16 (2004): 93–116, p. 99.

p. 106 'Indians top the list of all nations…', Pew Global
Attitudes Survey, 2007, available at pewglobal.org/.

CHAPTER 3

p. 108 Lise McKean, *Divine Enterprise: Gurus and the*

Hindu Nationalist Movement (University Chicago Press, 1996).

p. 108 Praveen Togadia, 'VHP to build a Hindu vote bank', *The Hindu*, February 9, 2006.

p. 110 'The Supreme Court has accepted the argument...', Duncan Derrett, *Religion, Law and the State in India* (Oxford University Press, 1999 [1968]).

p. 111 'According to Christopher Fuller...', Christopher Fuller, *The Servants of the Goddess* (Cambridge,1984).

p. 111 As the historian Franklin Presler describes it...',Franklin Presler, 'The Structure and Consequences of Temple Policy in Tamil Nadu', *Pacific Affairs*, 56, 2 (1967): 232–246, p. 235.

p. 112 The fabled Jagannath temple...', James Preston, *Cult of the Goddess: Social and Religious Change in a Hindu Temple* (Waveland Press, 1985).

p. 112 'The enormous wealth of Thirumala Tirupathi...', 'Court decree retired tirupati Temple's hereditary priests', *Hinduism Today*, June 1996.

p. 112 'The temple had fallen into disrepair...', Jagmohan, 'Don't allow meddling with Vaishno Devi Shrine', *The Tribune*, September 9, 1998.

p. 113 'Shri Amarnath Shrine Board...', 'Mired in controversies', *Kashmir Newz*, June 30, 2006.

p. 115 'The USA-based Global Hindu Heritage Foundation...', Global Hindu Heritage Foundation, http://www.preservehinduism.org.

p. 115 'Organizations like Bharat Jagran Forum...', see the website, http://www.bharatjagran.com.

p. 115 'The idea that temples need to be "saved"...', see the website of Hindu Janjagruti Samiti, http://www.hindujagruti.org.

p. 116 'Members of the National Commission on Religious Endowments...', Duncan Derrett, *Religion, Law and the State in India* (Oxford

University Press, 1999 [1968]), p. 501.

p. 116 'Temples may be defined as occult laboratories...', see above, p. 500.

p. 117 'As Joanne Waghorne observed...', Joanne Punzo Waghorne, 'The gentrification of the Goddess', *International Journal of Hindu Studies*, 5, 3 (2001): 227–67, p. 257.

p. 118 'The same sentiment in expressed...', 'End to government control of Temples demanded', *The Tribune*, December 27, 2006.

p. 118 'Every year millions of pilgrims...', 'Makaravilakku is lit by hand: Tantri', *The Hindu*, May 28, 2008; 'Sabarimala revenue put at Rs. 75.52 crore', *The Hindu*, January 15, 2008.

p. 119 'Writing in 1982...', Franklin Presler, 'The Structure and Consequences of Temple Policy in Tamil Nadu, 1967–81', *Pacific Affairs*, 56, 2 (1982):232–246, p. 245.

p. 119 'Chandi temple in Cuttack, Orissa...', James Preston, *Cult of the Goddess: Social and Religious Change in a Hindu Temple* (Waveland Press, 1985), p. 73.

p. 119 'Reports suggest that Tirupati...', 'Tirupati ousts Vatican, reigns at top', www.ndtv.com, September 13, 2007; 'The state of religion', *Indian Express*, January 23, 2005.

p. 119 'The number of pilgrims is up...', 'Vaishno Devi pilgrimage begins on healthy note', *Daily Excelsior*, February 2, 2009.

p. 119 'Sri Amarnath Shrine Board...', Gautam Navlakha, 'State cultivation of Amarnath Yatra', *Economic and Political Weekly*, July 26, 2008.

p. 120 'In just two years...', 'Shiv Khori shrine attracts lakhs', *The Tribune*, January 16, 2009; 'Pilgrimage to Shiv Khori shrine picking up', *Daily Excelsior*, September 4, 2008.

219

p. 120 'Ministry of Tourism of the state of Jammu and Kashmir...', 'Major boost for pilgrim tourism: Shiv Khori, Bawa Jito among 4 shrines to get huge central funds', *Daily Excelsior*, February 14, 2008.

p. 120 'There are calls to replicate...', 'Managing shrines', *Daily Excelsior*, January 21, 2008.

p. 120 'Even L.K. Advani is on record...', *Hinduism Today*, October 1997.

p. 121 'When the UGC, the highest educational policy-making body...', Pranab Dhal Samanta, 'Now, it is occult science', *The Hindu*, February 23, 2002.

p. 121 These schools are producing...', Christopher Fuller, *The Renewal of Priesthood: Modernity and Traditionalism in a South Indian Temple* (Princeton, 2003), p. 112.

p. 122 'In May 2002, the Sansthan...', 'Deemed University to Rashtriya Sanskrit Sansthan', available at the website of Rashtriya Sanskrit Sansthan www.sanskrit.nic.in.

p. 123 'Two other newly "deemed universities...', Swami Vivekananda Yoga Anusandhan , see the website at www.svyasa.org.; Bihar Yoga Bharati, at www.bihar.com.

p. 124 'A good example is Navi Mandal Veda Vidya Mandir...', 'Age old mantra: Vedic education schools', *The Times of India*, September 5, 2005.

p. 124 'A similar Vedic school...', 'Preserving a unique tradition', *The Hindu*, March 4, 2005.

p. 124 'Under the rein of the BJP chief minister Vasundhara Raje Scindia...', 'In Scindia's Rajasthan, temples get a shine', http://in.news.yahoo.com/040519/43/2d69k.html; 'Training camps for Rajasthan priests', *The Hindu*, March 20, 2004.

p. 124 'The state of Andhra...', 'Eight more Vedic schools will come up in state', *The Hindu*, December 25, 2007.

p. 125 'A case in point is Tamil Nadu…', 'Enter the Dalit priest', *The Telegraph*, April 26, 2008.

p. 125 'According to the official report…', see the official website of the Government of Tamil Nadu, www.tn.gov.in.

p. 126 'This is how the triangular relationship…', 'A saintly minstrel and his message', *Hinduism Today*, October - December 2006; 'The man Ambanis revere most', available at http://www.rediff.com. As for the land grant, the website of Sandipani Vidyaniketan contains the following information: 'The Shree Bharatiya Sanskruti Samvardhak Trust [the parent trust of Sandipani] then set out to acquire the existing piece of land. A request was made to the government of Gujarat who very generously granted 85 acres of land close to the Porbandar airport.' See the website of Sandipani Vidyaniketan at www.sandipani.org/trusts/index.asp.

p. 126 'Swami Ramdev…is building two universities…', 'Din in M.P. Assembly over land allotment to Ramdev', *The Hindu*, March 17, 2007; see also, Shantanu Guha Ray, 'Business of the Gods', *Tehelka*, June 24, 2007; 'Yoga guru Ramdev invited to tap Ayurvedic potential by Jharkhand government', at http://www.medindia.net; 'Ramdev gets university', *The Telegraph*, April 7, 2006; 'Swami Ramdev to set up world's biggest yoga and Ayurvedic centre', *The Organiser*, April 23, 2006.

p. 126 'The business elite, in India and abroad…', 'Shri Ramdev promotes yoga in UK', *The Organiser*, September 3, 2006.

p. 127 'Reports in the *Organiser*…', 'Promoting Hindu traditions in rural areas', *The Organiser*, July 11, 2004.

p. 127 'The popular Bangaru Adigalar Shakti "Amma",…', 'Spiritual revolution in Tamil Nadu', *The Organiser*, July 25, 2004.

p. 128 'Obey your guru!...', *Hinduism Today,* April–June 2004.

p. 128 'Agamic education, Fuller concludes...', Christopher Fuller, *Renewal of Priesthood*, p. 5.

p. 128 'According to G.K. Ramamurthy...', 'Preparing tomorrow's priesthood', *Hinduism Today,* January–March 2006.

p. 129 'Another priest training school in Pillaiyarpatti...', 'Keeping the faith', *Hinduism Today,* April 2003.

p. 130 'Even those who welcome these "swamiji schools"...', Dilip Thakore, 'The rising sun of the swamiji schools', *Education World,* April 2004.

p. 131 'the Sri Adichunchanagiri Mahasamsthana math...', ibid.

p. 131 'The Chinmaya Mission runs...', ibid.

p. 131 'The Art of Living Foundation...', Shantanu Guha Ray, 'Business of the Gods', *Tehelka,* June 24, 2007.

p. 131 'According to Edward Luce...', Edward Luce, *In Spite of the Gods* (Abacus, 2006), p. 177.

p. 132 'In 2006, the government of Orissa...', 'Varsity from house of guru', *The Telegraph,* December 11, 2006.

p. 132 'The AOL deal is puny compared to... Vedanta University...', 'Vedanta university in Orissa', *The Telegraph,* July 20, 2006.

p. 132 'But going by the past record...', '£ 10m state cash for first Hindu school', *The Guardian,* December 24, 2006. See also, 'Indian philanthropist behind UK's first Hindu school', Prasun Sonwalkar, London, September 11, 2007 (IANS), available at www.red-hotcurry.com/news/Hindu_school.htm.

p. 133 'I-Foundation, an ISKCON charity...', the website of I-Foundation www.i-foundation.org.

p. 133 'According to its own promotional materials...', see the website of Maharishi Mahesh Yogi Vedic Vishwavidyalaya http://mmyvv.com.

p. 134 'Career advisors in the magazine *Education World...*', Career Focus, 'Stars augur well for astrologers', *Education World*, November 30, 1999.

p. 134 'The proposed Keshav Vidyapeeth Vishwavidyalaya...', Nalini Taneja, 'RSSin action in Rajasthan', *People's Democracy*, March 6, year??.

p. 135 'To build a temple in Delhi...', see the description of 'shilanyas vidhi' under 'The making of Akshardham' on the website of Akshardham temple at www.akshardham.com. Quotes available at www.swaminarayan.org/news/2000/11/delhi/index.htm.

p. 135 'Yogiji Maharaj advised his followers...', see the description of 'shilanyas vidhi' under "The making of Akshardham", ibid.

p. 135 'Delhi administration under Jagmohan...', 'Land allotment to temple trust flayed', *The Times of India*, May 4, 2000; see also 'Whose Delhi is it anyway?', *Tehelka*, October 7, 2006.

p. 135 'The temple managed to acquire another 50 acres of land...', 'Akshardham temple to adorn river Yamuna bed', *The Times of India*, October 11, 2004.

p. 136 'In the state of Rajasthan...', see the power point presentation available on the Rajasthan Devasthan website (rajasthandevasthan.ppt).

p. 136 'In the state of Gujarat...', John Dayal, 'Financing faith,' *Himal Southasia,* October-November 2007.

p. 136 'In the state of Madhya Pradesh...', 'MP allots priests to conduct pujas', *Deccan Chronicle*, January 8, 2008.

p. 136 'In the state of Tamil Nadu....', HRCECitizens' Charter, 2007-08 at www.tn.gov.in/citizen/hrce.pdf.

p. 137 'the state of Himachal Pradesh...', 'Rs. 7.80 crore to boost pilgrimage tourism', *The Tribune*, January 17, 2007; 'Focus on temple tourism?', *The Tribune*, February 7, 2007.

p. 137 'Notable examples include...', 'Ford plans "Religious tourism" project in Bengal—Vedic Planetarium in Mayapur on cards', *The Hindu*, February 20, 2004; 'Nine temples on pilgrim circuit', *The Hindu*, March 4, 2002.

p. 137 'The state of Jammu and Kashmir...', 'Governor performs yagya, leads devotees to pratham darshan', *Daily Excelsior*, October 15, 2004; see also editorial title??, *Daily Excelsior*, August 6, 2007.

p. 138 'The state of Gujarat officially sponsors Navratri...', 'Vibrant Gujarat: Navratri tourism carnival', *The Organiser*, October 4, 2004.

p. 138 'Central government offered to spend Rs 7 crore...', Praful Bidwai, 'Kashmir turmoil and the Amarnath Yatra', *The News*, July 12, 2008, available at www.thenews.com.pk.

p. 138 'Hindu proselytization or Hindukaran...', Citizens' Inquiry Committee report, *Untold Story of Hindukaran of Adivasi's (Tribals) in Dangs*, January 3, 2006, available at http://www.milligazette.com/dailyupdate/2006/20060108-hindutva.htm.

p. 139 'The infamous Ekatmata yagna....', Lise McKean, *The Divine Enterprise* (Chicago, 1996), pp. 115–123.

p. 140 'The idea of banal nationalism...', Michael Billig, *Banal Nationalism* (Sage, 1995).

p. 140 'As Billig puts it...', ibid, p. 5.

p. 142 'According to the description provided by the organizers themselves...', see http://www.sandipani.org.

CHAPTER 4

p. 145 'Indians rank number one in the world...', Pew Global Attitudes Project, 'World publics welcome global trade —but not Immigration', available at www.perglobal.org; see also Meera Nanda, 'India in the world: How we see ourselves', *The Hindu*, December 11, 2007.

p. 147 'This rising self-awareness...', Samuel Huntington, *The Clash of Civilizations and the Remaking of World Order* (Simon and Schuster, 1998).

p. 148 'Against those like...', Francis Fukuyama, *The End of History and the Last Man* (Avon Press, 1992), p. ix.

p. 148 'Civilizations will clash...', Samuel Huntington, *The Clash of Civilizations and the Remaking of World Order* (Simon and Schuster, 1998), p. 67.

p. 149 'They attribute their dramatic economic development...', Samuel Huntington, see above, p. 93.

p. 153 'We proved by our history...', Gurcharan Das, *India Unbound* (Alfred A. Knopf, 2000), p. xvii.

p. 154 'The essential point is...', Pavan Varma, *Being India* (Penguin, 2004), pp. 109–110.

p. 155 'The arcane, impenetrable nature of Hindu lore...', Daniel Lak, *India Express: The Future of a New Superpower* (Penguin, 2008).

p. 155 'Consider the fact that...', P. Balaram, 'The Shanghai rankings', *Current Science*, 86, 10, May 25, 2004.

p. 156 'The number of research papers from India...', G. Padmanaban, 'Science education in India: Time to leapfrog with caution', *Current Science*, 95, December 10, 2008; see also, P. Balaram, 'Science in India: Signs of stagnation', *Current Science*, 83, August 10, 2002.

p. 156 'Even the much-hyped ITsector...', Gangan Prathap, 'Where have our young ones gone?: The coolieization of India', *Current Science*, 89, October 10, 2005.

p. 157 'A majoritarian is someone...', SDSA Team, *State of Democracy in South Asia* (Oxford, 2008), p. 76.

p. 157 'India's most reliable and respected pollsters...',

Suhas Palshikar, 'Majoritiarian middle ground?', *Economic and Political Weekly*, December 18, 2004.

p. 158 'A recent survey of the state of democracy...',SDSA Team *State of Democracy in South Asia* (Oxford, 2008), p. 101.

p. 158 'The voting trends...', Suhas Palshikar, 'Politics of Indian Middle Classes', in Imtiaz Ahmad and Helmut Reifeld (eds), *Middle-class Values in India and West Europe* (Social Science Press, 2007).

p. 159 'For the ordinary Indian ...', Dipankar Gupta, *The Caged Phoenix: Can India fly?* (Penguin-Viking, 2009), p. 214.

p. 160 'A relatively new, deeply Islamophobic and anti-Christian faction...', Meera Nanda, 'Hindu triumphalism in the clash of civilizations,' *Economic and Political Weekly*, forthcoming.

p. 161 'They go on to condemn the monotheistic God...', Ram Swarup, *Hindu View of Christianity and Islam* (Voice of India,2000), p. 39; Sita Ram Goel, *Defense of Hindu Society* (Voice of India, 2000), p. 20.

p. 161 'According to the VOI school of thought...', Abhas Chatterjee, 'Response', in Sita Ram Goel (ed.), *Time for Stocktaking: Whither Sangh Parivar* (Voice of India, 1997), p. 52.

p. 161 'The same idea is expressed by Koenraad Elst...', Ramesh N. Rao, 'Interview with K. Elst,' August 19, 2002, available at http://www.ramesh-n-rao.sulekha.com.

Elst made this statement in the context of the demolition of the Babri Masjid suggesting that rather than physically demolish existing mosques, Hindus should try to discredit Islam itself. This part of the interview is reproduced here:

Ramesh Rao (interviewer): *Are you saying that the demolition was a good thing?*

226

Elst: At the level of historic justice, I consider it perfectly normal that a Hindu sacred site is adorned with a Hindu temple. Hindus shouldn't overemphasize the history of Islamic destruction, the current victimhood culture is quite foreign to the Hindu spirit, but for once this focus on a temple forcibly replaced with a mosque has been instructive. At a more pragmatic level, from the viewpoint of saving lives, certainly a more pressing concern than the rights and wrongs of history, the demolition was a good thing, on balance. In the preceding years, India was tormented by communal riots over all kinds of issues, most of them unrelated to Ayodhya. The demolition led to a brief round of Muslim revenge actions plus the Shiv Sena retaliation in Mumbai, but then rioting stopped for nine long years. The demolition clearly had a cathartic effect on the rioters. To be sure, Islamic terrorism has continued, but Hindus refused to be provoked. They did not take out their anger on their Muslim neighbours after the Mumbai blasts of March 1993, nor after any of the numerous massacres of Hindus and Sikhs in Jammu and Kashmir, nor after the bomb attack in Coimbatore, nor after the attacks on the parliament buildings. Hindus have shown remarkable restraint.

At the most fundamental level, however, I am not too enthusiastic about the whole idea of campaigning for the liberation of historical temple sites from Muslim occupation. It is a well-attested fact that most historical mosques were built on the site of non-Muslim places of worship. This is true of thousands of mosques in India, but also of the Ummayad mosque in Damascus, the Aya Sophia in Istanbul, and even the Kaaba itself, where Mohammed smashed 360 idols venerated by the sanctuary's rightful owners, the Arab polytheists. *But trying to pull these sites out of the hands of the Muslims is the wrong approach. The Ayodhya campaign had the merit of drawing attention to this historic injustice, but henceforth the energy spent on it had better be redirected to a more fundamental objective. We should help the Muslims in freeing themselves from Islam, and then they themselves will release these places of worship. Every Muslim is a Sita, an abductee who must be liberated from Ravana's prison.* (emphasis added)

p. 162 'Supreme Being of monotheism...', Sita Ram Goel, *India's Secularism: New Name for National Subversion* (Voice of India, 1999), p. 17.

p. 162 'This kind of thinking is described as "designer fascism"....', Richard Wolin, *Seduction of Unreason: The Intellectual Romance with Fascism, form Nietzsche to Postmodernism* (Princeton University Press, 2004).

p. 162 'They prefer to call themselves *bauddhik kshatriya...*', David Frawley, 'A Call for Intellectual (bauddhika) Kshatriya', in Silá Ram Goel (ed.), *Time for Stocktaking: Whither Sangh Parivar?* (Voice of India, 1997).

p. 163 'The official website...', www.geocities.com/voi_publishers.htm.

p. 164 'All the arguments and evidence...', Michael Witzel, 'Ram's Realm: Indocentric Rewritings of Early South Asian Archeology and History,' in Garett G. Fagan (ed.), *Archeological Fantasies: How Pseudo-archeology Misrepresents the Past and Misleads the public* (Routledge, 2006). See also Meera Nanda, *Prophets Facing Backward: Postmodernism, Science, and Hindu Nationalism* (Permanent Black, 2004).

p. 164 'Islam and Christianity follow a path of adharma...', Abhas Chatterjee, 'Response', in Sita Ram Goel (ed.), *Time for Stock-taking: Whither Sangh*

Parivar? (Voice of India, 1997), pp. 59, 67.

p. 165 'As L.K. Advani put it recently...', 'Concluding remarks by Shri L.K. Advani', meeting of the National Executive, June 20–21, 2009, available at www.bjp.org.

p. 166 'The essential instinct of Semitic monotheism...', S. Gurumurthy, 'Semitic monotheism: The root of intolerance in India', *NPQ* (New Perspectives Quarterly), Spring 1994, 47–53, available on the website of the BJP, www. bjp.org.

p. 137 'On a visit to Chandigarh earlier this year...', Meera Nanda, 'Witness to a kidnapping', *The Hindu*, February 13, 2009.

CHAPTER 5

p. 171 'Evangelical churches...', Andrew, Higgins, 'In Europe, God is (not) dead', *Wall Street Journal*, July 14, 2007; Joshua Livestro, 'Holland's post-secular future: Christianity is dead. Long live Christianity', *The Weekly Standard*, January 1, 2007.

p. 171 'Europe has been described as...', Phillip Jenkins, *God's Continent: Christianity, Islam and Europe's Religious Crisis* (Oxford University Press, 2007).

p. 171 'Belief in reincarnation...', Michael Johnson, 'Europe's love of the occult', *International Herald Tribune*, August 16, 2007.

p. 172 'The Russian Orthodox Church...', Clifford Levy, 'Welcome or not, orthodoxy is back in Russia's schools', *The New York Times*, September 23, 2007; Michael Binyon, 'Russian roulette', *The New Humanist*, March–April, 2008.

p. 172 'Religious movements like...', Andrew Greeley, *Religion in Europe at the End of the Second Millennium* (Transaction Press, 2003).

p. 173 'The once atheistic China…', Fenggang Yang, 'Between secularist ideology and de-secularizing reality: The birth and growth of religious research in Communist China', *Sociology of Religion* (2004); Xinzhong Yao, 'Religious belief and practice in urban China, 1995–2005', *Journal of Contemporary Religion*, 22, 2 (2007).

p. 173 'A recent study of Indian scientists…', Ariela Keysar and Barry Kosmin, *International Survey: Worldviews and Opinion of Scientists, India, 2007–08* (Institute for the Study of Secularism in Society and Culture, 2008).

p. 173 'In the US…', E.J. Larson and L. Witham, 'Scientists are still keeping the faith', *Nature*, 386 (1997):435.

p. 173 'Recent data from the UK…', Richard Dawkins, *The God Delusion* (Houghton Mifflin, 2006), p. 102.

p. 173 ' "Vedic creationism" is a new trend…', Meera Nanda, 'Vedic creationism in America', *Frontline*, January 14, 2006; Deepak Chopra, 'Intelligent design without the Bible', August 23, 2005, http://huffingtonpost.com; Deepak Chopra, 'Rescuing intelligent design—but from whom?', August 24, 2005, http://huffingtonpost.com

p. 174 'Scientific creationism is spreading…', Ehsan Masood, 'Islam and science: An Islamist revolution', *Nature*, online edition, November 1, 2006.

p. 175 'An "Einsteinian God"…', Richard Dawkins, *The God Delusion* (Houghton Mifflin, 2006).

p. 175 'A secular society is one…', Peter Berger, *The Sacred Canopy* (Doubleday, 1967).

p. 176 'A liberal society like the US…', Meera Nanda, 'Secularism without secularization?: Reflections on God and politics in America and India', *Economic and Political Weekly*, xlii, 39–46.

p. 178 'Religion "stops at the factory gate"…', ibid., p. 129.

p. 179 'As there is a secularization of society...', ibid.,
107–108.

p. 182 'The freethinkers of the 1840s...', Owen Chadwick,
*The Secularization of the European Mind in the
Nineteenth Century* (Cambridge, 1975), p. 88.

p. 183 'During the heyday of progressivism ...', Susan
Jacoby, *Freethinkers: A History of American
Secularism* (Metropolitan Books, 2004).

p. 183 'If we want to change men's ideas...', Owen
Chadwick, *The Secularization of the European Mind
in the Nineteenth Century* (Cambridge, 1975), p. 59.

p.186 'The original secularization theory was flawed...',
Jose Casanova, *Public Religions in the Modern World*
(Chicago, 1994), p. 19.

p. 187 'Some Indian critics of secularism...',T.N. Madan,
'Secularism in its Place', in Rajeev Bhargava (ed.),
Secularism and its Critics (Oxford University Press,
1998), p. 302.

p. 188 'The death of secularization theory...', Peter Berger
(ed.), *The De-secularization of the World* (Eerdmans
Publishing Co., 1999), pp.2–3.

p. 188 'Religious movements dripping with reactionary
supernaturalism...', ibid., p. 4.

p. 188 'Take the work of Steve Bruce...', Steve Bruce, *God
is Dead: Secularization in the West* (Blackwell, 2002).

p. 189 'They become gentle prosperity religions...', Alan
Wolfe, 'The coming religious peace: and the winner is...', *The Atlantic*, March 2008.

p. 191 'Staring with a provocative essay...', Rodney Stark,
'Secularization, R.I.P.', *Sociology of Religion*, 60, 3
(1999): 249–273.

p. 193 'Stark offers telling data from Iceland...' , ibid., p. 264.

p. 193 'Europeans believe without belonging...', Grace
Davie. 'Europe: The Exception that Proves the
Rule?', in Peter Berger (ed., *The Desecularization of
the World* (William B. Eerdmans, 1999).

p. 196 'One such nuanced defence of secularization...',
Pippa Norris and Ronald Inglehart, *Sacred and Secular: Religion and Politics Worldwide* (Cambridge University Press, 2004).

p. 197 'They predict that...', ibid., p. 18.

p. 197 'They summarize their conclusions...', ibid., pp. 107–108.

p. 198 'They wanted more than...', Michael Lerner, quoted here from Alan Sokal, *Beyond the Hoax: Science, Philosophy and Culture* (Oxford University Press, 2008), p. 304.

Bibliographic Essay

This essay is intended to be a guide to further reading. It is not an exhaustive survey of literature.

The available literature on the history and nature of globalization is vast. Jan Aart Scholte's *Globalization: A Critical Introduction* (Palgrave, 2005) provides an excellent overview of contending theories of globalization. Other books that left a significant impression on the analysis offered here include: Colin Leys, *Market-Driven Politics: Neoliberal Democracy and Public Interest* (Verso, 2003), David Harvey, *A Brief History of Neoliberalism* (Oxford, 2007), and Gabor Steingart, *The War for Wealth* (McGraw Hill, 2008).

The analysis of the changing political economy of India offered here has been influenced by the following authors: Achin Vanaik, *The Painful Transition: Bourgeois Democracy in India* (Verso, 1990), Jean Dreze and Amartya Sen, *India: Development and Participation* (Oxford, 2002), Amit Bhaduri, *Development with Dignity* (National Book Trust, 2005), Barbara Harriss-White, *India Working* (Cambridge University Press, 2003), Ronald J. Herring and Rina Agarwal (eds), *Whatever Happened to Class?* (Dannish Books, 2008).

Those interested in developing a better understanding of the arguments of Indian neo-liberals can learn a lot from Arvind Panagariya's data-packed book, *India: The Emergent Giant* (Oxford, 2008). Gurcharan Das's *India Unbound* (Knopf, 2000) is indispensable. Other useful references include Daniel Lak's *India Express* (Penguin, 2008), and Edward Luce's *The Strange Rise of Modern India* (Doubleday, 2007). Dipankar Gupta's *The Caged Phoenix: Can India Fly?* (Penguin-Viking, 2009) is a thoughtful meditation on India's inability to convert economic growth into development.

Deepak Lal's survey of the economic philosophy of the Hindu right is somewhat dated but still useful: 'The Economic

Impact of Hindu Revivalism', in Martin Marty and Scott Appleby (eds) *Fundamentalism and the State* (Chicago, 1993). Richard Fox's book *Gandhian Socialism* (Beacon, 1989) on the shared ground between Gandhian socialism and the Sangh Parivar is thought-provoking.

While one can fill a large enough library with books about Hindu philosophy and spirituality, there are not enough books on the contemporary trends in popular religiosity. This reflects the fact that Indian universities don't have a tradition of a serious and rigorous sociology of religion. Milton Singer's well-known *When a Great Tradition Modernizes* (Chicago, 1972) contains many useful suggestions. By revisiting the same Chennai industrialist families that Singer had studied 25 years earlier, John Harriss has done a wonderful job of bringing us into the 21st century and debunking some of the erroneous assumptions made by Singer. His 'When a Great Tradition Globalizes', *Modern Asian Studies* (2003) is a must-read.

Christopher Fuller's *The Camphor Flame* (Princeton, 1992) remains an indispensable guide to contemporary Hinduism. Those interested in understanding modern gurus cannot afford to ignore Lawrence Babb's *The Redemptive Encounters* (Berkeley, 1986) and Lise McKean's *Divine Enterprise: Gurus and the Hindu Nationalist Movement (*University of Chicogo Press, 1996). Agehananda Bharati's writings, even though slightly dated, offer crucial insights into modern Hinduism. His *Hindu Views and Ways and Hindu–Muslim Interface* (Ross-Erikson, 1981) and *The Ochre Robe* (Ross-Erikson, 1980) are essential reading.

The literature on the Indian middle class is beginning to grow. Pavan Varma's *The Great Indian Middle Class* (Penguin India, 2007) is a popular and useful book to start with. A good analysis of the changing cultural tastes of the great Indian middle class can be found in: Christopher Jaffrelot and Peter van der Veer (eds), *Patterns of Middle-class Consumption in India and China* (Sage, 2008), Jackie Assayag and Christopher Fuller (eds), *Globalizing India: Perspectives from Below* (Anthem Press, 2005), and Imtiaz Ahmad and H. Reifeld (eds), *Middle-class Values in India and West Europe* (Social Science Press, 2007). There is simply no better guide to the political/electoral behaviour of the middle classes than Suhas Palshikar, whose essay 'Politics of Indian Middle Classes' appears in the volume edited by Imtiaz Ahmad and H. Reifeld.

The idea of banal or everyday nationalism is from Michael Billig's *Banal Nationalism* (Sage, 1995). How this everyday nationalism works in India is beginning to be explored. Some recent representative writings include: Badri Narayan, *Fascinating Hindutva: Saffron Politics and Dalit Mobilization* (Sage, 2009), Christopher Fuller, 'The Vinayak Chaturthi Festival and Hindutva in Tamil Nadu' (*Economic and Political Weekly*, May 12, 2001), and Meena Kandaswamy's online essay, 'Doing it Everyday' at boloji.com.

Moving on to the literature on Hindu nationalism, two books by Jyotirmaya Sharma are very illuminating: *Terrifying Vision: M.S. Golwalker, the RSS and India* (Penguin-Viking, 2007), and *Hindutva: Exploring the Idea of Hindu Nationalism* (Penguin-Viking, 2003). Essays by Cynthia Mahmood in her *A Sea of Orange* (Xlibris, 2001) are worth reading. Christopher Jaffrelot's *The Hindu Nationalist Movement in India* (Columbia University Press, 1993) is a classic.

The phenomenon of 'ethnocratic liberalism' is of crucial importance in understanding the dangers of Hindu nationalism which uses the language of liberalism to assert Hindu supremacy. Important are the writings of Roger Griffin, 'Interregnum or Endgame? The Radical Right in the "Post-fascist" Era' (*Journal of Political Ideologies*, 5[2], 163–178), and Richard Wolin, *Seduction of Unreason: The Intellectual Romance with Fascism, from Nietzsche to Postmodernism* (Princeton University Press, 2004). Tamir Bar-On's *Where Have All the*

Fascists Gone? Ashgate, 2007) is an excellent critique of the European New Right.

Most of the classics on secularism have been discussed in Chapter 5. For the Indian context, Rajeev Bhargava (ed.), *Secularism and its Critics* (Oxford University Press, 1999) is indispensable. Mukul Kesavan's *The Secular Commonsense* (Penguin, 2001) is thought-provoking.

Acknowledgements

This book has benefited greatly from the good counsel of friends and colleagues.

I am indebted to Professor Bipin Chandra who got me started on this project. He encouraged me to take on the project on scientific temper, out of which has emerged this book.

My thanks go out to my good friend Alan Sokal who has inspired me to put up a good fight in defence of a well-reasoned, principled, and open atheism.

My colleagues Barry Kosmin and Ariela Keyser at the Institute of Study of Secularism in Society and Culture at Trinity College, Harford, Connecticut, provided excellent company and stimulating conversations.

Rukun Advani of Permanent Black stepped in at just the right moment to pull me up when I was down and out. I could always count on intellectual and moral support of my good friend Achin Vanaik.

Chiki Sarkar of Random House has been simply amazing: I've yet to meet someone so young and yet so wise. Her suggestions have added a lot of clarity to the content and the style of the book.

It is a source of great joy to me that I am completing this book in New Delhi. I am extremely grateful to Professor Aditya Mukherjee for inviting me as a fellow of the Jawaharlal Nehru Institute of Advanced Studies at Jawaharlal Nehru University, New Delhi. I couldn't have asked for a place more conducive for writing. Many thanks to the gracious staff of the Institute for making my stay here so pleasant and comfortable.

My friends in the fourth dimension of the Internet were good conversation partners. Special thanks go to Ophelia Benson (Butterflies and Wheels at butterfliesandwheels.

com), Ralph Dumain (Autodidact Project), Caspar Melville and Laurie Taylor (New Humanist), and Ajita Kamal (nirmukta.com).

My friends and comrades from India kept me informed and provided a home away from home on my many visits to India. I am especially grateful to my good friends Asad Zaidi, Nalini Taneja, S. Anand, and Puran Mongia in Delhi; Lallan, Daljit Ami and their associates in the Critique group in Punjab University, Chandigarh; Parthasarathi Mondal, Kanchana Mahadevan, M.C. Arunan, and T. Jayaraman in Mumbai; Vidyanand Nanjundiah and Sundar Sarukkai in Bangalore; and Harjinder Singh in Hyderabad.

As always, my life partner Ravi Rajamani and our daughter Jaya have been there, steady like a rock. This book is for them.

A Note on the Author

Meera Nanda writes on science and religion. She is a philosopher of science with initial training in biology. She has received research fellowships from the American Council of Learned Societies and the John Templeton Foundation, USA. She is a visiting fellow (2009–10) at the Jawaharlal Institute of Advanced Studies, JNU. She is the author of, award-winning book, *Prophets Facing Backward: Postmodernism, Science, and Hindu Nationalism.*

CPSIA information can be obtained at www.ICGtesting.com
Printed in the USA
BVOW011909230112

281065BV00001B/3/P